"One of the most frustrating situations in p: when you don't know what to do. Jon Winde is based on his many years of experience, techniques, interventions, and perspectives that ensure you will build your professional and personal confidence so you will likely never get stuck again."

— *Bill O'Hanlon, Author*
Change 101 and Do One Thing Different

"*Getting Unstuck* will guide you through tough therapeutic dilemmas and help your clients on the way! No matter what your theoretical approach or level of experience, this book will improve your clinical confidence and professional expertise. Highly readable and filled with heart."

—*Clifton Mitchell, Ph.D., Author*
Effective Techniques for Dealing with Highly Resistant Clients

"I love it. Every therapist has faced those moments of not knowing how to proceed with a client whose problems or personality seem daunting. Winder, from his more than 40 years of counseling experience, has put together a wonderful compendium of stories and strategies for dealing with just these situations. In addition to a trove of practical advice, his book is full of compassion, heart and wisdom from a seasoned counselor—a great reference book for any therapist's bookshelf."

—*Joe Kort, Ph.D., CST, Author*
Is My Husband Gay, Straight, or Bi?

Getting Unstuck

Practical Guidance for Counselors

WHAT TO DO WHEN YOU DON'T KNOW WHAT TO DO

Jon Winder

LICENSED PROFESSIONAL COUNSELOR

LMP

LOVING HEART PRESS

Loving Heart Press
1142 Inspiration Drive
Bedford, Va. 24523

Website: jonwindercounseling.com

Designed by Country Mouse Design

Getting Unstuck / Jon Winder. —1st ed.

ISBN 978-0-9979612-2-5

Library of Congress Control Number: 2016921367

To Sh Ahmed Abdur Rashid,

who opened the door to inner knowledge, which goes much

deeper than anything I could write about here. Hopefully,

however, it is reflected in the spirit of my writing.

Contents

CONTENTS

CONTENTS

Preface

If you bought this book, I congratulate you on your humility. This is probably not the kind of book that you proudly display on your desk or bookshelf. Who wants to admit that they do not know what to do? The reality is, however, that all therapists, no matter how seasoned, get to a point where they do not know what to do. Maybe you bought the e-version, so you are covered.

Counseling can often be frustrating, and those times when we don't know what to do with the client are probably the worst. We feel like we are failing our clients and ourselves. This book is an attempt to arm counselors with perspectives, as well as a compendium of skills and strategies that will guide them through these tough times.

Counselors have a job like no other, one with awesome responsibility. The decisions we make, the words we say, the concern we show can have a lasting and often profound impact on individual's lives. We cannot take this trust lightly. We are called upon to deal with the greatest of tragedies, major catastrophes, unspeakable cruelties, and mind-boggling situations for which there are no easy or even plausible explanations. From 9/11 to Hurricane Katrina to the Sandy Hook Elementary shootings, we are the ones people turn to for solace, understanding, compassion, and, if we're lucky, some sense of meaning or perspective that lessens their burdens. As the caretakers of human pain and suffering, we are asked to perform monumental tasks—to soothe the unsoothable, comfort the uncomfortable, answer the unanswerable, and manage the unmanageable.

Counseling is not only a matter of mind and consciousness; you have to have the *heart* to do this. We must go to the core of the matter to find out how the person thinks and feels, and empower them to do better. We must see the good in our clients that no one else sees and reinforce that in them.

PREFACE

...

I became a therapist with a lot of interest and few skills. As a teenager, I read many psychology books. I was fascinated by the mind and how it worked. My career began as a volunteer in a crisis center. My training consisted of about four hours of basic training in crisis management. As a volunteer, I often would have to cover the night shift sleeping on a little sofa in an office about the size of a small bathroom. In the middle of the night the phone would ring, and someone would be on the other end in crisis, usually suicidal. Since I am a sound sleeper, I was not exactly at my best or in the best frame of mind when the phone rang. The first minute was usually figuring out, "Where the hell am I?" But necessity required that I respond to potentially life-and-death situations. I managed to engage with the callers, and I am not sure how well I did, but I did not lose anybody...to my knowledge. This may not be the best way to learn, but it is one of the most powerful and one that sticks with you—you do what you do, because you have to.

My formal training did not prepare me for the vicissitudes of doing therapy. Starting out in counseling can be mind-boggling; you often don't know what to do. Much of it is trial and error, which is part of the learning process. However, I had the opportunity to work in the ER at the local hospital as a mental-health consultant. Having lived a rather sheltered life, my initial concern was that I would be "freaked out" by the blood, pain, agony, and gore that I would witness. But I saw none of that—an ambulance would pull up to a separate ER door, the patient would be rolled in on a gurney wrapped in a blanket, taken into a bay, and the curtains drawn. A nurse would go in, often followed by the ER doctor. Then a variety of other health professionals such as the lab tech or pulmonary specialist would be called in. After the initial evaluation, the patient was either discharged, admitted to ICU or another hospital floor, sent to surgery, or in some sad cases to the morgue.

But something soon became apparent to me: THERE IS NO EMERGENCY IN THE EMERGENCY ROOM. Why is that?

And in this lies the one answer to the question, "What do you do, when you don't know what to do?"

And the answer is: ***protocol.***

Each person had a role and specific duties and carried them out. Though there are an infinite number of situations that cause people to end up in the Emergency Room, there are finite systems that are affected. There are wounds, breaks, infections, overdoses, mental incapacitation, breakdown of organs (heart attacks, strokes, diabetic coma, etc.), colds, flu, etc. Each category of emergency has a procedure used to assess and treat the infirmity, and each treatment team member has a role and responsibility for his/her area of expertise in the process.

And so, it is with counseling. Clients present us with an infinite number of situations, but protocol provides us with specific procedures, or a specific model or combination of therapy models to treat the situation. Experienced therapists generally follow a protocol either consciously or unconsciously. So, what you are *supposed to do* will often get you through *what to do*.

Of course, the practitioner's experience, knowledge and skill are important ingredients for the success of the protocol. There is no book that can give you this. The ideas presented here cannot compensate for this, but this book *can* give you ideas and a direction to deal with the most perplexing of situations. Doing therapy is often analogous to being lost at sea. In the distance, you see a lighthouse. With the rough seas and intense rain, you may lose sight of it, but you have an idea of where it is and the direction you need to go. And so, it is with counseling. We can all get lost at times in a session, but if we know where to take the client and how to get there, then we will eventually arrive at the goal.

So, this book is meant to help counselors establish a sound overall approach to their craft-protocols and a frame of mind to deal with uncertainty and seemingly *impossible* cases and situations. It also offers a systematic way to handle specific kinds of problems presented by clients. These are some of the tricks of the trade. Much of what I share here is the result of having been involved in the field of psychology nearly my whole life, and having read hundreds of articles, books, and blogs, as well as attended many conferences and workshops. I am indebted to those who have inspired me with their thoughts and insights. What I hope to have done is offer some new perspectives on these ideas that have guided my life and my profession. I hope this will open new doors of discovery for you both professionally and personally.

Jon Winder

Acknowledgements

First of all, I would like to thank all of the amazing people who have been my clients. You have taught me so much more than any course or book. I also would like to thank the many therapists I have supervised, who challenged me, educated me, and inspired me. It has been my honor to have worked with all of you.

Thanks to Deborah Berkley, who never stopped believing in me, and in fact, believed in me more than I believed in myself. I would like to thank Kate Knapp, whose enthusiasm, generosity, and dedication have made a lasting impression on me. Thanks to Linda Fowler, editor extraordinaire, who kept me on my toes and spent hours reading and commenting on my book helping me to find the perfect word. I would also like to thank James Denny Townsend for never giving up on me and guiding me through the rough waters of writing a book. Thanks, also to Bill O'Hanlon, who is so dedicated to helping other therapists pursue their writing dream, and Clifton Mitchell, who gave me the psychological go-ahead to write this book. Thanks also to Ron Klein, the first person I ever encountered, who really knew how to do therapy and made learning it a joy. I would like also to thank my friend and confidante, Ira Kaufman, who challenged me to be clear about my reason for writing this book and gave me hours of advice on how to market it. Thanks to Genevieve Whittemore for her help with the section on neuro-feedback, and being such a wonderful example of a therapist, who does not give up, until she finds the answer. I would also like to thank, Ms. Stang, my fifth-grade English teacher, long gone, but who taught me grammar by having our class do hours and hours of diagramming sentences. I have carried that knowledge all these years.

Finally, I owe thanks to my incredible wife, Lila, who gave me the space, encouragement, sagely-advice, and love to continue.

PART ONE

Perspective

Introduction

It's not that I am smart, it's just that I stay with problems longer.

—Albert Einstein

What do *you* do when you don't know what to do?
What makes you think you have to do anything?
What is it that you do when you *do* do something?
Why is it OK to not know?
What are the situations when we don't know what to do?

These are all questions therapists face daily consciously or unconsciously. One does not have to do counseling long before being confronted with these concerns. One of my first "oh, no" experiences as a counselor happened during my internship. I was a young grad student, and had as a client a lady who had volunteered to see a counselor on a pro bono basis. Naturally, I was a little nervous, since she was my first client, but even more so since she had a stern and imposing presence. I became much more nervous, because I soon realized she was staring at my crotch. At first, I thought was she just curious. But as I tried to get her to answer questions, she just kept staring at my private area. Soon it appeared she was more than just a little curious. As if that were not unsettling enough, every two or three minutes she would lick her lips. I don't think I ever squirmed so much in my whole life. I had no idea what to do or how to address this with her. If I mentioned it, she might say I was imagining it, so my only option was to endure it. However, looking back I realize that was the time that I learned to take notes during the session with the notebook in my lap. I have done so ever since. I have no recall as to what her problem was;

I only know that she made a very lasting impression on me.

So, not knowing what to do can manifest in many ways. If we examine the therapeutic paradigm, we can see, however, that situations fall into a few categories, and there are procedures that we can use to manage them. There are five main categories where problems can arise:

- The problem
- The relationship between therapist and client
- The difficult client
- The therapist
- Outside forces

The Problem

The most obvious situations in which we get stuck are when we are confronted with a problem that has no apparent or suitable solution. There are times when no matter what we know or what we say, we cannot make the situation better. The loss of a child, a diagnosis of a terminal illness, property being destroyed by a tornado, the trauma of being abused, facing prison time for a moment of indiscretion, and many more situations with which we are confronted daily may have no easy answers.

When I received training for hypnosis therapy, the class was ironically warned about **being hypnotized by the client**. As clients are describing their situation in a monotone and sinking deeper and deeper into their chair as they talk, therapists may find themselves falling hook, line, and sinker into the same sense of hopelessness and helplessness that the clients have–we become hypnotized by their sense of devastation. The class learned that to break a trance we must be mindful of our state realizing when we find ourselves engulfed, to shake it off and step outside of the situation to get a fresh perspective. In this way, we will not be hypnotized by the clients' problems. If nothing else, we can know that there are always other possibilities or ways of looking at situations to make them more bearable and understandable for the client.

The Therapeutic Relationship

Another group of situations in which we often don't know what to do is when we are not able to establish a therapeutic relationship with the client. Sometimes this means that the client is fearful, not ready to change, or alienated by something we have done or said. Establishing a therapeutic relationship is a balancing act. It requires the ability to balance being open and friendly, and at the same time, being willing to confront the client's shortcomings or challenge him risking pushing him away. Most all therapists pride themselves in their ability to build rapport and connect with the clients. It is very hard for therapists to see ways in which they may alienate the client. When there is a disconnect, the tendency is to blame the client. After all, the clients are the ones with the problems, and their inability to connect in a therapeutic way can easily be placed on them, since therapists are *masters of relationship*. So, when counselors find themselves at odds with clients or not being able to fully engage with them, ironically, one of the easiest ways to change is for counselors to be introspective and change their attitude, even apologizing if necessary.

Difficult Client

Clients come in many shapes and sizes; some with personality disorders, some lacking confidence to improve, some combative and aggressive, some lethargic and lacking motivation, and some beaten-down and overwhelmed. Each situation presents a unique challenge to the therapist. Helping people who do not want help, are afraid of getting help, or who have decided they're not ready to change tests the therapist's skill and flexibility. For example, most therapists have had an experience with a client diagnosed as having a narcissistic or borderline personality disorder, and many times just having that diagnosis will lead therapists to feel anxious. Of course, this is the product of counter-transference. Certain kinds of people just push our buttons. Personally, I have difficulty with clients who are overtly prejudiced. A certain part of me shuts down, and I have to fight with myself to overcome or put aside my personal feelings.

Other types of clients who may push buttons are the entitled, the quitter, the aggressor, the show-off, the complainer, the avoider, the competitor, and the rigid. In many of these situations, we may find ourselves at a loss as to how to respond. We feel challenged and uncomfortable, which adds to our inability to respond favorably to the client's needs.

The Therapist's Personal Difficulties

The fourth situation is when the therapist is having personal difficulty—physical, mental, or emotional problems occurring in his or her own life. Generally, most therapists can overcome or compensate for this, but to do so, they must be honest with themselves and be willing to explore their own role in the process. Certain clients may present problems that we as therapists have not worked through, or we have a similar problem and feel hypocritical telling the client what to do when we are not willing or have not followed through with what we know is right. These situations may highlight our own inadequacies as a person. We need to be up front and admit this in a professional manner, when appropriate. Otherwise, we run the risk of looking inept or deceitful.

Outside Forces

Clients obviously exist in a broader environment than the therapist's office, which can have a tremendous effect on them and the success or failure of therapy. Despite our best attempts, we may find that the environmental influences can either undermine or support the therapy, and often have a greater effect on the outcome than the therapy itself. For instance, the support may come in the form of a teenage girl telling her boyfriend to stop using drugs, or she will leave him, and he stops. On the other hand, one of the biggest challenges in doing therapy with children is that despite all the efforts made by the counselor and the child, if the parents are not on board, they can easily sabotage any therapeutic gains.

Add to this the prevailing culture in which the person exists. Culture can be positive, such as when certain behaviors are not tolerated or don't even happen. Community support may be the best force for healing that can occur. On the other hand, if the person grows up in an environment of hate, aggression, and fear, and where going to jail is a badge of honor, then any attempt to install positive values can be seen as weakness and vulnerability. These are the forces over which the counselor has no obvious control, but which counselors and clients have to battle to overcome.

CHAPTER 1

Not Knowing

I see my path, but I don't know where it leads. Not knowing where I'm going is what inspires me to travel it.

—Rosalio de Castro

How can not knowing what to do be okay?

Therapists faced with situations in which they don't know what to do may feel stuck, stymied, or inadequate. How can "not knowing" be a positive? After all, your client is coming to you for answers, and it is easy to become worried that you will not meet his or her expectations.

Counseling is More Than Answers

People come to therapy not just for answers to questions or issues in their lives, but also to be heard, understood, and accepted by another person. It could be said that what they are also seeking is *therapeutic wisdom*—wisdom generated from a combination of knowledge and experience. This comes not just from sitting in hundreds of therapy sessions, but also from life experience. And it manifests not just as saying the right thing at the right time, but it can come through in a smile, a wink, or thumbs up, or in not reacting to a situation. At other times, it could be exhibiting a peaceful composure, expressing a kind thought at the right time or having a sense of humor. Having weathered some of the vicissitudes of life and learned from the hard knocks, a therapist gains practical experience that can serve every day as a basis for helping others. In each counseling situation, we bring everything we have learned to date as a resource. Many counselors decided upon a counseling career after having survived some ordeal or trauma that gave them some insight, inspiration, and/or courage to help others.

I believe that every client comes into our life for a reason, and that there is a lesson to be learned from each one. Perhaps we see a quality in them that we admire—their example of courage or perseverance, or how they arrived at a solution we had not thought of. On the other hand, I have had clients where the lesson was, "I am so glad I am not like that," or "I can appreciate my life more, since I have not had to go through that." Maybe our clients were placed into our lives to teach us some important lesson and not for us to impart some great wisdom to them. When we can share in their victories and gain a greater understanding of human nature; that is the joy of counseling.

There is sacredness in not knowing. It becomes our teacher, which compels us to have faith and to seek out knowledge. When we can be quiet and honor that part of ourselves, we can learn to hear the answers. This requires trust and going beyond our normal ways of processing. Additionally, when we can share in that space with our clients, it is a mutual experience of discovery in the ultimate experience of therapy, which has been expressed as being in the flow. In this place, there is no sense of you and me, but only us being, interacting, and discovering. It is not about me, the therapist, knowing, but rather it is two human beings coming together to explore their potentials. This is a paradigm shift from the traditional idea of counselor-client relationship.

What Makes a Good Counselor?

As a former director of a residential substance-abuse program, I once needed to find someone to do the maintenance of the facility. We had quite a few applicants and set out to interview the top five. Most of the applicants, in an attempt to get the job, indicated there was no job they did not know how to do. They were proficient in plumbing, electrical, carpentry, heating and air conditioning, landscaping, etc. However, one candidate indicated that while he knew a lot of things in these areas, there were things that he did not know and would have to consult with friends or colleagues. He also stated he did not think that he knew enough about heating and air to make any promises about that. We ended up hiring him, the main reason being that he was honest about his abilities, and he had the humility to admit that he did not have all the answers.

Just as there are factors other than *knowing* that are more important in choosing a maintenance man, the same is true for therapists. While knowledge is an important criterion for being a good therapist, there are other criteria that end up being as important or more important than the therapist's degrees or specialty. The main criterion is: What kind of person is this therapist?

> **A therapist is only as good a therapist as he is a person, so if we want to be a better therapist, we need to be a better person.**

A therapist is only as good a therapist as he is a person, so if we want to be a better therapist, we need to be a better person. In the final analysis, all we have to offer others is the quality of who we are as a person. If we are burned-out, frustrated, and over-worked, that is what we are offering. If we are balanced, optimistic, and energetic, that is what we are offering. We have to be able to put aside our personal issues and feelings, so that we can be fully present with the clients. Not everyone has that ability. What I have found is that even if I am down or upset, once I connect with a client, my own problems seem miniscule.

So, what are some of the qualities of a good person that are also essential for being a good counselor? The most obvious are the ones cited by Carl Rogers—empathy, genuineness, and unconditional positive regard. These form the cornerstone of a solid therapeutic relationship. Often when a counselor I am supervising is having difficulty connecting with the client, these are the first areas to investigate.

Empathy

Suzanne came for counseling to deal with problems from her marriage. One of the points she described as a problem was that she was unhappy her husband bought her a new Lexus and expected her to drive it. This is a situation that would probably not elicit much empathy from most counselors, including myself—that is until I learned the circumstances behind it. Suzanne's husband was controlling and verbally and physically abusive to her. He always wanted to know where she was. Part of the reason he had bought her a Lexus was so that he could trace her whereabouts on the car's GPS. Another was to prove to the neighbors and his relatives what a caring husband he was for "providing" such a wonderful car for his wife. Suzanne said she felt like she was being forced to drive a "lie," and besides, she was more of a Subaru-station-wagon type of person, especially with three kids.

The ability to empathize is obviously very high for people in the counseling profession. Sometimes the problem becomes being too empathetic and not establishing appropriate boundaries. This can lead to the counselor becoming overwhelmed, then distressed, and eventually experiencing burnout. Tania Singer at the Max Planck Institute for Human Cognitive and Brain Sciences wrote:

> "Brain scans have shown that similar areas of the brain are activated both in the person who suffers and the one who feels empathy. So empathic suffering is a true experience of suffering, so in order to avoid this, we need to transform empathy into compassion. Compassion is a warm, caring emotion that does not involve feeling sadness if the other person is sad."

> *(Science 12 July 12 by Olivia Solon, http://www.wired.co.uk/news/archive/2012-07/12/tania-singer-compassion-burnout)*

Empathy often results in taking on the other's pain as though it were your own. Compassion, on the other hand, is offering love and concern, but not absorb the other's pain. So, it is possible and even desirable to be compassionate.

Another problem with empathy is that the counselor can develop counter-transference in which the client's appearance, attitude, behavior, or beliefs are so repugnant or antithetical to the counselor's moral or ethical beliefs that empathy seems to not be possible. While driving down the street one day, I realized a way to help overcome this tendency to judge or inability to connect. I noticed a *bag lady* pushing a shopping cart with what appeared to be miscellaneous belongings. She was all dirty, bent over, had a tired, wrinkled face and scraggly hair. I thought, "Once this woman was a beautiful little baby; what happened to her in her life to cause her to end up in such a condition? Was the spark or remnants of that original soul still present in her? What had life dealt her that she ended up in this condition?"

Since then, I see similar people on the street, and I am curious about that person's life story. I think how cruel life can be and wonder how this person has endured. This helps to create compassion instead of judgment. Now this may not be possible for all people. We all have our limitations as human beings, some of which are the result of personal trauma in our lives. There are counselors, for example, who cannot work with child sex abusers, especially if the counselors were abused as children. If you explore the abuser's histories, you discover, however, they too were victims. By cultivating an attitude of curiosity with the goal of understanding how this person became this way, it is possible to develop compassion, or at least to suspend judgment to render help to the person.

Genuineness

Sometimes it is difficult for the counselor to determine the balance between being genuine, saying what he truly thinks and feels (especially about the client), and being professional, which implies a certain detachment or air of authority, and therefore lack of genuineness. The goal is not to be popular with our clients, but be genuine and real.

Carl Rogers describes genuineness this way:

> It means that within the relationship he is freely and deeply himself, with his actual experience accurately represented by his awareness of himself. It is the opposite of presenting a facade, either knowingly or unknowingly.
>
> It is not necessary (nor is it possible) that the therapist be a paragon who exhibits this degree of integration, of wholeness, in every aspect of his life. It is sufficient that he is accurately himself in this hour of this relationship, that in this basic sense he is what he actually is, in this moment of time.
>
> It should be clear that this includes being himself even in ways which are not regarded as ideal for psychotherapy. His experience may be "I am afraid of this client" or "My attention is so focused on my own problems that I can scarcely listen to him." If the therapist is not denying these feelings to awareness, but is able freely to be them (as well as being his other feelings), then the condition we have stated is met. Certainly, the aim is not for the therapist to express or talk out his own feelings,

but primarily that he should not be deceiving the client as to himself.

("The Necessary and Sufficient Conditions of Therapeutic Personality Change," Rogers, Carl R., University of Chicago., 1957 Journal of Consulting Psychology, Vol. 21, pp. 95–103)

Clients often are very adept at picking up insincerity, phoniness, or haughtiness in some professionals. They are put off by it and feel demeaned by it. Genuineness, on the other hand, creates trust and gives credence to the words of the counselor. In such an environment, the counselor's pronouncement of *not knowing* is usually met with understanding and respect, rather than disappointment and questioning the therapist's ability or reliability.

All of this should be tempered considering the client's personality and need. For instance, some narcissistic clients only value a therapist who will challenge them and "give them a go for their money." They would not respect humility. Some oppositional clients may challenge your "lack of knowledge" and use it against you. There is no one approach that is suitable for all clients. One must develop the discernment and knowledge to know when to be and when not to be forthcoming.

Unconditional Positive Regard

We tend to *like* people who are *like* us. So, these two meanings of the word, *like*, reveal a connection or reality that we all experience. To connect with people who are unlike us without disliking them can be a challenge. Often when counselors are asked to describe the client they like to work with best, the profile is like the counselor's. They are bright, articulate, well-dressed, verbal, interactive, and motivated. When asked to describe the client with whom they have the most trouble, they describe the opposite.

I had a fraternity brother whose favorite saying was, "You might not like 'em, but you gotta love 'em," which I think is a wonderful attitude to develop unconditional positive regard. Nowhere does it say that you should like all the people you work with, and the reality is that there are some that you just won't click with. But if you have the attitude of unconditional positive regard, you can find some quality in that person to like.

Other Factors

In the development of the therapeutic relationship, a bond is created that helps to bridge the gap between those moments when the answer is not forthcoming. Building and maintaining that loving relationship is the safety net that fortifies the times of uncertainty, confusion, and temporary helplessness. The kind and depth of that relationship are based on the power of the therapist's self-knowledge, certainty, and personality. While the therapist has to have professional confidence, this needs to be balanced with a sense of humility. Being humble does not take away from a therapist's expertise; rather it can enhance the client's belief in the therapist's ability.

Ideally, the counselor is a model for the client. There is a Marshall McLuhan saying that was famous back in the 1960's: "The medium is the message." As a counselor, how you think, how you process situations, how you react or not, and how you express yourself are all part of the therapy and message to the client. You should model the most positive qualities–trustworthiness, integrity, patience, optimism, sincerity and a love for life. You show you are invested in the client by your innate curiosity about the client and his/her life, and your desire to learn and grow from any experience. You show by example how a person can operate out of love and not fear, and how to gain the peace that comes from learning to live with uncertainty and not having to have the answers.

You don't have to be super-human; you can exhibit vulnerability, frustration, disappointment, even anger, but always in a constructive therapeutic way, which means that you must put yourself aside and maintain a balance when expressing yourself, not at the expense of the client. Any self-disclosure or exposure you do should only be for the sake of moving the therapeutic process forward. You should set aside your own wounds from the past. If you are triggered by a client who cuts into your own emotional pain, then you need to seek out supervision and/or possibly get counseling for yourself.

Counseling is a matter of the sum total of what you bring to the table. What do you bring to the table?

- What do you have that the client needs?
- What is your capacity as a human being?

- To what extent is your life something people could model themselves after?

I often think when I am working with an adolescent or someone who is philosophically, culturally and demographically opposite me (young, Latino, female, for instance), what do I have to offer them? Even more importantly, what do I have that they want? My default is all the qualities stated above. Who, deep down, doesn't want more peace, hope, understanding, and love in their lives? Again, what I have to give is who I am as a person.

Not Knowing as a Door

I was reminded that of all the knowledge in the world, what we know is as infinitesimal as we are as a person. Someone said we are only one grain of sand on the beach of life. So how could we know everything? Well, you could say, "I don't need to know everything, just what is needed to help people who come to me for help." I attended a psychotherapy conference in Washington, D.C., where there was an exhibit hall with booksellers from many different psychological/counseling publishers. There were easily 1,000-2,000 different books there, and at least 50-75 books that looked so interesting, and I wished I knew the information in them—and those were only the ones in which I was interested! I realized there are tons of things I don't know and wish that I did. On the one hand, I could feel down on myself for not knowing all these things, or I could see it as "Life is a great experience of gaining knowledge, and look at all that I can still learn after 40+ years of doing therapy."

And so "not knowing" can be seen not as a wall, but as a door...to new learning.

CSI Detective

In a way being a therapist is like being a CSI detective, but instead of looking for answers through clues, the therapist looks for answers through the symptoms. Each client has a life, and if the story of that client's life was written down, it would be a 500, 1,000 or maybe even a 10,000-page book. As therapists, we only get to see a few paragraphs or maybe a few pages. If clients are in therapy for a longer time, we may get to see a whole chapter. So, in a way, we are shooting in the dark with their problems. But if we want to get to the source of a problem or to understand the dynamics that created the behavior, we need to explore where it originated.

And so, we become detectives not settling for superficial answers. We ask more probing questions such as:

- At what point did the client develop those traits? Why?
- Is the problem related to childhood trauma?
- Is it a brain disorder or learned behavior?
- Is it related to some belief the person developed at some event in his/her life?
- What is the client really angry about?
- What were the factors that went into that?

It takes an amazing curiosity and the perseverance of a detective to ferret out the nature and origins of these symptoms. It requires us to dig deeper and go beyond pat answers like,

"I've always been that way." (Even as a baby?)
That's just how I do things (Where and how did you learn to do that?)
I just don't care (Why don't you care? When and why did you stop caring?)
I don't want to talk about it. (Okay, but just tell me why you don't want to talk about it.)

With these kinds of statements or situations, it is helpful to keep asking, "… and why is that?" even if you just think it to yourself.

Bobby does not like school.
And why is that?
He doesn't care about it.
And why is that?
He is not motivated to do well.
And why is that?"
He just gave up.

CHAPTER 1: NOT KNOWING

And why is that?"
He got behind and never figured how to catch up.
And why is that?
He was sick in third grade and missed a lot of school. When he went back, he was way behind the others. He has never been able to make up the deficit.

So, the question, "And why is that?" had to be asked five times to get to the real reason. Being asked that question can be very irritating to the client, so you can mix it up with other statements or questions like:

- Tell me more about that.
- What's the reason behind that?
- How did that come about?
- What do you think caused that?
- What made you think that?
- I'm curious about how that happened.
- What's your guess about why that is?

Each response is designed to go deeper into the situation, until you can get to the core. In a way, what you are doing is sorting through symptoms as exemplified by the example above. I call this process breaking through the glass floor (which obviously is the opposite of the glass ceiling). By asking one more question, we bust through the *pat answers* to the next level and eventually to the root cause or causes.

One clue that you have not arrived at the core cause is if the answer contains the word, *just*. This is a dirty little four-letter word in the counseling lexicography. "He *just* wants attention," or "He is *just* being manipulative," are common examples. No one is ever *just* anything. *Just* in a sentence implies that the answer is simple, you have it figured out, and there is only one factor, and that automatically rules out others. Human behavior is way too complex to think a person's problem is the result of one factor. Even if a situation could be reduced to a *just* statement, it does not lead to any solution. For example, if a client is ascertained to be "*just* faking it," how does that help in determining the corrective? It may sound astute, but it is not helpful. Why is he faking it? Why does he feel like he needs to fake it? Why and when did he start faking it? What is the payoff for faking it? What are some alternatives that would work besides faking it? These are the kinds of questions the detective/counselor might use.

A New Way to See Failure

Counselors may think that their not knowing what to do in any particular situation means they are a failure. But there is a saying in Neuro-Linguistic Programming (*NLP, the science of modeling and treating the patterns of human behavior*) that states, "There is no failure, only feedback." Basically, what that means is that if you try something and it does not work, this is just feedback that it is not working, and you need to do something else.

> *I learned of a local private school that does not fail any student. And the school doesn't promote students onto the next grade, if they can't keep up. Rather, students are given a unit of information to study and then tested when they feel ready to take the test. If they get an 80% or more on the test, they go on to the next unit of study. If they made only 60%, for example, this does not mean they failed, but the score indicates there is 40% of the material they have not yet mastered. This way the test is a feedback mechanism of what they did not understand. They are then given the material to re-study and keep taking the test until they reach 80%, and then they can go to the next section. This way they are not forced to go on to harder concepts having not understood the simpler ones. This approach takes into consideration that not everyone learns at the same rate, and students have differing abilities to master different subjects. So, the test is not set up as a situation for the student to fail; it is only a feedback instrument. "You have not learned this yet. This is the part you do not know. Try again." This more enlightened way of teaching is being incorporated into software teaching programs, such as Aleks©, which embraces this model of teaching.*

How is this relevant to counseling? If a counselor chooses a particular intervention or assignment for a client and it does not work, or the client does not do it, that does not mean the therapist, the client, or the assignment were failures. Rather, there are several alternate things that it can mean:

- The client was not ready to do this process at this point in the therapy.
- The client did not see the relevance or the validity in it.
- It was too difficult for the client.
- It was not what the client needed.
- The client had other priorities.
- The client was inexperienced and did not have the self-confidence to complete it.
- The therapist did not adequately communicate the purpose of it.
- The therapist did not communicate clearly the nature or directions of the assignment.
- It was not what was needed at this point in the therapeutic process.

So, if one has an attitude of curiosity instead of self-defeat, the "failures" can often reveal as much or more about the client, than if the assignment had been completed.

Surrender

Counseling sometimes seems like a thankless profession. There are periods of time in which it seems like we pour our hearts out, rack our brains, come up with brilliant solutions and great wisdom, and we're not sure anyone hears us or is affected by our efforts. Early on in my counseling career if I had a good session, I would feel good about myself, and then I would have a good day. But if I had a bad session, I would feel terrible about myself and think that I had no business doing therapy, and it would ruin my day. Since I was new and my batting average was not so good, I seriously considered switching to physical therapy as a profession. My reasoning was that if someone came in with pain, and I did physical therapy on it, they would leave without the pain, hence I would get immediate feedback. In counseling, however, it seemed like the client comes in with pain and leaves either still having the pain, or even if it had been abated, I did not know it. I felt like I could not tell whether I'd helped him or not. I didn't realize that change is often *slow and subtle.*

But I hung in there, and soon former clients would come up to me in the grocery store or library and share how their lives had changed due to the therapy and what I had told them. Naturally, I was always curious about what I said that was so great ... so I could use it on more clients. They would tell me, and I would think, "Gee, I said that to a hundred people, but it didn't change their lives ...that I know of."

Sometimes I would have what I considered a terrible session—feeling lost most of the time and like I had failed the client–and then the client would come back the next week and tell me how wonderful the session was, and how it changed their whole outlook on life. Other times, I would feel like it'd been *a masterful session*, and I was so proud of the work I had done, and the client never came back. I realized it was different strokes for different folks, and all I can do is put forth the effort, and understand the results are not in my hands.

I realized what I could do was to attend to each client, be sincere and caring, giving each one my fullest attention and energy, and surrendering the outcome to my Higher Power or God. Many times, a client had come to the session in crisis, and we would try to resolve it. I would do my best to help always wondering, "Could I have done more?" "Do I really know what I'm doing in this case?" "Am I missing something," or dozens of other doubts. But by the end of the session as they were leaving, I would look up and think. "God, they are in your hands now. I did all that I knew what to do today. Bestow grace upon them."

I learned how important it was not to let my ego get all wrapped up in the outcomes of the sessions. It also allowed me to go home at night and not obsess about what would happen. This is not to say that I didn't have second thoughts or wouldn't try to review the session to analyze what I could have done better. It was that I learned to accept and let go, and it was okay not to always know.

CHAPTER 2

Knowing and Change

Setting goals is the first step in turning the invisible into the visible.

—Tony Robbins

T HERE IS THE STORY of the master mechanic, who was called to fix a vital piece of machinery that broke resulting in several production lines having to be shut down. He spent only a short time studying the machinery. Then he got out his hammer, went over to a particular gear and whacked it, and the equipment started running. He then presented the foreman with a bill for $1,000. The foreman was astonished at the bill and complained to the mechanic that he had spent less than five minutes fixing the equipment. The foreman said he would need a breakdown of the bill to justify it to the accountant writing the check. The mechanic then wrote him an invoice with the following:

Repairing the equipment	*$15*
Knowing where to hit the equipment	*$985*
Total	**$1,000**

While the last chapter supported the right and value of not knowing what to do, this chapter focuses on the importance of knowing what to do and how to go about it.

Change Agents

How many therapists does it take to change a light bulb? Only one, but the bulb has to want to change.

People come to treatment because they cannot deal with their situation or state. They may not know what is wrong, what they need to change, or how, and they often resist change. As counselors, we must have the expertise of identifying, motivating and creating change; we are change agents. Many of the problems of not knowing what to do are related to not knowing how to get people to change.

This simple understanding dawned on me early in my career, and I was surprised I had never encapsulated what I do is being a change agent. I wondered if other therapists had done so. I called up several colleagues and asked if they would be interested in discussing this. They were intrigued by the idea, and we met for lunch and began by asking questions:

- What is the process of change?
- What are the factors that cause people to change?
- What promotes change?
- What inhibits change?
- Change happens that is good for us and change happens that is bad for us. Are the same forces at work in both situations?
- What are the forces that cause change for the positive, and what are the forces that cause change for the negative?

As change agents, we need to understand the answers. One way to figure this out, we decided, was to examine our own lives. How did change come about for us personally?

Think about a major change you have made in your life.

- Was it a conscious or unconscious change?
- Did you make a decision to change, or were there events that caused you to make the change?
- How long did it take for the change to come about?
- What was the process you went through to create the change?
  - Did it take a lot of effort such as preplanning and

preparing, or did it happen spontaneously?

In many ways, we take these factors for granted, and yet understanding them is critical to doing effective therapy.

One of the group's conclusions was that the factors that cause positive change are much different than the factors that cause negative change. We determined that positive change can come through education, inspiration, values, necessity, and the desire to survive and thrive. Negative change can come through illness, trauma, physical and emotional pain, desperation, carelessness, greed, selfishness, vulnerability, being overwhelmed, lack of energy, chemical imbalance, and addiction, among others.

Change can be brought about consciously or unconsciously. Most change requires a catalyst of some kind. Sometimes we can create that through an impact in therapy.

Phyllis was a police officer in our therapy group serving as an undercover narcotics agent. While on the surface she seemed hardened, underneath she was a caring person, and there was nothing she would not do for others. She was taking care of her biological parents, who were elderly and feeble, and her husband's mother, who was in the nursing home. On top of that, her job required long hours and was very stressful, but she was determined to do whatever was needed to arrest the drug dealers she was tracking. It was obvious that she was in way over her head. She looked drained in every group, and yet she denied that she could not handle all her responsibilities, no matter how much she was challenged.

As a therapy assignment, she was asked to make a list of her burdens. She listed five and was told the next week to bring five bricks to group and put the name of a burden on each of them. The next week she arrived with five painted bricks each with a name on them. She was then given each brick one on top of another to hold. These represented the burdens she carried. Then six sofa pillows were placed on her back—each one representing a responsibility that she had. Then the members of the group lined up behind her in a chain holding on to her representing people in her life making demands upon her. She was then told to walk around the room carrying the bricks, while stooped over balancing the pillows on her back and pulling eight people. She walked and walked and walked for almost ten minutes with the bricks weighing her down almost to the floor.

Finally, the group leader confronted her and asked her how long she was going to do this. She said until she was told to stop by the group leaders. The members asked why she just didn't stop, and she said an amazing thing—she never thought of it! It never occurred to her that all she had to do was stop and tell the group and the leaders, "I'm not doing this anymore." It took this concrete activity to dawn on her that she needed to change. Having been raised to be obedient and to put others before herself and trained as a police officer not to give up, she never realized that she had the right to say "No, I'm not doing this anymore," to the people in her life. By the end of her treatment, she had not only divested herself of many of her responsibilities, she put in for vacation, and she and her husband spent a week at the beach.

Fix vs. Change

Much of the difficulty we encounter with our clients is that they often want a fix instead of to change. A fix is a one-time intervention by an outside force (person, prescription or illegal drug, or intervention) that, hopefully, has permanent lasting effects. Encouraging the client to take the slower, more stable route is more difficult in our age of quick fixes. But fixes may be a house of cards. While they look good and can have flashy results, they often fade or collapse over time.

Change, on the other hand, is evolutionary a step-by-step process that requires a personal commitment of time, effort, and energy. It necessitates motivation and willingness to change, self-examination and evaluation, goal setting, learning new skills, and trial and error. It is difficult, because there is always the possibility of uncertainty (will it work or not?). This is also uncharted territory in that many have never consciously experienced or dealt with the raw emotions that may surface. But clients become empowered to go on and deal with even deeper situations, once they navigate through this difficulty and realize they are okay. It is like peeling back the layers of an onion—when one layer of hurt is discovered and discarded, often there is another layer. Sometimes clients feel as if they are making no progress because these new layers arise. "I was doing so good, and today I am a wreck." Generally, that means something else is surfacing, and this deeper revelation or emotional disturbance is the fruit of progress (though it often does not feel that way).

Bryan was a pipefitter, who came for treatment for marital therapy. He was a big burly man with a gruff exterior, but his complaint was that he was not able to be affectionate with his wife. He expressed having tender feelings towards her, but could never express them. He would tend to either freeze up or break out in a sweat. Sexually they were compatible, but neither was particularly interested in sex, and according to Bryan, this was not a problem.

In exploring his history, Bryan shared that he was not popular with the girls in school and avoided most of them. He would feel very nervous around them, and whenever he started to get close to a girl to or thinking of her as his girlfriend, he would have symptoms of a panic—rapid heartbeat, racing thoughts, sweating, and sometimes even nausea. His wife was the only person with whom he did not feel this way, but they had worked together for several years, before he allowed himself to get interested in her.

We tried several relaxation techniques and desensitization that unfortunately, had a paradoxical effect. He would actually get more anxious, when he was relaxed. Luckily, his wife was very understanding and patient with him. Bryan was convinced that his problem had nothing to do with her; it was all about him.

We then began to search his childhood history. When did he first remember feeling so anxious? He immediately said, "Six." Given the certainty with which he said it, it was clear that something happened at that age. He could not, however, recall anything out of the ordinary happening to him then. He recalled his father being away for weeks at a time and always feelings relieved when he returned home. When asked why this was, Bryan stated that he felt protected, but he did not know from what. Later he uncovered that he was fearful of his mother but had no idea why.

In one of our sessions, I suggested that he write a letter to "Little Bryan" from "Big Bryan" telling him that Big Bryan would help little Bryan by asking what he needed. I then had him write a response from Little Bryan using his non-dominant hand, which he did. I asked him to read both letters. When he read the one from Little Bryan, he began shaking, and then tears came to his eyes, and he started crying. "What did he write?" I asked. He said, "I honestly don't remember writing this, but Little Bryan says that mommy is always rubbing my pee-pee and sucking it. I don't believe it; but somehow I think it must be true. I don't remember this at all. Do you think Little Bryan is making this up?"

I said, "I seriously doubt it. Why would he make that up? Take some time and just be with this and see how it settles with you."

25

The next week he came back and disclosed that during the week, he did start having actual memories of his mother molesting him. "I can't understand why any mother would do this to her child, especially my mother. But as I thought about it, it started to make sense; this was the reason for my fear of intimacy and females."

●●●

I work with families who want a fix for their children. Dissatisfaction with the child's *bad* behavior is the problem most often identified by parents. Ideally, they just want some pill or therapeutic intervention to fix their child. There are situations in which certain medications will drastically improve a child's ability to gain control of his/her behaviors or emotions. So it does not seem unreasonable for the parents to have such an expectation, but generally, medications are limited in what they can ameliorate, and in some cases, they are of no use, or in fact, can add to the severity of the problem due to side effects.

Medication cannot solve relationship problems. Many parents do not understand this. Better relationships solve relationship problems. Parents often do not see the role they play when there is a problem in the parent-child relationship. They tend to place all the blame on the child for being disobedient or for being defiant, without looking at their part of the process.

Medication does not resolve relationship problems. Better relationships resolve relationship problems.

In fact, parents can be quite defensive when told their interactions with the child may contribute to the child's dysfunction and taking a new approach to their parenting must be a part of correcting the behavior. The reality is that, even if the child changes his/her behavior, and the parents do not become involved as part of the process, chances are the child will eventually revert to the identified "bad" or even worse behaviors.

So, for situations to improve in people's lives, they have to change and, in order to change, people have to overcome their *fear* of change.

Fear of Change

Counselors assume that when people first come to therapy, that they will open up and talk about their innermost feelings and thoughts. For a person starting out therapy, that can be a very scary proposition.

I was mortified when I first participated in group therapy as a client, thinking the group is going to force all these deep secrets out of me that I was not ready to share. So, I was very nervous about my first excursion into therapy-land. But I realized early in the process that nobody could force me to say anything I didn't want to share. The only way they were going to learn about me was if I told them. I was in charge of the words or information that came out of my head and mouth. So, that realization gave me a certain amount of comfort and willingness to participate and to go forward. As others shared their information, I was more comfortable sharing mine.

Change tends to create fear. The irony is that many clients are more willing to settle for the *uncomfortable known* than to put forth the effort to attain the *comfortable unknown*. In other words, some people are miserable and know they are, but they have learned to cope with it, rather than changing and risking the unknown. One of my female clients was extremely agoraphobic. When her 10-year-old daughter discovered that her mother was being treated for this, she exclaimed, "She doesn't need treatment; she just doesn't need to go outside." Hey, problem solved … but it just wasn't that easy.

We are obviously creatures of habit. Part of the fear of opting for the unknown is the possibility that the change will not work or create an even worse situation.

Martha had a 14-year-old daughter who was quite beautiful. Martha was very protective of her. She basically would not let her out of her sight, except when her daughter went to school. Martha had been sexually molested, when she was in her late teens and vowed that nothing like that would happen to her children. She tried to build a wall around her daughter, wouldn't let her go to parties, and practically forbade her talking to boys. Her worst fear was that her daughter would be raped.

Tragically, the boy next door did rape her daughter about two months after Martha started therapy. Martha was devastated. What she did not realize and could not handle at this point is that she actually contributed to it happening.

How could this be? It was a classic case of "be careful of what you are afraid of, because you may actually create it." Instead of allowing her daughter exposure to boys, which could have helped her learn how to deal with their flirtation and come-ons, she shielded her daughter, and therefore, the daughter did not even know what was taking place, let alone know how to defend herself.

One of the first steps to creating change, therefore, is to reduce the client's fear. Clients coming to therapy, especially the first time, are usually experiencing fear, either from the situation that is bringing them to therapy or from being in therapy itself. This fear may be perceived as resistance, but is more accurately:

- fear of a new situation
- fear of being exposed
- fear of not being able to be successful
- fear of feelings that may emerge
- fear of not pleasing the therapist
- fear of being vulnerable
- fear of counseling being the last hope and it not working
- fear of surrendering control to another person

Failure to acknowledge and understand these fears can undermine the therapeutic process. One way to overcome fear is to talk to clients at the beginning about their *stuff*. Tell them, "One of my roles as a therapist is to listen to your stuff. We all have stuff; you have stuff; I have stuff. Some stuff we are willing to share with others. Other stuff we are not willing to share, and there is some stuff we don't know that we have, because we have stuffed it so far down, it is not part of our conscious retrieval system. My job as a therapist is to listen to all kinds of stuff. I don't judge people by their stuff. Your stuff is only important to me to the extent that it is an obstacle for you. We all tend to stuff our stuff, and stuffing our stuff is what makes us sick and unhappy. My goal is to help you unstuff your stuff." This usually brings a smile of relief.

That does not mean to take it lightly. The process of therapy is to uncover and discover certain aspects clients' lives or trauma that cause them to act or respond in ways about which they were not even aware. Often when people think about their stuff, they feel ashamed—afraid if others knew about this stuff, they would not like them. And yet, ironically, the people you are closest to are the ones who know the most about you, and therefore the most about your stuff. One of the wonders of group therapy is that when people begin to share their stuff, they develop a bond, and in many ways, that bond is as strong or stronger than the bond with their families, because it is based on mutual sharing of the most intimate details of a person's life.

Uncovering this *stuff* is often challenging. Discovering long buried feelings related to traumatic experiences is not much of an incentive to continue in therapy. However, when the clients realize they can experience and overcome these feelings, it is tremendously rewarding.

Jennifer's husband asked her to come to therapy. The couple had been having difficulties to the point that they were considering divorce. One of the main problems was that the husband had to travel out of town at least one week a month. Each time he was about to leave, she would get very irritated and would hound him about his job, accuse him of seeing someone else, and insist that he did not love her. He was tremendously frustrated, because he loved his job and loved his wife, but was unable to convince her he was being faithful. After a huge confrontation, he persuaded her that, whether she believed him or not, she needed to get some counseling. She agreed to counseling to "save the marriage."

However, Jennifer spent most of her beginning hours in therapy sessions complaining about her husband. Any time the therapist tried to turn the conversation towards her, Jennifer would deflect it by blaming her husband or discounting what the therapist was saying. The therapist let her vent for several sessions, but by the fourth session, he just stopped replying verbally to all her concerns. Halfway through the session, Jennifer realized the counselor was not responding to her.

"Am I boring you?" she asked.

"No," said the counselor, "I am just wondering what you want out of coming here. It appears that you just want me to believe your side of the story, and I am not sure how that will help you."

"What do you mean?"

"Well, during the last session, I realized that I think I understand what you are going through, but I am not sure how my understanding you will make your relationship with your husband better, and it seems like anytime I try to get you to focus on your part, you change the subject. "Why is that?"

He then gave several examples. At first, Jennifer denied that was happening, but gradually conceded that perhaps the counselor was right.

"I don't know. I panic at the thought of my husband leaving me alone, and yet I realize I am pushing him away permanently." At that point, she began to cry. "All my life I have felt alone, and I just can't bear that feeling. My dad left when I was

eight, and it was just me and my mom. She had to work and would leave me alone telling me to call the neighbor, if there was an emergency. I never learned how to deal with that, and I still haven't. I feel so foolish; I'm a grown woman and afraid to be left home alone. I always felt that if could just tell my mom how bad I felt, she would cave in and quit her job. She never did. I guess I am using the same lame approach with my husband, and it doesn't work with him either. I don't know of any other way to deal with it. I guess that is really what I need help with." Having just discovered and sharing that, she felt like she could look at the situation with her husband in an entirely new light.

Sometimes it is healing for the client to just admit to another person what they know, but could never face. Learning to live with the truth can be liberating—creating a new sense of authenticity, and knowing one no longer has to hide or cover up.

Stages of Change

It is commonly believed that the first step in changing is admitting to having a problem, but the process of change starts way before that. James Prochaska and Carlo DiClemente of the University of Rhode Island have outlined a five-step process to change called the **Transtheoretical Model of Change**. While these steps were originally designed to describe the process that alcoholics and drug addicts go through to overcome their addiction, they can also apply to efforts made to change one's mental or emotional state, lifestyle, way of coping, or behavior. One of the major ways counselors get stuck and don't know what to do is that they assume that the client is at the stage for action. But as you can see from the chart below, action is the fourth step in the process. So, for example, prescribing Narcotics Anonymous Meetings for a drug addict, who is not even aware of the severity of his illness, can be a waste of time.

1.	Pre-contemplation
2.	Contemplation
3.	Preparation
4.	Action
5.	Maintenance

Let's briefly look at each of these stages:

Pre-contemplation is the stage at which individuals are unaware or barely aware of their problems and have no intention to change in the foreseeable future. Family or friends may confront them, but they deny having a problem. Or they may be aware of it on some level, but believe they can manage it. It is as though there is an incubation period for a problem to take hold and rise to the level that demands action.

Problems are often solutions that no longer work, and because of that, it is difficult for the person to accept them as problems. A primary example is drugs or alcohol for the substance abuser. Many people believe that in drugs they have discovered the most wonderful way to manage their stress, improve their sociability, join with other like-minded people, and possibly even improve their sex life. While it takes differing times for the benefits of using to run out, for true addicts, they must endure much pain and suffering before finally accepting that such an initial *godsend* could turn into such a curse. It is common not to know what to do with people at this stage, because they are so insistent that they do not have a problem and resent those who insist they do—including the therapist. At this stage information given with compassion and respect is much more effective than coercion and threats.

Contemplation is the stage in which people are aware that a problem exists and are seriously thinking about doing something about it, but are either not sure how to go about it or have not yet committed to taking action. It takes time to internalize and come to terms with the impact of their situation. They tend to weigh the pros and cons of changing, either consciously or subconsciously. They often try to negotiate half-steps or alternatives with themselves and others. "Maybe I'll just cut back," or "I will apologize to my wife and promise to never hit her again."

Fear has its greatest hold at this stage. The therapist has to tread cautiously. Pushing clients too fast can result in their balking and backing out of therapy. This stage requires patience. Most counselors feel like a failure, if they cannot get a firm commitment from the client to change. The indecision is often seen as resistance. Be aware that deciding to change is a process…and often a long drawn out one. Sometimes it will take a crisis to force the person to change. Many have to hit bottom, though this is not always the case. Some clients have the foresight to realize that without change, their lives are not going to get better. What is helpful at this stage is having these clients evaluate their own life situation as opposed to telling them how serious their situation is.

Preparation is the stage that combines intention and planning. Clients accept they have problems and acknowledge they need to begin the process of exploring options for help. Individuals at this stage determine what steps they need to take, develop plans, and take some preliminary steps. For example, they may decide they need counseling, consult with friends about who is the best counselor to work with, do research online about their mental illness and treatment possibilities, and then call for an appointment. If living in a bad situation, they may start exploring the housing market and saving money to move out of their home. This is the stage where the counselor and client can cooperatively develop a treatment plan.

Action is the stage in which individuals modify their behavior, experiences, and/or environment to overcome their problems. Action involves overt behavioral changes and requires a considerable commitment of time and energy. It takes a lot of momentum to engage at this level, the result of either a long period of suffering or a crisis. It is like a teeter-totter—as soon as the pain of not changing outweighs the fear of changing, then the commitment to make a change emerges. What often complicates this process is that the person will make a little change, see some improvement, justify to themselves it was not as bad as everyone said, and then slowly relapse into the old behavior believing they are okay. Or the opposite happens: the person makes a little effort, sees no change, believes the action is not working, and then gives up. To get the momentum going, it is important to take *baby steps* setting small attainable goals. Learning to stay the course is critical, and the counselor can play a crucial role in monitoring this process and giving encouragement and support.

Maintenance is the stage in which people work to prevent relapse and consolidate the gains attained during the action stage. For addictive behaviors, this stage can extend from six months to an indeterminate period. In this stage change becomes a new habit and then, hopefully, a permanent state. There is a subtle shift in the locus of control from external factors (family, friends, job, etc.) to internal factors (self-satisfaction, healthy outlook, sense of peace, etc.) This is a maturing process in which the client is willing to forgo the previous payoff of the old behavior or attitude in order to get a greater reward. For example, the person stops being the victim and having others feel sorry for him and regains his/her personal power. This can also be the stage of "no choice," meaning that the client arrives at a place where the use of drugs, food-binging, suicide, or other forms of self-destructiveness are no longer choices, even when faced with a situation, which in the past might have led to such behaviors. The change then becomes an integral part of the person.

It is easy to assume that people coming to therapy want to change. If interventions do not seem to be working, clients may be in the pre-contemplative or contemplative stage. Clients may even subconsciously look for reasons *not* to change. If they feel too much pressure, they may give up and blame the therapist, providing them with a reason to quit therapy. Internally generated motivation is much more effective than externally imposed.

Motivation

Motivation is the steam that runs the engine of change. Behaviorists tell us there are two main reasons people are motivated to change—fear of punishment or anticipation of reward. Many people will be motivated by both, but there are some people who will not be motivated to change, no matter how great the reward. And there are others who no matter how great the punishment will not change. As an example, I worked with a heroin addict and son of a prominent businessman. My client worked for his father, who was a recovering alcoholic and had some knowledge of the disease of addiction. He would give his son significant bonuses for going a certain number of weeks without using and presenting lab results proving that he was clean.

However, that approach backfired. It soon became apparent the son would work for the bonuses not to stay clean, but to save up for drug binges. It was only after he was arrested on a DUI charge that he decided to take his drug problem seriously. So, fear of punishment was his only motivator.

In contrast, many youthful offenders have become so immune to punishment that it no longer is a motivator. It is not uncommon to hear one of them say, "Lock me up; I don't care." No amount of punishment seems to faze them. However, if they were truly rewarded in a meaningful way, they might respond quite differently.

A severely depressed 15-year-old was failing in school and physically attacked his younger siblings, shoving them down, punching them, and even kicking his little sister who had to be taken to the emergency room. His grandmother, who was very strict, was raising him. She would ground him, yell at him, take away his video games, and even lock him in his room for hours at a time, but this made no impact on improving his behavior; in fact, it only made it worse.

A different approach was necessary. To redirect him and encourage him, his counselor needed to find something in his life that sparked him. She discovered that he had two dogs, and that when he was upset, he would calm down by taking the dogs out into the woods. As he talked more and more about the dogs, she realized that he had a real commitment to them. He took sole responsibility for them, and his grandmother confirmed taking care of the dogs was the one thing he did conscientiously and consistently.

The counselor made a deal with him: if he could go six weeks without being mean to his siblings and raise his grades up to a C average, the counselor promised to help him get a volunteer job working with dogs. She took him to a local veterinarian, who gave him a pep talk and a chance to work as a veterinary assistant. As a result, he changed tremendously. He saw that to become a vet, he needed to do better in school. His work with the animals helped to lift his depression, and his compassion for the battered animals helped him to realize the impact his bullying was having on his brother and sister. With skills training, he could establish a new relationship with his siblings and set an example as big brother.

Lack of motivation is often cited as a reason for a client's lack of progress. The staff in the drug rehab residential program where I worked would often come to me and want to discharge a resident, because he was not motivated to change. All he wants they said is "three hots and a cot." My response was that part of our responsibility was to motivate the clients. Their standard response was, "If they don't want help, you can't help them. You can lead a horse to water but you can't make it drink." And my response was, "Yes, but you may make it thirsty."

Motivation is a big factor in treating alcohol and drug addiction, and in the beginning the motivation is almost always external. It is said that addicts don't come to residential drug treatment of their own accord. They are ordered by the courts, threatened with divorce by the spouse or with job loss by the boss, or warned of physical deterioration or death by the doctor. They don't come because they want to be clean and sober. After all, what did a person who had been addicted to drugs and/or alcohol every day for the last 10, 20, or 30 years know about a sober lifestyle, and why would they want it? Quitting in their minds meant facing possible painful withdrawals, removal of the one thing that they believed would help them tolerate their lives, and totally changing their lifestyle. This was made clear one day in group therapy:

Jack had been arrested for his fourth DUI and was facing major prison time. He had been in a car wreck after running a red light. The people in the other car, a mother and her six-year-old daughter, ended up being hospitalized with severe lacerations and bruises. Jack had pled guilty and had come to treatment to try to mitigate his sentence.

I asked him in group therapy what he would do when he finished the 28-day treatment and was awaiting going to prison. He freely admitted that he was going to get loaded every day before he went in. I was surprised, and in hopes of helping him change his mind, asked the rest of the group what they would do if they were in a similar circumstance. There were eight members in the group, and they all agreed they would do the same.

I was shocked and disappointed, but it became apparent to me the staff and I needed to educate the residents about the benefits and rewards of sober living, in addition to the disease concept of addiction and its effects on their lives. We had to paint a picture of recovery to which they could relate. So creating motivation was a big part of our mission.

10,000 Hours

Knowing what to do in therapy is extremely important. Malcolm Gladwell in his book, *The Outliers*, proposes that to be successful at anything, one must do it for at least 10,000 hours. People who do this are often outside the main stream, and hence the term, outliers. Gladwell gave numerous examples—from the Beatles to Steve Jobs—of people who spent hours and hours perfecting their profession. The Beatles played 6-7 hours a day, seven days a week, in a little nightclub in Hamburg, Germany, before they became famous. Steve Jobs spent almost every spare hour of his teenage life doing programming at a local college computer lab. If you're a counselor who sees twenty clients a week for an hour, that's a thousand hours a year. So, it would take ten years of doing counseling on a consistent basis to become effective

Hours, in and of themselves, do not necessarily make a good counselor. What they do, however, is give you exposure to many people and problems, expand your knowledge base, create the opportunity to try out different therapeutic approaches, and provide feedback in a way to learn about yourself and your ability to form relationships. (If you really want exposure to people, try working the ER at a hospital. It was there that I met a man who tried to circumcise himself, "trim it up a little bit," and an alcoholic who was tired of falling, so he had wrapped himself in bubble wrap, and that was all he had on when the police picked him up.)

Deliberate Practice
What are other factors that differentiate a good therapist from an excellent one?
What is the best predictor of a positive outcome?
How does one go about becoming an excellent therapist?

One person who set out to find answers to these questions is Scott Miller, founder of the Institute for the Study of Therapeutic Change, an organization composed of mental health professionals advocating excellence in behavioral health. Miller, along with Barry Duncan and Mark Hubble has spent the last 20 years studying what works in therapy. The trio began in an interesting way by taking on "impossible clients", who were referrals from other therapists of their most difficult cases. In this way, they started to learn what worked and what was not working, to find out how and why others failed, and what needed to be done to create successful outcomes. The tendency is to think the model of therapy made the difference. However, one of his discoveries was that the model of therapy and techniques used accounted for only 15% of the effectiveness of the outcome.

In an article in the *Family Therapy Networker*, Barry Duncan describes what they learned:

> Far more statistically significant to successful outcomes are what researchers label extra therapeutic factors–what clients bring into the therapy room and what influences their lives

outside of it. These factors might include persistence, openness, faith, optimism, faith, supportive grandmother, membership in a religious community or sense of personal responsibility: all factors operative in a client's life before he or she enters therapy. They also include interactions between such inner strengths, happenstance or luck at a new job, a marriage, a change in the weather, the crisis successfully negotiated that brings a husband and wife together. Lambert's 1992 analysis ascribes 40% of improvement during psychotherapy to such client factors.

Barry Duncan, Mark A. Hubble, Scott Miller "Stepping off the Throne," Family Therapy Networker, July/August 1997, pp. 22-35.

After reading an article written by a Swedish professor at Florida State University, K. Anders Ericsson, the world's leading authority on expertise, Miller became curious about how Ericsson's theories could be applied to the field of counseling. Miller contacted him to specifically see, if he could shed some light on what distinguished top performers in the counseling profession. Ericsson had conducted similar studies on the effectiveness in several populations, such as pool players, ballet dancers, health professionals, and athletes. In 2009, Ericsson worked to determine what creates top performance in counseling. One of the ways Ericsson arrived at this was by studying top-performing chess players. What created their effectiveness was determined by their willingness to analyze and come up with alternative options for each move, and not by how many games they won or how many chess books they read.

The key to both (and other fields of expertise) was what Ericsson labeled "deliberate practice," which means the therapist takes a concentrated approach to consciously improve his ability to do therapy. This involves building skills, being mindful, getting feedback and reflecting on it, and developing strategies for improvement. It means acknowledging limitations, pushing knowledge to the limits, and being willing to step out of our comfort zone to test and expand one's knowledge and skills. Deliberate practice requires among other things: good supervision, a desire to learn from each client, willingness to do research, and conscious evaluation of one's performance in an objective way.

Deliberate practice takes a lot of discipline. Most therapists may not be willing or even desirous of improving in this way. We have what Scott Miller calls a "risk-aversive error-phobic culture," that causes us to not want to leave our comfort zone. If we only deal within the realm of knowing, we will never learn new ideas or skills or grow personally or professionally. By taking this risk, the door from not knowing to knowing is open.

Developing Your Tool Kit

What do counselors have in their toolkits to help clients? There are two schools of thought. Some therapists have a single set of tools they use very proficiently. These tools work well for them and their clients, and are often evidence-based practices. Under pressure from managed care and nationally-funded programs administered by SAMHSA (Substance Abuse and Mental Health Service Administration), evidence-based practices have flourished. The advantages of such therapies are that they have a proven track record, a data base from which to operate, and a standardized procedure that has proven to work well. The disadvantages of some of the evidence-based practices are that they are too rigid, do not take into consideration the client's individual needs and circumstances, and the focus of therapy is on faithfulness to the model, not necessarily the client.

The other school of thought is eclecticism, which espouses tailoring the therapy to fit the client, since every client is different. At the far end of this continuum is a comment by Milton Erikson that you invent a new therapy for every client. Of course, that does not preclude having a specific framework from which to work—however generalized that might be. Beginning therapists usually described themselves as eclectic. Partially, this is due to the fact that they have not matured into any particular mode of doing therapy, or they don't have the experience or exposure to the different tools. The advantages of the eclectic approach are the flexibility to address each client's specific needs, and it operates on the principle that one size may not fit all. Disadvantages are that what is being done may not be effective, has neither history nor a method to measure its effectiveness, and may include too many therapeutic biases and idiosyncrasies.

Therapists often use tools that best match their personality and make-up. Interestingly, those tools are usually the ones they feel the most competent using. For example, a cerebral person may be drawn to cognitive-behavioral types of therapy. Therapists, who operates best on an emotional level, may be drawn to Gestalt Therapy. People, who are dramatic, might like psychodrama. Those who are musical might be drawn to music therapy, and people who like working with children might be drawn to play therapy. This is neither good nor bad.

Many novice therapists rely on their personality as their main therapeutic tool, since they are not particularly drawn to any one model of therapy. They tend to rely on caring, encouragement, and positivity as their approaches. This is not usually a problem as a beginning approach, unless they become content with this level of functioning and do not pursue expanding their skills into more defined therapies.

As Miller's research has shown, a therapist's technique or theoretical approach only accounts for 15% of the positive outcomes. Perhaps, the technique's degree of effectiveness may be more tied more to the therapist's belief and comfort with using the technique, rather than its efficacy. For example, I've been trained in hypnotherapy, but don't feel particularly effective using it. However, I am more comfortable using deep-relaxation and guided-imagery, which are cousins to hypnosis. They are both very effective in helping the clients change their state of consciousness, and subjectively, the state of consciousness reached by each of these techniques is comparable, if not the same.

Having specific tools in your tool kit can be both a blessing and a curse. If your tools give you the confidence and the approach you need to deal with difficult clinical situations, then they are a blessing. However, if your tools are limited, they may not meet client's needs. So, the key is to cultivate a variety of tools to cover a variety of situations.

PART TWO

Strategies

CHAPTER 3

Redefining the Solution

Nothing is impossible. The word itself says, "I'm possible."

—Audrey Hepburn

YOU'RE A THERAPIST, RIGHT? It's your job to find solutions to problems. But your client is sitting there presenting you with a problem for which you know no solution…or at least an *easy* solution. What now?

Often we cannot find a solution, because we are looking in the wrong place or thinking a solution should look a certain way or meet certain criteria. But there are many ways to arrive at solutions to problems.

Helping clients arrive at solutions by developing their goals or desired states and identifying the steps to achieve them is the key to effective therapy. Sometimes when the goal cannot be achieved directly, we must help the client to view the situation from a different perspective—to look for the unexpected.

Picture the Goal

A client once told me that when he and his wife went out to eat, they both try to be accommodating. One would say, "Where would you like to eat tonight?" and the other would say, "I don't care. Wherever you would like to eat is fine, honey." Unable to come up with a solution, they decided they would drive until they came upon a restaurant that both agreed was suitable. They ended up driving all over town considering various restaurants, still not able to decide, and never arriving at a final destination.

"How about that one?"

"Yeah, okay."

"It sounds like you really don't want that one."

"No, it's okay if you want to go there."

"Well, I don't want to go there if you don't."

"Well, where do you want to go?"

"I don't care, it's up to you."

And so it went. The lesson is if you don't know where you are going, it is pretty hard to get there.

The same is true for therapy. Not knowing what to do is often the result of not knowing where we are going. Some clients have no idea that there is a goal in therapy; they often just want to talk or unload their emotional burdens. Others may want the therapist to decide for them what they should do. In other cases, the therapist has one goal and client another. The therapist may see clearly what the client needs and push the client in that direction. For example, the client may not want to end a romantic relationship, while the counselor, seeing how destructive it is, tries to convince the client to let it go. Arriving at an agreeable goal is not always easy.

One of the most basic concepts in counseling and the foundation for treatment planning is the establishment of goals, and yet it can easily be overlooked. It is surprising how many times sessions seem to be going nowhere, and the reason is the loss of focus on the goal. When supervisees are having difficulty with a case, I often ask, "What is the goal?" This frequently draws a blank stare.

***

Many clients are neophytes with no concept of what is possible in therapy. When I first began doing therapy, there were times when, session after session, clients would just talk about their problems. I realized they had no idea there was much more that we could be doing in therapy besides talking about problems. To streamline the process of their figuring it out, that I developed a handout that I gave clients at the end of the first session, asking them to pick their desired level of therapy. The choices are:

a. **Just talk** – At this level, clients feel a need to just get things off their chest or know that someone else knows and understands what they are going through.
b. **Reality check** – Clients are looking to get some honest and impartial feedback about themselves and the ways in which they are living their lives.
c. **Problem-solving /decision-making** – Clients are conflicted and seek guidance in making life-changing decisions.
d. **Psycho-education** – Clients want to learn specific skills or acquire certain information.
e. **Change work** – This is the level of more intense therapy in which clients strive to resolve past trauma or overcome certain engrained, destructive or unconscious patterns.

Clients may start out at one level and progress to a deeper level. Additionally, I ask them to write goals using the following instructions:

Please write at least three goals using the following criteria:

1. *State each goal in a positive way, i.e., what you will do, not what you won't do. For example, a positive goal would be, "I want to be positive and strategic in my interactions with my children," instead of, "I need to quit yelling at my children."*
2. *State the action that you need to take, not what others need to do. For example, "Get my spouse off my back," would not be something you could do, but to state the goal as, "I need to detach myself from my spouse's complaining," would be something you could do.*
3. *Be specific. For example, "I want to develop a positive attitude towards myself and my family, and express it daily," is better than, "I want to be happy."*
4. *Apply to a specific time, place, or circumstance. For example, "I need to express to my father the next time I see him how what he said hurt me so much."*

By clearly stating their goals, the clients and I will know what we are working on, and more importantly, when we have achieved their goals and completed treatment. The most effective therapy happens when there is a meaningful vision of the future and a cognitive understanding of the process. In other words, clients know where they are going and how to get there. Ideally, arriving at the goals is a collaborative process requiring exploration with the client. The counselor becomes like a coach, creating energy and ideas that spur the person on. When clients are stuck or wavering, encouragement and enthusiasm can help them break through their inertia.

Many times, clients ask how they will know when they will be done with therapy. I tell them that when they are confronted with a difficult situation and can answer the question, "What would my therapist suggest I do?" they are ready. Even better is when the clients come up with suitable answers and are no longer dependent upon the therapist for solutions.

A Matter of Perspective

As counselors, we are presented with situations involving great tragedies with irreversible effects and consequences. There is no way to make these painful events just go away. Even when there are no apparent solutions or correctives, there are still options. One such option is to change the perspective of what happened.

Tony Robbins, a motivational coach, was interested in finding out the difference between people who were successful in their personal lives and careers and those who weren't. In other words, he wanted to determine the nature of excellence. One characteristic of these highly successful people was their resilience in the face of life challenges. One way people processed challenges in their lives, he observed, was to ask themselves questions. The kinds of questions successful people asked were significantly different from those asked by less successful or less resilient people. He determined that unsuccessful people operate from a set of questions that do not lead them to helpful conclusions, questions such as:

> Why does this always happen to me?
> What did I do to deserve this?
> How did I get so screwed up?
> Will this ever end?
> Why me?

Our minds are like computers that try to answer these questions. A question such as, "Why does this always happen to me?" is a rhetorical question to which there is no real answer. Consequently, the mind's computer spins out of control trying to find a suitable answer to solve the impossible. This process expends lots of energy and leads down a dark path to despair, confusion, and discouragement—all features of self-defeat.

The questions successful people ask do the opposite; they lead to clarity, solutions, and corrective actions. In other words, they create a new perspective. What are these questions? Good question! They are questions like:

What can I learn from what has happened?
How can I come out of this a better person?
What is the lesson for me to learn?
How can I use this to better myself?
How would successful people handle this?

Even a question such as, "What is funny about this?" automatically begins to change our perspective when asked sincerely. Finding the humor in a traumatic experience is a way to begin detaching from the negative impact of trauma and discovering that many perspectives are possible.

Ironically, some people hold onto their negativity as if it was a badge of honor. Convincing clients they can stop struggling and accept what has happened to them is a great challenge, because they have invested so much time and effort into the struggle. In his book, *Love is Letting Go of Fear*, Gerald Jamplosky gives the example of a person at sea holding onto a boulder that is causing him to sink. He is calling for help. People are yelling at him to drop the rock, but he argues, "I really worked hard for this rock. It is my rock, how can I let go of it?"

"But it is pulling you down," comes the reply.

"I know, but it's all I've got."

It is difficult to work with people who seem so invested in holding onto their misery. Identifying the secondary benefits is sometimes crucial to helping them overcome it. Using a metaphor like the one above can often help them see how they are sabotaging their own recovery.

Another interesting story that is very useful:

Once there were five-year-old twin boys, one a pessimist and the other an optimist. Wondering how two boys who seemed so alike could be so different, their parents took them to a counselor. The counselor took the pessimist to a room piled high with new toys, so that he could play. Next the counselor took the optimistic child to a room piled high with horse manure.

After ten or fifteen minutes, the counselor went back to check on the pessimist, expecting the boy to be thrilled. But instead the boy burst into tears. Puzzled, the counselor asked, "Don't you want to play with these toys?"

"Yes," the little boy bawled, "but if I did, I'd only break them and get in trouble, and there are no Legos, and they are my favorite thing."

Next, the counselor checked in on the optimist, who yelping with delight, had scrambled to the top of the pile, and was digging out scoop after scoop, gleefully tossed the manure into the air. "What on earth are you doing?" the counselor asked.

"Well," said the boy, beaming, "there's got to be a pony in here somewhere."

Teaching clients how to *find the pony* takes a good sense of humor, imagination, and optimism.

One of the counselors, whom I supervised, told me that he and his wife were distraught, because she had to have a hysterectomy to prevent her from contracting cancer. This was a huge disappointment; in that they had been undergoing fertility tests for many months. In a very interesting turn of events, he was present the same time I was doing an intake with one of his prospective clients. In sharing her medical history, she disclosed that a year before she had had a hysterectomy and gave a hearty laugh, "It was the best damn thing that ever happened to me!" she exclaimed. I snuck a look at him, and he gave a little grin and a slight nod of his head. It was a matter of perspective. Even though the irony was obvious, it did not erase the pain.

So, one of the goals of therapy is to help the client gain a new perspective— one that brings meaning to the issue, peace to the heart and mind, and a greater purpose in life. This is easier said than done.

The Farmer's Judgment: A Tale

Once upon a time there was a farmer who had some land a way outside the village. He had a son to help him and one good horse. Indeed, it was a magnificent horse. So magnificent, that when the King passed through the village, he heard about the horse and asked to see it.

The King was so impressed that he offered the farmer a considerable amount of gold for the horse. But the farmer would not part with his horse, and the King went away. The next day, the horse ran away! The villagers rushed to the farmer and exclaimed, "Oh, how awful. Your horse is gone and you don't have the gold! What a bad thing has happened to you!" The Farmer replied, "Well, I don't know that it's a bad thing, but I do know my horse is gone and that I don't have the gold."

A few days later, the farmer's horse returned. And, not only did the horse come back, he brought six wild and beautiful horses with him. Each would be worth a great sum once they were broken and trained. When the villagers heard, they rushed out to see the horses and to say to the farmer, "Oh, you were right! It was not a bad thing that your horse ran away. Now he has returned and brought you six more fine horses. It is a good thing! I don't know if it's a good thing or not," the farmer said. "I just know that my horse has come back and brought me six more horses." The following day the farmer's son was trying to break one of the wild horses and he fell off and broke both his legs. Again, the Villagers visited the farmer and they exclaimed, "Oh, you were right! It was a bad thing that your horse came back with six more horses. Now, your son has broken both legs and cannot help you with your crops. Surely you will suffer great losses. Oh, what a bad thing!"

And the farmer said, "Well, I don't know whether it's a bad thing or not. I only know that my son was thrown from a horse and that both his legs are broken."

The next day the King returned to the village. He was leading his soldiers to the border where the kingdom was engaged in a terrible battle with a neighboring country. The enemy was fierce and most of the young soldiers were marching to their death. As the King passed through the village he rounded up all the young men to join in the fighting. Of course, the farmer's son, with his broken legs, did not have to go. After the King and his men left, the villagers rushed to the farmer and exclaimed, "Oh, you were right! It was a good thing that your son fell off the horse and broke his legs. Now he will certainly not die in this war as will so many other young men.

The farmer replied, "Well, I don't know if it's a good thing, or not. But

I know that my son did not have to go with the King to fight this battle.

And so, the story goes.... Who knows if this is good or bad?

—www.cyber-key.com/mj/sufi.html

One can choose one's perspective, you see.

Changing History

Much of therapy is dealing with emotional wounds from the past. These can range from relatively mild to extremely abusive situations, but both can have an impact.

I remember coming home from school in the second grade very excited about something that had happened. My brother was there, and I enthusiastically blurted out, "Hey, guess what happened to me today!" Rather annoyed, he looked at me and said, "Aw, who cares?" It was as though he stabbed a knife into my heart. It never occurred to me that no one cared, something he basically affirmed. As a result, for many years as a child I did not share much with others thinking no one cared what I had to say. Still today, there is part of me that reverts to the message, even though I know it is not true. But that little statement had a tremendous impact on my life. And yet, the message seems so miniscule compared to the abuse suffered by many of the children with whom I have worked. I can only imagine the impact on a child who is daily being berated and belittled, and frequently beaten.

We cannot change the actual events that have happened, but we can change the way they are remembered, gain a new perspective, and neutralize the mental and physical effects of what happened.

Things of the past, while they may seem very real, exist in our memory and, as we know now, in our body. This seems obvious, but it is a very important fact when doing trauma therapy. When clients begin to re-experience childhood trauma, reminding them it is not happening now gives them a sense of control and a way to begin distancing from the historical experience. Additionally, when reminded they are now in a physically safe place (counselor's office), and they have gained knowledge and new coping skills unavailable to them at the time of the trauma, they can feel emboldened to revisit the painful experience.

Is it possible to change our history? Obviously, we cannot change the actual events that have happened, but we can change the way they are remembered, gain a new perspective, and neutralize the mental and physical effects of what happened. A classic example: a woman walks by the neighbor's house and sees the husband and wife yelling and screaming at each other. She draws a reasonable conclusion they must be having marital problems, and perceives them as very aggressive. Later she learns that what she witnessed was their rehearsing for a play. They were not actually fighting. So, in a way, we can say history was changed. What she thought and experienced as two people fighting was actually two people rehearsing for a play.

How does this relate to therapy? Seeing past experiences in a new light can diminish the negative impact on the person.

One of my clients shared that she had felt greatly rejected by her mother. Under hypnosis she recalled an incident in which her mother severely rebuked her for bringing flowers home for her mother and instead of welcoming the gesture, her mother yelled at her to get out told her to leave her alone. What was meant as a loving gift to her mother turned into a traumatic experience of rejection. I encouraged her to discuss it with her mother, since it seemed to still be so impactful. The next session she told me she had brought up the issue with her mother, despite her fearful anticipation of how her mother might respond. Recalling the incident, her mother apologized profusely telling my client, this was the day she found out her mother had cancer. The mother remembered feeling like her world was falling apart and did not want her daughter to see her so distraught; that was why she had wanted her to leave. Her mother was trying to protect her, not reject her, and had no idea her daughter had experienced her actions as rejection.

It is possible that much of our past is built on many false assumptions. This is not to say we should deny the experience, but that we should open to the idea that what happened may or may not have been as bad as we remember. Learning the truth, or at least another perspective, can have a profound healing effect. If the client can talk to others who were present at the time, a different perspective might become available.

We know that people's memories of the same situation can vary greatly, as research involving crime-scene witnesses has revealed. Recently, a teenage brother and his sister witnessed a suicide scene in which a friend had shot himself. Seeing the blood splatters on the bed and wall upset the brother tremendously, while the sister, who was preoccupied looking for a suicide note, barely noticed them. They were side by side, but had quite different recollections of the scene.

There are other ways of changing history. Another way is having the client see the past as a movie. This creates a whole variety of ways to modify the story and thereby ameliorate the impact. One can slow it down or speed it up, insert new scenes, and delete old ones.

Jake, a pediatric physician, loved to sail, but had a tremendous fear of bodies of water. He wanted desperately to overcome his fear. After investigation, we determined that his fear of the water related back to the time he was around 6-years-old, swimming in the ocean. A huge wave came, and he was caught up in it, tumbling and tumbling, getting scraped as he did. He was terrified thinking he was drowning. Luckily, he was near the shore, and his father rescued him. As he remembered the scene, he again became agitated. I suggested that he should relive the incident, but see it as a movie running in slow motion. While doing this, I suggested that as he was tumbling, he could get his bearings by paying attention to the lighter water, that indicated the direction of the surface and the darker water that indicated the bottom of the ocean. In this way, he could orient himself and know which way to aim his body. He also learned he did not have to fear for his life while he was re-experiencing it, because he now knew the outcome: he would be all right.

In another session, he watched the movie in his mind after having completed a deep-relaxation exercise. This was like watching a scary scene in a movie while being relaxed. The combination of relaxation and being able to slow down the movie helped him to overcome his fear. We were then able to have him do some desensitization at the pool, and finally, he could practice on the dock at the lake. He no longer had the original fear and gradually could get in and out of the water with no anxiety.

So, the once-unmanageable situation now became manageable. We did not change his past, only how he re-experienced it.

History can also be changed by inserting a new scene or situation into the memory. This can change the impact of the memory, even though the new scene is fictional. It is like when music was recorded on vinyl records; if the record got scratched, every time you listened to it, you heard the scratch. With the fictional insert, every time the person remembers the incident, they think of it in the new way. For example, people who felt helpless can imagine a friend or relative coming to their rescue or guiding them through the experience.

One of the more appalling stories I heard came from Lennie, a client whose father punished him by making him strip naked and lie spread eagle on the bed as he beat him with a belt. Lennie was so traumatized that he could barely get out the details of the story. I asked him if he would be willing to revisit the scene again, but this time bringing in whomever or whatever he could have had to help him. He immediately said, "Yes, I would bring in Superman. He would burst though the wall, grab my dad and push him up to the ceiling, telling him if he ever did it again, he would crush him with his bare hands." So we replayed the scene with the new insert, and he started smiling. He said that he felt as though he was no longer alone, and that someone was sticking up for him.

Well, this was a wonderful discovery. Now every time he remembered that situation, it was paired with Superman coming to his rescue. Even more importantly, it was **a child's solution to a child's dilemma**. It would not have been effective, if it had been his adult cognitive mind trying to come up with some rational way to handle it. This way the little child in him could be satisfied that he no longer had to endure that punishment alone.

Any way you can change the remembrance of the past can change the impact. This is one of the main principles of Eye Movement Desensitization and Reprocessing (EMDR). Having the client remember a traumatic incident, while moving his eyes in certain directions discharges the emotional impact of the situation. In a training session Ron Klein, director of the American Hypnosis Training Academy, had a participant tell a traumatic story of physical abuse by her stepfather, which was quite impactful. He then had her tell the same story using a high falsetto voice. She started laughing while telling it. Now every time she remembers it, she has a different response.

Break It to Me Gently

One way to soften the blow of the truth is what Dave Waters, retired psychiatrist at the University of Virginia, calls the "stroke-kick" approach. This involves giving the client feedback, but coating it with positive intention. Usually it goes something like, *"I know you have good intentions and want to do the best thing (stroke), but when you do that, there are all these negative consequences (kick)."* When working with parents, a common example is, *"You obviously care deeply for your children and want the best for them (stroke), but when you are so harsh in your approach, they come to resent you, rather than respect you"* (kick).

Another way to impart the truth harkens back to the early days of family therapy when a supervisor or team of colleagues would watch the therapy session through a one-way mirror giving helpful instructions by calling in by telephone to the therapist. For example, they may say, "Tell the father, the team believes he is hiding his true emotions, and they think deep down he is very regretful for the way he handled the situation." Sometimes the team was divided over what they saw and would call this in to be shared with the client. More strategically, sometimes the team would mirror the client's ambivalence by saying half the team saw the situation one way (often benignly or even beneficially), while the other half of the team saw it much more critically. For example, they might say part of the team did not believe the mother was putting forth effort to protect the children (the real message), and part of the team felt like she was doing the best she could. The family member could hear the critique, and at the same time, feel understood. This is like the stroke-kick technique above, but with the additional authority of "the experts behind the mirror."

Well, this kind of supervision is rare these days, and one does not always have the luxury of getting feedback from a team of experts. However, the same dynamic can be applied without the use of a mirror and a team behind it. This is done by saying, **"Part of me sees you this way, and another part of me sees you another way."** Thus, you can encapsulate the client's ambivalence and acknowledge the self-destructive pattern the client is exhibiting and still be seen as being encouraging and not judgmental.

The Answer vs. Answers

Many clients come to counseling looking for an answer to their dilemma. Many of them do not know exactly what to expect from counseling. Their hope is that counseling will provide a quick solution to their problem. Often clients want someone else in their life to change–a child to behave better, a husband to communicate more, a wife to be more affectionate, a boss to be the less demanding, etc. Clients can, therefore, be disappointed when they discover there's no easy answer. As stated before, change takes effort and people are often not willing to put forth the effort.

Then there are clients with dilemmas for which there are no easy answers–a mother who's recently lost a child, a wife who remembers the first time being sexually abused, a person diagnosed with terminal illness, a child who has been given a complex diagnosis such as autism or bipolar disorder, or a couple who cannot resolve their differences. Many times there is no one answer. Generally, however, answers evolve over time as the client explores the different dimensions of the problem without being able to directly resolve the situation.

I have several friends and family members with complex medical diagnoses, including cancer. No one medication or treatment will cure the illness, but a variety of possibilities can be explored. Each one can bring a little hope, and perhaps a little progress in the person's condition. The same is true for psychotherapy; clients come in with situations that are overwhelming to them. Instead of looking for **the** answer, it is more productive to spend time looking at different alternatives and selecting the best among them. These could be techniques for coping, adopting a new perspective on the situation, or learning how to manage the symptoms.

One of my core counseling beliefs is that **the answers are out there somewhere**. I may not know them, but there are always new ideas, techniques, or just ameliorating ways of looking at a situation. My wife had multiple chemical sensitivities, such that she could be around certain kinds of perfumes or scented products. This limited where she could go and how she could travel (e.g., she couldn't stay in hotels, nor travel on a plane, etc.). For years, we hoped we could find one treatment or therapy that would *cure* her. As we have learned, there is no such cure. There were, however, a plethora of little steps she learned take to help her situation, such as avoiding certain places, wearing a mask, utilizing alternative therapies, such as acupuncture, homeopathy, etc. While none of these alone was a cure, together they did improve her condition and allow her to keep going. Luckily, she has could build up her immune system to the point that now many of her symptoms and reactions are minimal.

Betty, who had a long history of sexual abuse as a child, began to have memories of those situations as she approached menopause. At first, she did not believe or want to accept what had happened, thinking her mind was just playing tricks. But as she began to dream and even have nightmares about the situations, she realized that they really had happened.

Initially, she wanted an easy answer. She asked to be hypnotized to make the thoughts go away. This was not easily done, because any one trauma can affect many different aspects of one's life and just making the thought go away does not dissolve the tangle of emotional web that the trauma weaves. She soon realized the memories would not automatically go away. However, there was a way to manage and heal from them.

The first step was to help her access a place within herself of peace and safety, a place of retreat, where she could go to counteract the fear and anxiety she felt when these thoughts came back. As she did this, she felt encouraged, but at the same time, she began having more flashbacks. She realized that overcoming the pain and healing from these events was a multi-step process.

We then focused on all the things she could do in her intimate relationship with her husband, and worked on strengthening those aspects. She also joined a support group, which helped to break down her walls of loneliness and isolation. She learned relaxation techniques and to take better care of herself by changing her diet and taking baths with soothing music and candles. She read inspirational books, and even tried her hand at writing some poetry. This led to her journaling and daily processing the things she was grateful for in her life. No one of these activities gave her the relief she so desperately wanted, but each one helped to chip away at the block of fear and hopelessness she had felt at the beginning of therapy.

She would come for counseling for a couple months, make some progress, then take some time off to process what she had learned and experienced. In this way, she became less discouraged and more motivated to continue. As she learned that she was in charge of her progress, she became more empowered, accepting that there was no magic wand to take away her pain and heal her. She could see counseling as a journey with progress and setbacks, and seeing herself on the road to recovery.

Skills vs. Problems

Doing therapy with children often involves working with parents who want to give the therapist a long list of problems and complaints about the child. Long ago, I adopted a rule that I don't allow the child to be present, when the parents talk about these problems. I did not want the child to associate counseling with a litany of the problems he is having, which could reinforce these problems and lead to a self-fulfilling prophecy.

Ben Furman, author of *Kids' Skills*, developed an approach to work with parents in this situation, which was to have the parents make a list of the problems and then prioritize them. Then they list beside each problem the skill that is needed for the child to overcome the problem. For example, if the problem is angry outbursts or aggressiveness, the skill the child is lacking is expressing anger in a constructive way. If the child is disobedient and refuses to cooperate or participate in an activity, then the skill that is lacking is the ability to get motivated or the ability to negotiate.

Furman suggests that the therapist lists the problems on the left side of the paper and the skills on the right. Then the therapist tears the piece of paper in half, wads up the *problem* half, and tells the parents the focus of therapy is not going to be on the problems, but the *skills* the child is lacking. It is difficult for the parents to accept that the skills are more important than the problems. They find it much easier to complain about the problems than to provide solutions by teaching children new skills.

Jerrod was 14 and had gone to live with his grandmother, since his mother was on drugs and could not manage him. Grandmother, in contrast, was very accomplished and lived in a very nice home in the country. The grandmother asked little of Jerrod, only to cut the grass. No matter how much she urged, begged, or threatened to get him to do this one simple chore in return for all that she had done for him (bought him new clothes, provided him a decent living environment, and gave him a weekly allowance), he refused. After all attempts to get him to respond had failed, the counselor finally asked, "Why won't you cut your grandmother's yard after all she has done for you?" It took a lot of coaxing, but finally, he sheepishly replied, "I don't know how to start or run the lawn mower." He was ashamed he did not know, but the reality was that his mother's house had no grass in the yard, only dirt and weeds. He had never learned how to run a mower, and there had been no one to teach him. So, he not only needed the skill to start and run the lawn mower, he also needed the skill to express his needs and shortcomings without fear of reprisal.

The skill-building approach can be very effective with adults. Improving communications, managing feelings, building self-esteem, relaxation training are examples of skill-building that are beneficial.

Normalize and De-pathologize

People with a history of mental illness not only have to deal with their problems, but also the stigma of having these problems, which in and of itself becomes a problem. They begin to redefine themselves in derogatory terms using such expressions as crazy, dysfunctional, weak-minded, and screwed-up.

Emergency room staff see some of the most critical mental health problems. Drug overdoses, suicide attempts, and people who have reached the bottom and have nowhere else to turn are common situations. It is not uncommon for people in the middle of crisis to ask, "Do you think I'm crazy?" When I put myself in their situation, my standard response was, "I don't know how you have managed as long and as well as you have." I could say this honestly and sincerely, because I have not suffered from the depths of mental illness. Living life with mental illness can be compared to running a race with a cement block tied to your foot. While I am no stranger to adversity, given some of the horror stories I heard in the ER, I don't know if I could endure the conditions in which some people are forced to live or have chosen out of necessity or ignorance.

I told them, "You need to know it takes a lot of stamina, perseverance, and determination to go through what you've been through." They are usually surprised, because in no way do they see themselves as strong. What they could not see was…the fact they had survived was a positive, and despite all the serious crises in their lives, they were still struggling to survive. I asked what kept them going, thus turning the focus away from their dysfunction to whatever coping skills they had developed and utilized. This was not to minimize the struggle and seriousness of their situation, but rather to depathologize the situation by having them identify and reinforce their ability to sustain themselves and persevere.

I focused on their resiliency by asking a few questions like, "In the face of so many tragic situations, how have you managed to continue after all that you have been through?" or "What keeps you going?" I would get answers like, "I had to be there for my child," or "I am not a quitter," or even "I keep hoping I will get a break," and "I don't know; I guess I am just stubborn" This gave me great clues about what to work with, i.e., about their inner resources. Much of this thinking comes from solution-oriented therapy, which looks for what is working and tries to normalize the difficulty. I say to the patients "If I had to deal with what you have had to deal with, I might ask the same question."

This approach gives them a base from which to operate by focusing the spotlight on their strengths, rather than their weaknesses. For example, people may tolerate and/or try to deal with the situation for many months or years and see little progress. Slowly, it may take a toll on them to the point they consider suicide. I want to focus on how they could manage the situation for as long as they did. I want to be able to identify the specific skills that enabled them to endure whatever the situation was.

By identifying the clients' strengths and skills, the therapist begins to build a construct that allows them to take charge of their lives, rather than dwelling in the state of victimization.

By identifying the clients' strengths and skills, the therapist begins to build a construct that allows them to take charge of their lives, rather than dwelling in the state of victimization. It gives them hope, where there is seemingly little hope. It gives them a sense of wellness, rather than illness. So sometimes, the solution to the problem of not knowing what to do is to focus not on solving the problem, per se, but rather on building on the client's strengths. This way they can approach their problems with a new sense of empowerment, perspective, and tolerance.

Another way to normalize or de-pathologize a situation is to redefine its "meaning." It is easy for clients to get very worried about their plight. For example, one of the difficulties with anxiety disorders is that people get anxious about being anxious, which compounds their fear.

This became apparent when I worked with an accountant who was having panic attacks. He shared with me that he was under a lot of pressure at work to turn out lengthy monthly reports, as well as deal with routine purchases, and manage crisis situations that arose daily. He was a typical Type-A personality, very eager to please and willing to do whatever for the sake of the company. Even though he complained senior staff didn't read or even review many of the monthly reports he was asked to do, he berated himself for not being able to keep up. I asked him what his limit was, and he looked at me totally befuddled.

"What do you mean?" he asked.

I said, "How do you know when your boss is asking more of you than you can deliver?"

"I have no idea. I never even considered that. If he asked, I assumed I had to do it."

"Do you?" I asked.

"I don't think I have a choice," he replied.

"So even if the workload he is giving you is stressing you out to the point that you are having panic attacks, you still have to do everything?

"Absolutely," he exclaimed, "Your brain is telling you that you should be able to do anything and everything that is expected of you no matter what, because you are a committed, excellent employee. However, you do have a limit. Luckily, with these panic attacks, your body is telling you that you have reached your limit, even though your brain may be saying otherwise. So you can be thankful that you are having these attacks, because now you know when you have reached your limit, and you can utilize this to convince your boss you need to cut back."

Armed with this information and a little coaching, he could confront his boss about his workload and negotiate eliminating many of his reports. Normalizing and seeing his attacks as *friendly warnings*, reduced much of his fear and concern about them.

How can we de-pathologize depression? Part of depression is that people get depressed about being depressed. To get started, we need to revise the statement, "I am depressed," based on the principle that *how you verbalize or conceptualize a situation determines how you experience it.* What this statement implies is that everything I am is depressed. In an equation format, it would be: I = depression. It is impossible for depression to deal with depression. In order to cope with the depression, one needs to separate out some part of me that is not depressed. So, begin by changing the statement,

> "I am depressed," to
>
> "I have depression," to
>
> "I have depressed feelings or thoughts," to

"I am having depressed thoughts and feelings right now."

Having depression instead of *being* depressed places space between yourself and the disorder. It is much easier to recover from depression, if you have a self that has to give it up or let it go, rather than it being your total self. Reducing it to feelings and thoughts further reduces its impact. Finally, being able to conceptualize that it is only happening *now* implies that may not always be present. The phrase, "This too shall pass," is tremendously helpful.

A similar approach from Narrative Therapy can be used. Whatever problem the person is having is described in third person. So, for depression, the questions might be:

> When did depression come into your life?
> What is depression trying to do for you?
> How is depression your friend?
> How is depression your enemy?
> What would it take for you to say goodbye to depression?
> What would you lose if depression left you?
> What would you gain if depression left you?

These questions also convey the idea there is a "you" that is separate from and, therefore, can control the depression, which is a major step in overcoming it. They also hint that depression is temporary and may not always be around.

Thinking Outside the Box

One problem clients have is not being able to see beyond their own situation and how to get out of it. It's as if there is a heavy burden on top of them, and they cannot figure out how to turn it around so that they come out on top of the burden. Because they are so engrossed in the problem, they are blinded to the alternatives.

Mullah Nasrudin lost his house keys and was standing under a street light looking for them. His best friend came by and said, "O Mullah, what are you doing?"
"I am looking for my keys," he replied.
"Where do you think they might be? I will help you," his friend proffered.
"Oh, I lost them over there," and he pointed to a dark field.

CHAPTER 3: REDEFINING THE SOLUTION

"Well, why are you looking for them here?"
The Mullah replied, "There is more light here."

According to the Mullah's thinking, his solution seems logical, yet he is not seeing the whole picture. How does one go about thinking outside the box? The first thing to consider is that there are always other ways of thinking about the situation. Just because you haven't thought of them does not mean they don't exist. Obviously, this involves keeping an open mind and being receptive to seeking out other's ideas. Part of the process of therapy is to cooperatively brainstorm and develop other ways of conceptualizing the problem and solution.

Jersey was a fellow psychologist who felt driven to write. He had written several articles only to have them rejected by publishers. This had a profound impact on him, and he developed writer's block. He came to me to overcome this problem, so that he could continue to write. We did several exercises to help him relax before he started writing, as well as visualizations in which he could imagine the words flowing out of his mind onto the paper. These had some impact, but he was still not satisfied with the amount or quality of his writing.

One day I decided to step back and ask him the bigger question of why he felt compelled to write, and what he hoped to get out of it. He hesitated and seemed to think long and hard before answering. Finally, he said that he had certain feelings and ideas that he wanted to communicate to others, things that he had learned and experienced over the years and felt would be useful to share.

Thinking outside the box, I asked him if there was some other way he could communicate these thoughts and feelings besides writing. He was totally intrigued by this idea and said that in the back of his mind he thought he could do this with art. I had no idea he was an artist. He said he wasn't, but that he thought he would enjoy experimenting with it. I encouraged him to explore this. The next session as we began to talk, he pulled out two amazing drawings. One was a very intricate Mandala with major aspects of his life symbolically embedded. He also had drawn a truly remarkable picture of a man's life in different stages struggling with alcohol. He said he felt like a new person, and that he had uncovered a whole new aspect of himself that not only had lain dormant, but which he had no idea even existed. Several years later, I got an invitation to an art gallery show displaying his latest drawings and paintings.

The old saying, "There is more than one way to skin a cat," (why on earth anyone would even want to skin a cat is beyond me) holds true in therapy.

Trial and Error

> *I have not failed; I have just found 10,000 ways that it won't work.*
>
> —*Thomas Edison*

Trial and error is one of the least favorite techniques, but one of the most common. When seen in the light of "There is no failure only feedback," it is integral to the counseling process. Even the most scientific of approaches involves trial and error. The use of psychotropic medications is a clear example. Each medication has the potential to affect each person differently. The process of trial and error is the only way to know how a medication will affect the person. Part of this process is progressive approximation. Each step in the process gets you a little closer to the answer.

Trial and error is not necessarily the avenue of last resort; just encouraging people to talk about themselves and their situation involves trial and error. You try to have them to understand and be open to the process of therapy; sometimes they are receptive and sometimes they are not. One way to gauge the success of trial and error is through direct feedback from the client.

I once saw a couple with marital problems who were referred by the employee assistance program. One of my approaches, based on solution-oriented therapy, was to talk about the positive experiences they had in their marriage. (Most people who come in for marriage counseling expect to talk about their problems, and they usually have their defenses up. I have a big couch in my office, and I am often amazed at how far apart two people can get on that couch. One of the subtle ways I measure progress is how close together they start sitting as therapy proceeds.)

So, I had them to talk about their successes, and even more directly, what drew them together, what they liked about each other. This often warms up the room for further discussion. It also gives them a message that there is more to counseling than just airing problems.

I spent most of the hour exploring what they loved about each other, how they met, and what was significant in their lives. They could share a lot of very positive things. When the session was over I thought it went well, and I was looking forward to our next meeting. Later that week, however, I got a call from the EAP counselor, who stated they were not interested in coming back. I told him I was surprised, because it seemed like we had a very good session. They were receptive, and we talked about many positive things, and they left seemingly in a good mood. He said they had shared all of that with him, but what they wanted was to talk about their problems, and it seemed I was not interested in hearing about them.

Well, this was feedback of a surprising nature, and I told the EAP counselor that I would definitely focus on the problems, if they were willing to come back and give me another chance. Fortunately, they were, and they ended up continuing therapy for several months.

So, this is trial and error. I tried to do solution-oriented, talked about strengths, and got feedback that this was not what the couple wanted. I did not feel bad about that. I felt good that the couple could share what they wanted out of therapy, and that I could shift gears. Not many clients will be so forthcoming to give the therapist that kind of feedback. Since then, especially after at the of the first session, I always ask, "Does what we did today meet your expectations and needs?"

Self- Healing Tools

> *Give a man a fish, he can eat a meal. Teach him how to fish, and he can eat for a lifetime.*
>
> *-Unknown*

The use of psycho-education is integral to therapy. People not only benefit from answers to their problems, but also the means, i.e., the tools of change. We can teach these tools of change by introducing the principles, modeling them, and applying them to different situations. What are these tools?

1. **Understanding** – I had a college professor say if you want to hate someone, don't try to understand them. One of the best ways to overcome anger and resentment is to understand why a situation happened.

2. **Communication** – You can clear up years of frustration by learning how to express your thoughts, feelings, and ideas in a constructive, non-harmful way.

3. **Processing** – Taking a critical, yet non-judgmental look at situations and playing out new scenarios empowers the people to gain new insight and skills to manage their difficulties.

4. **Serenity/Acceptance** – This is something for which we all struggle. Yet during a crisis, especially if we have been harmed, it is not possible, unless we have taught ourselves to turn our concerns, hurts, and worries off. Little prayers or saying such as, "Change me O Lord, not my circumstances," "Let go and let God," or the Serenity Prayer help us put things in perspective.

5. **Forgiveness** – Forgiveness is not about saying what happened in the past was okay, but it is about letting go of situations *for our own healing*, and that holding onto resentment only poisons us; it does not affect the person who wronged us. They may be oblivious to it, in total denial of it, or discount it as your overreacting. In many cases, they are not the ones suffering; we are.

6. **Self-disclosure** – The general fear is that if people know what I think and feel, they will reject me. And yet expressing these inner feelings and thoughts often endears others. I have often thought that, if I could get a group together and have members write down their deepest, darkest secrets, the messages would not be too dissimilar. We all have much more in common than we know.

7. **Catharsis** – Holding on to resentment, anger, and bitterness is like an emotional cancer that eats away at us. Sometimes the only way to get over something is to go through it. Being able to "get it out" is healing. This takes trust and time to develop the courage to express these deeply held emotions.

8. **Service to others** – Don't underestimate the healing power of helping others. Twelve Step programs derive much of their effectiveness from recovering people helping others. The saying, "The best way to get it, is by giving it away," exemplifies the spirit of this approach.

9. **Goal setting** – As stated before, setting goals is integral to the therapeutic

process, but it also can help in the day-to-day process of making gains.

10. **Compassion** – In the midst of feeling terrible about our life and our self, if something happens to a loved one, like an accident, all our self-absorption immediately is replaced by compassion for the other person. Likewise, if we can learn to develop compassion for ourselves and accept our trials and failures, we can begin the journey to recovery. Certainly, there are other tools, but utilizing the above tools can go a long way in overcoming our difficulties and arriving at effective solutions.

CHAPTER 4

Difficult Clients

Be kind whenever possible. It is always possible.

—Dalai Lama

ASK ANY THERAPIST ABOUT THEIR MOST DIFFICULT CLIENTS, and you will almost always get an immediate groan, loud laugh, or expletive. These clients stick in our minds and cause us to question why we ever became counselors. They can be humiliating, puzzling, challenging, and embarrassing. More than any other situation, they are the clients who activate our insecurities about what to do. Finding the middle path to work with them is one of the greatest challenges of counseling.

I often think when working with a difficult client that there are therapists who work with these kinds of clients and do not find them at all difficult. This leads me to two questions: 1. What am I missing that I find this client so difficult? and 2. Where are those therapists, so I can refer this client?

It is important not to confuse difficult clients with complicated clients. Just because a case is complicated does not mean the client is being difficult. Very cooperative clients can have very complicated cases.

There is a certain protocol to develop in working with people who are difficult, and when followed, the net difficulty tends to disappear ... or at least becomes manageable. The key is an effective therapeutic relationship. When working with difficult clients, the saying, "A rising tide lifts all boats," should be applied.

In other words, **the more effective the relationship with the client, the less difficult the client.**

The Ideal Client

Jackie comes in for therapy. She is bright, attractive, well-dressed, intelligent, able to articulate her problem, insightful, and eager to try anything asked of her, pleasing personality, straight-forward, totally appreciative of any help you give her, makes major progress with little guidance, and pays her bill in cash before the session. Who could ask for anything more? The problem is…well, good luck. If this is your hoped-for client, you will be sorely disappointed. This kind of person either doesn't exist or doesn't need a counselor.

But if your ideal client is someone who has a variety of problems, has his defenses up, lacks trust in anyone (especially "shrinks"), challenges you along the way, confuses easily, and is not motivated to change, then you are in luck. How could this be your ideal client? It could be, if you enjoy the challenge, want to test your limits, and expand your expertise.

One of my ideal clients was Garth, a 16-year-old client with black-painted finger nails and eye shadow, dog collar, ripped jeans, black spiked hair, and all kinds of chains. My first impression of him was not very favorable. What made him ideal, however, was the he helped me see and overcome my prejudice and tendency to make assumptions. Because as I got to know him, I discovered he was an honor-roll student, never did drugs, was president of a state Christian youth organization, and was incredibly intelligent, articulate, and insightful, which contradicted all my stereotypes of him. When I asked him what the deal was with his appearance, he said, "I am very aware of how I present and my impact on people. And you know what, Jon? If they can take the time to get past my appearance and find out who I am as a person, then those are the people I want for friends." Wow.

He taught me about myself and helped me grow, and I could help him overcome some emotional trauma. And even if he did meet all my stereotypes, I had no reason but to give him the greatest respect as any other person, which was the bigger lesson. For me, the ideal client is one I can learn from, and whose life I can significantly impact.

How to Make a Difficult Client

How to make a difficult client may sound a little strange, because 1. it seems like they already come difficult and, 2. I am understanding and compassionate; how can I make someone be difficult? It is a subtle process that no one sets out to do, but there are several ways we do it. Some of these items come from my own experience of having received counseling. Being on the other side can be quite enlightening, because we experience what the client experiences. I found myself becoming difficult and resistant in reaction to some of the counselor's suggestions or observations. Here are some of the ways we may contribute to a client being difficult:

Lack of Sensitivity to the Clients

- **Not tuning into them and jumping to conclusions.** To prove our prowess as a therapist, we may push to come up with ideas and answers without really taking time to truly understand what the questions are.
- **Taking them in a direction they don't want to go.** No matter how sensible or rational an intervention is, if the client is not on board, it will result in a power struggle and/or the client's refusal to cooperate.
- **Having an agenda that overrides their agenda.** Therapists tend to not be aware of having an agenda with clients. It is easy to think, "I am only trying to help," or "I only want what is best for the client." The assumption is that the therapist knows what is best for the client. For example, if a client seems to be in a troublesome relationship, the counselor may see how this is a pattern related to the client's belief that they don't deserve anyone better. However, it may be the client is not ready to accept that and wants to work on the relationship no matter how dysfunctional it is.
- **Being too authoritative.** It is well-known that many adolescents have difficulty with people in authority. Unfortunately, this attitude exits beyond adolescence. Many clients do not want or respect the therapist being commanding or imposing. While being

authoritative may seem benign to the therapist, it may stimulate negative feelings from the client's past. Clients may feel belittled and grow resistant to any further interventions.

- **Glossing over significant points.** When clients talk about their situation, therapists can easily make assumptions about what is important and what is not, based on their own experience and the need to appear knowledgeable. To make sure you are on track, you need to check in with the client. For example, "You have talked about several concerns. Which one would you like to focus on first, or is most important to you?"

- **Not consulting with them about solutions.** Counselors will come up with ideas and try to sell them to the client, thinking the client is looking to the counselors for answers. Clients can see this as coercion, or at least, not relevant. A simple question like, "Do you think that would work for you?" allows the client to be a co-creator of the solution. Even better is just to ask, "Given what we have talked about, what do you think would work for you in this situation?"

- **Getting into a power struggle.** I tell the counselors I supervise if you get into a power struggle with a client, you have already lost. Counseling should be a cooperative effort, not a *winner-loser* situation. If the counselor *wins* the power struggle, the *a priori* assumption is that the client lost and therefore, the counselor made him/her a loser—not a situation in which any professional should be.

Seeing Clients in a Negative Light

- **Doubting their truthfulness, when they are telling the truth.** Nothing can destroy a client-therapist relationship like accusing clients of lying when they are telling the truth. Even if you think they are in denial and are just pointing this out, it can be offensive. If they are lying and it is pointed out, this can destroy the relationship. It does not mean you don't address what you perceive as untruthfulness, but better to take it on as your problem. Say, "I'm sorry I have such a hard time believing you."

- **Not trusting them.** The best rule in working with clients regarding trust is, "You need to trust the person until you have a reason not to trust." And even if this happens, the issue is not whether clients can be trusted, but what causes them to be distrustful? Maybe you have not won their trust, and you are the one that needs to change. Maybe they have a long history of being hurt, when they trusted others, and they are testing you. Some therapists get highly offended if a client "gets over on them." This is bound to happen, especially when working with addicts and sex offenders. The goal is to build the best relationship, so these issues can be addressed.

- **Misjudging their character.** Often clients' reputations precede them. Some counselors prefer not to review any information from outside sources, until they have met with the clients, so as to not prejudice themselves. I have many times been surprised when a client did not match the description or degree of difficulty I was told to expect. We all have some prejudices and a tendency to be judgmental. I once took an inebriated client to the ER, who was very calm when we walked in, but within minutes of being there, the triage nurse and he were yelling at one another. He had been in counseling with me previously and never caused a problem. However, he immediately took offense at the way this nurse addressed him and interacted with him. I too was surprised by her tone and manner. I thought later she has must have had bad experiences with alcoholics, maybe even grew up in an alcoholic family, and automatically put up her guard. A great corrective for overcoming judgmentalness is a saying from Alcoholics Anonymous, "There, but for the grace of God, go I."

- **Siding with others against them.** One of the trickiest situations you can encounter in doing couples or family counseling is making sure that you are not only seen as impartial, but also as supportive, even when one person is obviously the instigator of the problem. You should toe a fine line, and if the balance shifts too dramatically, there is a good chance you will lose one of the participants. If this happens with a couple. it is a good idea to separate them and do individual sessions until the issue can be resolved.

- **Siding against them**. This is often a problem when dealing with adolescents, who automatically assume you are on the parents' side, especially if parents are paying for the counseling. However, if they see you are on their side (which is many times a new situation for them), they will be more open. Parents may react when they see this bonding and say, "He is just pulling the wool over your eyes." It is important at this junction to say in private, "I know it seems like I am siding with your child, but I have to do this to win her trust and find out what the real issues are. Just bear with me until I can find out the truth."

Poor Therapeutic Practices

- **Being inconsistent.** Comments from clients about past experiences with counselors often contain complaints like, "I never knew what kind of mood he would be in," or "I could never get a straight answer from her," or "I often did not know what he was trying to tell me." These kinds of inconsistencies undermine the effectiveness of therapy. Consistency builds trust and establishes some safe boundaries. Inconsistency leads to confusion, uncertainty, and insecurity. Repetition, structure, follow-through and asking for feedback are key to developing consistency.
- **Sarcasm.** Any attempt to get back at the client or cast them in a poor light, no matter how subtle or justified, will surely back-fire on the therapist. This will break the bond of trust and cooperation.
- **Giving up on them.** Some clients, especially those with personality disorders, may test the therapist by being obstinate and challenging. They may tell you they are no good and not suited for therapy, or therapy is not working, or that you are no good and don't know what you're doing. If you agree and decide to discharge them for lack of progress, they can become deeply hurt and offended. It is

better to set some mutually-agreed-upon goals and a time frame within which to reach them. Make sure that some of the goals are easily attainable, so the client can get some experience of success. If they don't meet the goals and timelines, that becomes the deciding factor for discharge, not the therapist's frustration level or clinical judgment.

- **Taking it personally.** When challenged, disrespected, or otherwise provoked by a client, it is easy to take it personally. The attitudes and behaviors clients present to you at these times are often the source of many of their problems, and certainly did not originate with you. I constantly have to remind supervisees, "It's not about you." Therapists often become the receptacles of client's resentment, frustrations, and anger. "Deep down inside the difficult client is a very anxious person who is trying to cope with a painful and vulnerable existence" (Kottler, 1992). That is not to say that you should take abuse from clients. This calls for setting strong barriers with the client, but in a respectful and, hopefully, teaching way. You may say, "I understand your frustration right now, but that kind of talk is disrespectful and not acceptable. Let's look at some other ways to deal with what you are going through right now."

Counselors can get drawn into all the above without even realizing it. It takes counselors with humility and integrity to admit they are part of the problem, and they need to change and/or apologize. The travesty is not that any of the above happens, since we are all human, but that counselors refuse to accept their part, or even deny it, and place all the blame on the client for being difficult.

What's the Difficulty?

Clients are difficult not only because of what they do and how they do it, but also because of how they are perceived and labeled by their therapists.

—*Jeffery Kottler*

Tess was a prideful, middle-aged woman who had become a crack addict. She came from a very good family, but ended up becoming addicted to drugs after an auto accident, and eventually turned to crack. She was spurned by her family, ended up on welfare in public housing, and supported herself by selling her medication, which she could convince several doctors to prescribe for her.

While waiting for her daughter, who was seeing another counselor in our practice, she spotted me in the waiting room and said that she was drawn to me. Later she described it as feeling a mystical connection to me. I agreed to see her, and she soon became very dependent, seeing me at least once a week and often calling for additional sessions. While she was receptive, kind, and humorous, she was very frustrating, since she would sabotage almost every effort that I made to rescue her (which was my goal—not hers). I wanted to restore her to her former lifestyle, but she was resigned to her current way of life. It took me many sessions to realize that though she suffered a lot, she seemed to take pride in her ability to endure adversity, which also gave her reasons to continue with therapy. Yet, when I finally caught on and began to validate her need to live in crisis, she accused me of giving up on her. It was like I was her source of hope that kept her going while allowing her to self-destruct, knowing I would be her life-line. I ended up feeling trapped.

One day, l realized that since she had cast our relationship as "mystical," I subconsciously felt I needed to meet all her expectations of me. When I could truly let go of that and give myself permission to start distancing myself from her, then she could gain some independence. She escalated into a crisis and was hospitalized with an overdose. She called for help, and I was able to coach her through the situation over the phone, emphasizing all that she had learned and gained as a client. I told her I would only see her again in a month, if she got into Narcotics Anonymous, got a sponsor, and stayed clean, so we could celebrate her success. She did all of that and came in for a session. We could talk about all the positive things that happened and wonderful lessons she had learned. We had two more sessions about three months apart each time sharing her insights and blessings that were now part of her life.

What made her difficult to treat? Like I said she was pleasant and eager to participate in treatment, but it was her willingness to suffer rather than change, that proved so frustrating, and that I failed to recognize and to accept that as her reality.

So, let's think of some ways clients are difficult:

- The client, who seems to enjoy coming to therapy, but is not interested in changing.

- One who challenges the therapist and feels like he must always have the upper hand.
- Someone who is verbally aggressive.
- Someone who is nonresponsive and determined not to engage in the process of therapy. This is often seen with adolescents.
- Someone who thinks he/she are always right and have all the answers.
- Someone who complains and whines about the therapy not working.

There are so many ways to classify difficult clients—almost as many as there are negative characteristics of clients. Any behavior or personality trait, if taken to the extreme, can be difficult. Take friendliness, for example. It is hard to believe that being overly-friendly could be difficult. I call it the "warm-puppy syndrome." We all love and adore cute little puppies. They are so cuddly, energetic and lovable. We love to hold them, give them kisses, and let them lick our face … for a time. But after about five minutes, we are done with all the cuddly stuff, and they are not. They still want to jump in our lap, no matter what we do to discourage them, slobber on our faces, squirm all over, and if too excited, pee on our clothes. Enough of the friendliness! We have all experienced people like this who are out-going, complimentary, and super-sweet, but that is all. After a while, it seems like a show, not very genuine, and then becoming irritating.

> **There are so many ways to classify difficult clients—almost as many as there are negative characteristics of clients. Any behavior or personality trait, if taken to the extreme, can be difficult.**

Difficulty by Diagnosis

Diagnostic categories are another way to think about difficult clients. Certain diagnoses are notorious for being difficult to treat. Almost any counselor, psychologist or psychiatrist will tell you that people with borderline personalities are one of the most difficult. Closely associated with this are narcissists and sociopaths, as well as many of the other personality disorders. Eating disorders, severe depression, bi-polar, schizophrenia, PTSD, and dementia would probably round out the category. It is not the diagnosis, per se, that makes such clients difficult to treat, it is the manifestation of specific traits, symptoms or qualities that make them difficult to treat, i.e., what do they do or don't do that makes them difficult?

Ten Characteristics of Difficult Clients

Here are some major categories:

1. Unmotivated

Meeting a new client always seems to be a great opportunity to make a difference in someone's life. When we start to work with clients and find they are unmotivated, it is easy to become disappointed or discouraged. There are many reasons for lack of motivation. Some people come to therapy to please or appease others and are not invested in it. Others may not believe in therapy or do not believe therapy will work for them. Some do not believe in themselves and their ability to make changes, and some are heavily defended and do not want to accept that they need to change. Clients who are not motivated for therapy may also be unmotivated in many other areas of their lives. They have had little success with their own efforts. It is easy to become discouraged with them, but if we could see the process by which that person became unmotivated, like time-lapse photography, we would be more compassionate. This can sometimes be seen when working long-term with children. It is sad, frustrating, and even heartbreaking, to see a child being barraged by constant criticism give up hope, adopt a sense of failure, and stop trying.

Solution – Generally, what is needed is some way to up-the-emotional-ante either positively or negatively. Clients are motivated by fear of consequences or anticipation of reward. By helping them to project into the future the positive and negative consequences of changing or not changing, you can find a tipping point that will engage them in the desire to change. Working with negative consequences can be more difficult, because people get used to the negative bit by bit, and it becomes semi-comfortable. It is like putting a frog into hot water.

If you place a frog into a pot of water and slowly turn up the heat, it will stay there until it boils. However, if you put a frog into a pot of boiling water, it will jump out. So, the shock of the consequence has to be severe enough that the person will not become complacent.

Working for the positive also has its downside in that often clients do not know what is possible. If you ask them, "If this problem goes away how would your life be different?" Often they are at a loss. Helping them develop an awareness of how their lives could be better is a critical step in the process of change. Next is giving them the encouragement and belief that change is possible, and a step-by-step approach to get there.

2. Complainers

These are the clients who seem to only want to vent their feelings and express how everyone else is wrong or doing them wrong. They complain about family, friends, and their job. If you try to help them, they eventually complain about you. The payoff for doing so is they feel self-righteous and can easily blame others for their problems. Other complainers take satisfaction in playing the role of victim, hopefully to elicit sympathy and concern. There is a Catch-22 with complainers: if you agree with them, then they are reinforced. If you disagree with them, that adds more fuel to the fire. Being able to find the middle path is a challenge.

Solution – The first step (as always) is to build a relationship with them— based on mutual respect. It's not a matter of having to dispute or overcome their complaint or complaining. One can listen patiently and process their complaints with them. The next step is to have them define what they want. If you are using the NLP model, help them to determine what state they want and point out how complaining will not get them there. Also, help them to discover the payoff for complaining and explore other ways to attain that payoff without having to complain. Once they determine that you are on their side, they are much more likely to back off and cooperate. From a solution-oriented point of view, you may take another approach to help them find and discuss areas of their lives for which they have appreciation, which is the opposite of complaining.

3. Why don't you? Yes, but'ers

Eric Berne, who created Transactional Analysis, wrote *Games People Play*. In the book, he describes a whole set of transactions between people called games. Games are… "a series of interactions (words, body language, facial expressions, etc.) between two or more people that follow a predictable pattern. The interactions ultimately progress to an outcome in which one individual obtains a payoff or goal. In most cases, the participants of the games are unaware that they are 'playing.'"

—*www.ericberne.com/games-people-play/*

One of the games with which most counselors are familiar is "Why don't you? Yes, but." Basically, the game is: the therapist gives the client several suggestions and says, "Why don't you…?" The client responds with, "Yes, but…" followed by several objections about why the suggestion would not work. If this happens occasionally, it's no big deal, but if every suggestion is countered with "Yes but…," this can be a big source of frustration, since it seems like the client is not interested in your sagely advice. According to Berne, games have a payoff, and the payoff for this game is that the client proves that there is nothing that can help them. Therefore, they have been right all along—they are a hopeless case, or they don't have to change, because nothing will work.

Solution – Stop brainstorming solutions, since that only reinforces the idea that the situation cannot be fixed. Instead, there are other options:

1. Listen and give no advice.
2. Observe that this may not be the right time to change.
3. Suggest the fear or dread of change is so great that it cannot be risked as this time.
4. Explore the secondary benefits of not changing.
5. Build up their confidence and inner resources by identifying strengths that can be brought to the situation instead of solutions, and
6. Finally, toss the ball back into their court, asking what they think they should do, suggesting you don't have the answers, but can only help them find what will work for them.

4. Challenging

Counseling is an interesting profession. One assumption is the counselor must know more than the client about any given situation, but the reality is that *counseling is the art of knowing how to respond to others no matter what the situation*. Clients challenge counselors for a variety of reasons: 1. It is their personality—often to cover up their own sense of inadequacy. 2. They enjoy the intellectual sparring. 3. Their gruff exterior is a cover-up for poor self-esteem. This can happen with the small-man syndrome, men who are physically small who come across as very challenging and 4. Challenging may be cultural. Some clients developed this persona to survive in the environment in which they grew up. They are very cut-to-the-chase people, and immediately want to know my credentials, how therapy is going to help them, and how much I am going to charge. One even tried to get me to agree to refund his money if he didn't improve, which made sense from his point of view. (I didn't take him up on it, since he could easily sabotage any efforts on my part.)

Solution – There are two directions to go when working with challenging people: 1. Avoid power struggles and being confrontational, disagreeable or authoritarian. This requires the counselor to discover the client's interests and/or line of reasoning and go with it. 2. The other approach is almost the opposite: to match them one-on-one, not backing down, yet at the same time remaining positive and constructive. Some clients respect this kind of assertive approach.

A technique that is often useful and disarming is . Someone who does not react to what they are saying throws off challenging people. Even just a long pause before responding, as though you are contemplating what they are saying, can change the rhythm of the interactions and "take the wind out of their sails." Or you can reflect back to them their concerns. This too can divert some of their energy and, hopefully, lead to some reflection.

5. Dependent

Another difficult category is the overly dependent. These clients are attracted to and/or endearing to the therapist, making it difficult to terminate therapy. For some, their relationship with the therapist is the only meaningful relationship they have, and the therapist is the only person who will listen to and understand them. Others may feel so inadequate that they do not trust taking any step forward, unless they have the validation of the therapist. They need a lot of hand-holding and constant reassurance. Often they are easy to manage because, they may always arrive on time, never miss an appointment, and are agreeable to anything you suggest. The problem is that they only make progress to a certain point, because if they are too successful, they fear therapy will be terminated. So, you end up dealing with the same problems, which can be quite monotonous, but they are easily offended if you attempt to cut short treatment.

Solution – At first, they may need a lot of encouragement and support. Next, they need to identify their strengths and how to apply them to their problems. Then they can benefit from very delineated and specific goals, which become criteria for success and discharge. The achievement of each goal is celebrated. Once the goals are met, the rationale to stay on in therapy no longer exits. If clients begin to create crises to sabotage treatment to stay in therapy, it is best to spread out sessions and provide additional sessions only to reinforce progress.

6. Organicity or impaired by chemicals

Clients who are cognitively impaired due to physical brain damage can include those with long-term use of drugs or alcohol, traumatic brain injury, and dementia. Many have co-occurring mental health diagnoses, which contribute to the difficulty of treating them. For example, clients may be suffering from depression, anxiety, and even personality disorders. Sometimes there is confusion about where to start—with the addiction, brain disorder, or the co-occurring disorder.

Solution – Patience and slow going are critical for any efforts with this population. Celebrate small steps in progress. Much of this takes constant repetition and reinforcement. For chronic alcoholics and drug addicts, it may take several months of sobriety to get them to focus on any significant issues, and relapses are not uncommon. But each relapse is to be considered part of the process of recovery and not a failure if it used to understand what still needs to be done.

While most efforts to work with someone while they are intoxicated go unheeded or forgotten, helping the person when they are not intoxicated is at least a place to start (even if they are still drinking/using). The most strategic approach at this point is to do an intervention by having family members confront the client with the impact of the drinking or drugging on the family, while at the same time expressing their love and concern for the client, but at the end demanding that the client seek help.

Traditionally, mental-health therapists have said they cannot help the person, until they get clean or sober, and the substance-abuse counselors have said the client cannot get clean sober, until they get treatment for their mental health problems. The solution is to treat both simultaneously, thereby treating the person, not the diagnosis.

7. Fearful and distrustful

As mentioned previously, many clients have tremendous fear of therapy either because of the process itself or what might be uncovered in the process. The fear can derive from three sources: 1. The client's fear of opening up to their feelings and past experiences, known and unknown. 2. Fear of what the therapist might think and feel towards the client, and 3. Fear of the therapeutic process and environment, i.e., talking in front of a stranger, not knowing what the process is, and not knowing what to expect.

Solution – Fully explain the therapeutic process—how it can be expected to go and the positive outcomes that can be achieved. A typical explanation might be something like this: "The goal of therapy is to achieve whatever goals you have. You oversee the process. It will go as quickly or slowly as you like. I will do what I can to help you clarify what the issues are and what the possible outcomes are. I am not here to judge you. I will explain any intervention before I do it, and you can let me know whether you are willing to do it or not."

8. Silent

Silence may be the ultimate resistance. Few things can be more unnerving than clients who refuse to respond to anything you present. Reasons for the *silent treatment* are varied. One is that they are extremely depressed and resigned to the thought that nothing will help. For others, it is a battle of the wills, especially adolescents. This is a variation of the "You can't make me" mantra they often present when asked to do anything. Other clients resent the invasion into their privacy, and some can't figure out what the therapist is asking and therefore shut down. Still others just do not operate on the verbal level, whether due to trauma, age, or intellectual capacity. For example, children who are raised in an environment where everything they say is challenged or discarded, eventually give up even trying to explain what they think or feel. So silence is their default.

Solution – With children and adolescents you have to "prime the pump" i.e., get them to talk about anything—computer games, pets, movies, heroes, cars, and music. For therapists who do in-home therapy, I suggest they view the client's room and see what kinds of posters, models, pictures, or themes are present. These, then can become the subject of discussion. Another approach is to talk about key issues the client's parents have brought up saying, "I think they may be a little unfair in their assessment of you. I would like to hear your point of view." For other children, working in a different modality is much more fruitful. Play therapy is the therapy of choice, and yet I am amazed at how many counselors work with children without understanding the importance and need for play as a means of communicating with children. (This may be the result of a weakness of counseling education.)

Sand tray is an excellent mode for non-verbally inclined clients and even adults. Other modalities include the expressive therapies: art therapy, clay therapy, music therapy, story-telling, arts and crafts, visualizations, relaxation training, and hypnosis. (for a further explanation, see Chapter 11). One of the most reluctant teens I had was totally transformed, when I suggested that I could teach him self-hypnosis. Many of these techniques also work well with adults.

Few clients deny experiencing stress. The higher the stress level the more likely they are to shut down, so doing deep relaxation is often a great way to get them started. Not only does it lower the stress level, but just as in hypnosis, the technique involves relinquishing a certain amount of control to the therapist. I have been amazed at the physical transformation of the clients' countenances when I do relaxation exercises. It is as though their true self tends to emerge; I have witnessed them actually looking younger when they do this.

Another approach to dealing with silence is to just let it be. After a short period, clients may challenge you by saying, "Aren't you going to do anything?" There are several replies that would be fitting:

I am not sure you are ready to proceed, and I am just trying to respect your space and timing.

You seem to have a hard time responding, and I thought you needed to go more slowly.

Sometimes silence can be very helpful. Is it helping you?

I am fine with the silence. I have some notes to do, and when you are ready to talk, I'm here for you.

9. I-Don't-Knowers

"Why are you here for counseling?"
I don't know.
"What would you like to get out of counseling?"
I don't know.
"How are you feeling right now?"
I don't know.
"What makes you happy?"
I don't know.

Ever had a dialogue with a client go this way? You do too know. Many therapists find this one of the most frustrating client responses. While it is easy to think that the client responding with "I don't know" is simply a form of resistance, there are many other explanations why a client may default to this refrain. Some clients **do not** know. They have little insight and perspective, and no one seriously asked them these kinds of questions. Some are clueless about what they want out of counseling or how they feel. Others who respond with "I don't know" are what I call lazy thinkers. They never take the time or effort to inspect their lives. In some cases, it is just an automatic verbal response like, "Ya know," with which people often pepper their conversations. And for others, it is a way of saying "Back off," or "Why should I cooperate with you?"

Solution – One of the easiest ways to avoid this response is to not ask questions that will elicit this response. Questions are often experienced as a form of interrogation and may feel intimidating to clients, so they block the process by not responding.

Clifton Mitchell also gives an easy way to respond (Mitchell, 2012). He suggests taking the position that the client literally does not know and to respond with statements such as …

"Right now, you really are stumped about what to do."
"It is difficult to see a way to deal with this, currently."

If you suspect a client has said, "I don't know," in order to avoid some threatening reality about him/herself, simply express your suspicion:

"It is difficult and scary to actually say aloud the truth about…"
"You seem really uncomfortable facing this aspect of your life."

He also suggests changing your question to something less threatening. For example, have clients think about what they wish they could do. This allows them to think about alternatives without feeling like they are committed to doing it. Mitchell explains that part of the process is learning to be okay with the clients' not-knowing, and equally important, our own not-knowing.

Mitchell further suggests that how you handle the "I don't know" response can be a critical juncture in therapy. He sees it as a way to open therapeutic doors, and something to be pursued with great curiosity. Instead of assuming the client is just being defensive, you can go forward with a statement like, "Help me understand your struggle as you search for an answer." Discovering the reason behind the not-knowing may reveal more about the client's internal dynamics than the actual answer to the question.

Another approach to "I don't know" answers that works amazingly well is to say, "Well, if you did know, what would be the answer?" or "What is your best guess?" These seems to work well with people who are lazy thinkers or who have experienced having their answers dismissed no matter what they say.

One way to help people who sincerely do not know is to change the perspective of the question. You can have them think about the question from a third-party perspective. For example, you could ask them what they would say to a friend who had a similar problem, or if they were the therapist, what would they tell themselves. An approach that works with children is to change the context of the problem. For instance, if there is a family situation that is bothering them, you can put it in the context of an animal family. You could talk about a baby rabbit that lost its mother and ask how the child thinks the baby rabbit would feel, or what the baby rabbit might need to feel happy again.

10. Secondary Gain

Clients, who despite tremendous efforts and creative interventions on their behalf, do not change may be stuck due to secondary benefits of maintaining the problem. For instance, anger can be a way to gain respect (though it is usually based on fear); depression may be a way to avoid having to take responsibility; complaining may be a way to gain sympathy; and addiction may offer an escape from having to deal with reality. When I discuss this in my workshops, I say, "What if one of the audience was drunk and out of control right now? Where would all the attention go?" There would be mumblings and concerns about how to handle the person, who would become the center of attention. For some alcoholics, the only way the get attention or be taken seriously is when they are drunk. Clients are usually not conscious of these secondary benefits, and in fact, may be in great denial about them.

Solution – Help clients to discover these secondary benefits and why they exist. Next, come up with alternative ways of getting these needs met. In this way, you end up creating a win-win situation in that the negative behavior is stopped and the benefits can be retained.

Resistance is Fertile

When therapy is not going well, and clients are not cooperative nor invested in treatment, the rubric of resistance is easy to invoke. This seems to out-rank even manipulation as a universal reason for lack of therapeutic progress. Resistance in most counselors' minds is the bane of their existence. Counselors usually think of resistance in therapy in a pejorative way rather than a descriptive way.

Resistance, in and of itself, is not necessarily bad; it can be positive—a fertile basis of information. For example, clients who are discriminating and want to have the best kind of therapy may balk or protest against certain kinds of therapeutic interventions that don't meet their needs. Explanations of resistance among professionals range all the way from thinking there is no such thing to believing that it is the source of all difficulty in therapy. Steve DeShazer postulates that, "Resistance is a figment of the imagination." He further insists that, "When clients do not cooperate with their therapists, it is not because they are resisting; rather they are teaching their therapists how to be most helpful, and also showing them the behavior they do not especially appreciate" (Kottler, 1992). Therapists who are unwilling to look at their own role in the therapeutic process place the onus on the client's resistance as the reason for no or little progress.

A true perspective of resistance should not center on the reluctant or fearful client; it has to do the therapist's role in the therapeutic process. What are we doing or not doing to create resistance in the client? How are we connecting or not connecting to the client? How are we responding to the client's reluctance to engage? Some experts believe that resistance is a result of the therapist not establishing the correct relationship with the client.

Resistance is particularly troublesome in that it can have a negative impact on the therapist. Clifton Mitchell in his book, *Effective Techniques for Dealing with Highly Resistant Clients,* states, "We often think it is our fault that our clients do not change. Resistance can result in feelings of insecurity, incompetence, frustration, hopelessness, stress and burn out." But he adds, "Resistance is a fact of therapy. All therapists experience resistance. All therapists go through periods where resistance gets the best of them. All therapists should learn to manage resistance. There is nothing personal about resistance, other than that which we allow to be personal."

There are many reasons for resistance by the client. Some of these reasons are listed in Mitchell's book.

Why Are My Clients So Resistant? It may be because:

They do not want to be in counseling; they are coming for someone else.
They may be having an "adjustment reaction" to a new situation.
They think that to come for counseling they must be crazy or they are seeing a "shrink."
They are having a reaction to the openness of the therapist.
They do not know how to be a client.
They are not used to talking about their feelings.
They are fearful they will not be a good client.
Need for perfectionism.
Shame related to not being able to resolve past issues.
Fear of taking risks.

Fear of loss of familiar things.

Poor social skills.

Desire to flex their individuality.

Passive aggressiveness due to transference.

Life has taught them not to trust anybody in authority.

Resistance may be the only expression of power.

They are psychologically drained.

Personality style that enjoys the battle of resistance.

They are avoiding responsibilities.

Over-dependence and sabotaging to maintain counseling relationship.

Healthy response to bad counseling.

From: Effective Techniques for Dealing with Highly Resistant Clients, *2nd Edition, by Clifton W. Mitchell, 2012.*

It is easy to forget what a strange experience therapy can be. Telling a complete stranger your innermost secrets and feelings is completely foreign to most. Therapy is obviously a process, and as such, takes time and effort to build the kind of relationship that will invite such interactions. From the clients' point of view, they have no idea what to expect and may feel very vulnerable. This natural reluctance is par for the course and should be acknowledged and validated.

Another perspective is that resistance is the person protecting a deep emotional hurt that probably stems from a traumatic experience. This deeply, buried emotion may be stored in the body for years. Resistance is the setting of a boundary to not let anyone in or to let out what may be an overwhelming experience. Therefore, the resistance should be validated and even honored. Only by acknowledging its protective stance, instead of challenging it, can the space open to bring it into the light.

How else can we reduce resistance in sessions? Pacing and timing are essential to prepare the client for counseling. Pacing means joining with clients, no matter what or where they are, and waiting for a time to introduce a new concept or explore a new subject such as a past trauma. Timing is like jump rope when two others are turning the rope, and the jumper has to find the right time to jump in. Resistance is minimized when a certain rhythm and trust has been developed.

Therapists need to be flexible in their approaches to clients. There is a saying in NLP, "The meaning of communication is the message the person receives." This places the burden of the communication on senders and their ability to *speak in a language the person can understand.* In other words, if the client responds in an unexpected way, you may have not communicated to them adequately. This requires insight and creativity on the part of the therapist to build the therapeutic bridge with clients. When asked for feedback about previous experiences in therapy, clients cite a major complaint about therapists' failure to respond, i.e., they just listened. Clients weren't sure the therapist heard what they said, and they didn't feel like they were getting any direction. On the other hand, some complained therapists talked most of the time and didn't show any real comprehension of their concerns. Therefore, some clients may require a lot of direction, and for the therapist to be assertive and challenging, while others may just need the therapist to be more passive-subservient, attentive, and understanding.

Probably the most effective way to deal with resistance is to ask informally and formally for feedback, about the current process: what is and is not working? Equally important is asking what is the client's expectation of counseling and how it is being fulfilled.

Time and again, questions arise about what works in therapy and how to measure it. Scott Miller in *The Heart and Soul of Change: What Works in Therapy* is convinced that feedback-informed treatment session-by-session increases success rates. In other words, asking the client how the session went and having them rate their progress between sessions are the most effective ways to measure outcomes in therapy. Miller developed two scales, the Outcome Rating Scale (ORS), which measures therapy effectiveness, and the Session Rating Scale (SRS), which measures the strength of the therapeutic alliance. These scales are available online at www.scottmiller.com.

Amazingly, just the process of asking for feedback from clients on the effectiveness of their sessions and their progress in between increases positive clinical outcomes.

Amazingly, just the process of asking for feedback from clients on the effectiveness of their sessions and their progress in between increases positive clinical outcomes. This direct feedback shows respect for the clients, and based on their feedback, therapists can have an open dialogue on what is working and what is not working in therapy from clients' perspectives. This can be a great learning experience for the therapist if he is open to the feedback and has the flexibility to change. This process increases one's effectiveness and reduces resistance.

11 Solutions for Working with Difficult Clients

1. Believe there is a way – No solution will be arrived at, unless you believe it can happen. Nothing happens unless someone thinks of it and believes it possible. No building would be built, no book would be written, and no food would be prepared, unless someone thought of it first. You may not know what the solution is or how to do it, but know that it can be done. Begin the process accepting the idea that there is an answer. This is not some Pollyannaish-kind of wishful thinking, but rather an openness and willingness to explore possibilities.

2. Build a relationship – The whole premise of counseling is based on establishing a respectful and trusting relationship. Without it little can be accomplished. Some clients have never had this kind of relationship. Therefore, they may have difficulty, since they have no reason to expect that a relationship with the therapist will be any different. If the therapist understands this, goes slowly, and does not push too hard, the relationship can blossom, and many of the perceived difficulties can be overcome. Therefore, the best hope for helping difficult clients is building the kind of relationship that will win their trust and respect. Without it, little can be accomplished,

3. Need to prepare client for a session – Clients often have no idea what to expect when they come for counseling. You should pave the way for clients by explaining what the process of therapy is—how the session should go, what each technique is, how therapy can help, and how they will know when they have completed treatment. If these issues are not explained and discussed, the client may develop fear. Clients are much more willing to go somewhere, if they know where you are taking them. Equally important is to get their permission for the go-ahead. Questions like, "Are you willing to go along with that?" or "How does that sound to you?" put the client more at ease, and give them a sense of control of the session. It is also helpful to model a technique or give examples to make the technique more relevant.

4. Be a "nudger" – Clients are often reluctant to disclose information about themselves, but will often open up more with a little "nudging." So, the first time you meet resistance and they balk, push a little harder by saying things like, "I am just really curious about that," or "It seems like a real critical piece of the puzzle." However, if they still refuse to talk or tell you to back off, then you must respect this. However, you can make one other subtler attempt by saying, "I understand this is difficult to talk about, but can I just ask you one question?" If the client says it is okay, then ask, "Can you just tell me why you don't want to tell me?" This usually has two results: they will either give in and start talking, or if they answer your question, they will tell you what the block is. That, then, becomes the topic to be addressed. All this must be done casually, as these moments can be delicate, requiring good timing and proper phrasing based on the needs of the client and the situation.

5. Avoid power struggles and taking comments personally – Clients can be challenging or even condescending towards the therapist, especially when they feel pressured. Don't take their comments or reactions personally. This is one of the hardest lessons for therapists to learn—that when clients are attacking or condescending, it may feel very personal, but clients have been this way for a long time, and what you are experiencing is their "stuff," which they learned to survive. Their challenging you can be of great benefit, since it allows you to observe a possible source of their difficulty, and it can be reframed as their expressing their feelings instead of holding them in. However, if you "get your hackles up" and say anything like "I'm not going to let any client ... (tell me what to do, act like that, think he can run the show, etc.)," then you are in trouble. Chances are you have just engaged in a power struggle that you will never win, because the only way to win a power struggle is for the other person to lose. Making your clients into losers is not sound therapeutic practice.

6. Teaching is counseling – Knowledge is power, and educating your client about their diagnosis and the ways and skills to manage and overcome it are essential to success. I worked at a drug treatment center that used a model of care developed at The Hazelden Treatment Program in Minnesota. One of its key components was to teach alcoholics and drug addicts the nature and treatment of addiction. This was revolutionary, because previously, almost all treatment up to that time was done with the attitude that the doctor or therapist knew best, and the patient or client just needed to follow directions. Today, clients have access to much more knowledge and often have researched their disorders.

Encouraging them to do so and giving them resources add to the validity and effectiveness of your therapy. Compliance and outcome improve by educating clients to understand the dynamics of their problem, and why and how the treatment can be effective.

7. Healthy modeling – There are levels to counseling. One of the ways in which clients can be influenced is on the meta-level. These are subtle, often implicit, and include such things as the counselor's demeanor, emotional state, and cognitive process. If there is good rapport and respect for the counselor, in-evitably the clients learn the way the counselor approaches problems, processes them, and acts. For example, the client may pick up on how the counselor reacts or does not react, remains calm, is systematic, and utilizes certain social and verbal skills. It would be presumptuous to tell the client, "Do what I do," but allowing them to go forth on an unconscious or conscious level gives them the freedom to choose which aspects of the counselor's approach works for them.

8. What the client wants – Probably one of the greatest reasons for failure in therapy is the incongruence between what the client wants and what the therapist interprets that to be. Often the therapist does not try to find out what the client wants from therapy or overlooks or misinterprets it. Verbally checking in with the client at each session helps to ensure you are on the same page. You can ask questions such as: "Is this the direction you want to go?" "Are we addressing what you think are the greatest priorities?" or simply, "Are you okay with the way therapy is going?"

9. Achilles heel – Every individual has vulnerability. Part of the art of counseling is being able to seek out and expose the client's vulnerability in a safe and caring environment. I often see the client as having a protective wall. Behind it, there is a real person, who is a scared child inside, but appears to be emotionally impenetrable on the outside. Looking for and exposing the defensive wall often starts the therapy process in earnest.

10. The movie of therapy – Getting bogged down or having a negative attitude about the client will not help, no matter what the client is presenting to you. In difficult situations, which you anticipate with trepidation, think of it as a movie in which the client is playing a role, and you are playing a role (this is not too far from the truth). Question whether you like the therapist you are playing—why or why not? In this way, you create a third-person perspective where you are an observer, and therefore, not so attached emotionally to what happens.

11. Clinical supervision and consulting – Clinical supervision provides therapists with critical feedback offering new insight into cases, identifying their strengths and weaknesses, and preventing burnout. For beginning therapists, clinical supervision is critical to upgrade their skills and knowledge and to address issues in the counseling session. Professionally and ethically, it is recommended that every counselor have either a clinical supervisor or a consultant with whom to discuss cases. In most reputable agencies, clinical supervision is built into the agency's structure. For therapists in private practice, it is important to establish such a practice, even if it is just meeting regularly with colleagues.

The Special Case of Borderlines

Have you ever wondered why therapists have such a reaction, when they hear that a client has a borderline personality disorder? Borderlines seem to be the pariah of the mental-health profession. This became clear to me one day during a group we started at the drug rehab center for clients with co-occurring disorders. One of our first exercises was to have each member of the group share the diagnoses they had been given over the years. Many had three or more diagnoses. Often they were relatively ignorant of what each diagnosis meant. One lady said she had been diagnosed as a borderline. I asked her what that meant to her. She said, "The only thing I know from what they told me is that I'm fucked up, and there is nothing anyone can do to help me." I immediately knew this had probably happened, and unfortunately, was not surprised by this response. Many therapists have this point of view. At the same time, I was horrified by the attitude that gives birth to this prejudice. How can this attitude possibly be therapeutic? That day was when I decided to rethink borderline personality disorder as a trauma-based disorder because, in my experience, almost every client diagnosed with borderline personality disorder has a history of terrible abuse.

Marsha Linehan, who is recognized as the most knowledgeable expert about borderline personality disorders, says that the name is unfortunate. It originated at a time when psychological disorders were categorized into two factions:

psychosis and neurosis. The term, "borderline" was used to describe someone who had characteristics of both. Linehan would prefer it be called, "emotional dysregulation disorder," given the clients' inability to manage their emotional responses. It is as if they have no governor on their emotions, either negative or positive. When seen in this light, a borderline seems more understandable and, therefore, more workable.

This is not to say that working with borderline personality disorders is easy. Therapy usually starts out as being a relatively rewarding experience for both the client and the therapist, since the clients are usually very appreciative and hopeful. They may think you are the best therapist ever, but the situation can turn difficult, when they feel any kind of disapproval, or when trauma is uncovered. They will often have deep emotional outbursts and are not easily calmed. Sessions can end up running over. After such sessions, clients may feel that they are too much trouble for the therapist, and/or fear the therapist will abandon them. If you reassure them that you can handle whatever emotional difficulties they may be having, they may ask for more frequent sessions. They may also become suicidal, and want even more reassurance from you. If for some reason, you do not respond in a way that puts them at ease or is encouraging, they may turn on you, saying that you do not care about them. Any little misstep along the line can be the spark that sets off an emotional firestorm.

Such clients may stop coming to sessions. The therapist may end up calling and apologizing and trying to coax them and reassure them that they should come back. Part of the clients' dynamics may be a passive-aggressive way of punishing the therapist for being so careless. This can force the therapist to be apologetic, while at the same time, resentful of being manipulated. If the suicidal feelings increase, the client may take even more drastic steps to get attention. Some clients will stalk therapists; some will park themselves in the lobby; some will call the therapist at home at all hours of the day and night pleading for help; and some have even slit their therapist's car tires.

This escalation can certainly cause a cascade of feelings in the therapist— helplessness, fear, resentment, worry, anxiety, confusion, and self-doubt. One can go from being a great therapist in the eyes of the client to one who is unsure, incompetent, impotent, and probably in the wrong profession. Being able to withstand this storm of emotional battering does not come easy. It takes a certain amount of ego strength and/or experience with the ability to detach to weather such assaults. Even then it can be stressful.

Underlying Dynamics that Cause Difficulty

It is at this point that the therapist should take stock of the internal dynamics going on within the client. The behaviors and emotional states are rooted in fear. This can easily result in the therapist's not knowing what to do. As I discussed earlier, the therapist must become like the CSI detective ferreting out the deeper dynamics at a pace that the client can manage. Reassuring and empowering the client should be the first step. The therapist must be able to co-create with the client a place of safety and security both outwardly and inwardly. Only after this safe place has been firmly established, can the client can proceed to uncover painful events from the past. *Each behavior should be seen considering how it serves to protect and meet the needs of the client.*

Before making any decision or acting on those feelings and thoughts, the therapist must guide clients through their angst and return them to their safe place. In this process, it is important for the therapist not to take what the client says personally, even though the client may say many harmful, hurtful personal things. On the other hand, we as counselors do not have to take abuse from anyone, and in standing up for ourselves in a kind, yet firm way, we can serve as a role model for how the client can protect themselves from others' abuse.

Finally, not every therapist can handle every client, and at some point—especially, if there is a large degree of countertransference, the therapist may have to refer the client to another therapist.

CHAPTER 5

Dance the Dance

Opportunity dances with those already on the dance floor.

— H. Jackson Brown Jr.

The right brain/limbic (unconscious, emotional, intuitive) interaction of the psychotherapist and client is more important than cognitive or behavioral suggestions from the therapist; the psychotherapist's emotionally-charged verbal and nonverbal, psychobiological attunement to the client and to his/her own internal triggers is critical to effective therapy.

"Attachment Theory vs. Temperament: Treating Attachment Disorder in Adults," http://daily.psychotherapynetworker.org/free-reports/attachment-disorder-inadults-become-an-attuned-therapist

ANOTHER WAY OF SAYING this is that therapy is like dance. When there is attunement, the magic of therapy can evolve ideally to the point where there is a flow and rhythm to the process, and no one is taking the lead; it is just happening.

Once the dance begins—therapists usually start it—therapists need to encourage clients to take the lead. If clients become distracted or fearful, refusing to engage, then the therapist takes the lead. Clients may not have the confidence, the understanding of the process, or even the knowledge of how to dance and take the lead. Therapists must guide them through the different steps, allow them to practice, and step in when needed. So sometimes the therapist leads, and sometimes the client leads. As the experience deepens, the therapist relinquishes control to the client, always willing to take the lead as needed. Gradually, a flow develops in which the two are just dancing with each other through different moods and situations, and this becomes an integrated, organic process.

There are other possibilities in the dance, however, that can contribute to not knowing what to do. One is that neither is leading; another is each wants to lead but go in different directions. It is also possible that the client does not want to dance, wants to dance by himself, wants to do a totally different dance, or has no idea that a dance is even taking place. In these circumstances, it is wise to talk about therapy and the role of the client and the therapist. This "therapeutic dance" requires skills, coordination, and cooperation. The more it is done, the better each become.

What is the Music?

If therapy is a dance, what is the music? Think of music. What is it that gives it impact? What is the nature of the impact? It is said that music moves the soul. It creates sadness, excitement, arousal, sympathy, and unity. It can also elicit reminiscence, appreciation, inspiration, and pride. What is the equivalent of music in therapy? The answer is emotions.

Emotions can inspire us, scare us, endear us, and encourage us. They can set the rhythm and the pace of therapy and determine the difference between success and failure. They can stir the passions to break through and overcome resistance and fear, or they can paralyze, overwhelm, or discourage the client from continuing. They are the source of energy that gives drive to the therapy. E-motion is often referred to as energy in motion.

The first emotion to arise is probably curiosity. The therapist is curious about the client's needs and background, and the client is curious about the therapist and the process of therapy. If all goes well in the first session, trust begins to break down the barriers of distrust, so that hope can emerge. Gradually a rhythm begins to develop and there is a flow. At times, the music is soft and calm; at other times, it is bombastic and clashing. Therapy generates relief, trust, affection, respect, courage, compassion, and excitement. But it can also elicit anger, grief, fear, remorse, and dread. Clients, and sometimes therapists, tend to avoid painful emotions. Some therapists, including many beginners, are hesitant to pursue deeper levels of emotions. They either fear that they will make the client worse, or that the client will get stuck, and the therapist will not know how to manage the emotion. Another reason is that they have not gone deeply to a level within themselves and fear arousing their own reactions. Doing therapy at this level and jumping into the traumatic experiences of the past takes a leap of courage. However, the only way to get around or over an emotional situation is to go through it. Just as in music, timing is also critical. Coming in too soon may create chaos; waiting too long may create lost opportunity. Luckily, the therapist can orchestrate a way for the dance to proceed.

Real change is driven by emotions. For example, most smokers know the dangers of smoking, but that knowledge alone rarely causes them to stop. However, if they find out they are in the early stages of lung cancer, or their young child begs them to stop, the emotional reaction to these situations can provide the motivation and determination to change. Many times, the emotions need to be ratcheted up to a crescendo to bring about the change, while other times the emotions are just under the surface waiting to be released.

Bert was in his late 60's and had been drinking himself into oblivion, feeling no purpose in life, and hoping that he would either die from drinking or something else. He was admitted to detox and slowly began to come out of his alcoholic fog. His room was along a narrow hallway with about ten rooms. The first room, however was the furnace room. In the early days, he would forget which room was his and later said in group therapy he never saw a place with so many furnaces. At times, he would languish and seemed to not care whether he got sober or not. One day, however, he got a phone call from his granddaughter, whom he had not seen or heard from in three years. She was 13 and so excited to hear him sober. He immediately perked up realizing that there was someone who still loved him. In group he stated, "I can't get sober for myself, but I can do it for my granddaughter." Any time he started to lag in his efforts, he was reminded of his goal to make his granddaughter proud of him.

So, learning how and when to tune and attune to emotions is often the key to success.

Aikido

In the East, there is a martial art called Aikido. In a way, it is a dance—a dance with an opponent, an attacker. It embraces an interesting point of view about conflict or aggressiveness and how to deal with it. In the Western way of thinking, if a person is challenging or threatening us, the basic approach is to either attack him, so as to overwhelm him, or at least to stand our ground. So, sports such as boxing, football, or wrestling have grown in popularity, because the goal is to overwhelm and defeat the opponent by being physically superior. One can say that there is *tissue damage* in this approach, because standing your ground or overpowering the other leads to physical contact or a clash. When this approach or attitude is reflected in day-to-day conflicts in relationships, it becomes problematic. It can cause harm on both emotional and physical levels. In attempting to defend ourselves from a perceived threat, we can cause injury to others and often ourselves by being so forceful or stubborn.

In Aikido, instead of overpowering your opponent or standing your ground, the goal is to merely step aside, possibly grabbing the opponent and using the momentum of his charge to trip him up and take him to the ground. There is no clash, per se, and no physically-damaging encounter. It is a more psychological and strategic way to deal with conflict. Applying this principle to verbal or personal attacks by another person, the point would be not to out-argue him or stubbornly resist his ideas, but to figuratively step aside, possibly agree with him or at least concur that he is entitled to his ideas. In this way, you avoid fighting force with force, but rather take the energy out of it rendering it harmless. Here is one Aikido master's way of describing it:

> Aikido is the realization of Love. If you think that "martial art" means to have opponents and enemies and to be strong and defeat them, you are mistaken. The true spirit of the martial arts is to be one with the universe and have no enemies. The essence of the martial arts is the spirit of loving protection of all beings in the universe. Never defeated means never fighting. This is not mere theory. You practice it. Then you will accept the great power of Oneness with Nature.
>
> It is not a technique to fight or defeat an enemy. It is the way to reconcile the world and make human beings one family. The

secret of Aikido is to harmonize ourselves with the movement of the universe and bring ourselves into accord with the universe itself. Aikido is non-resistance. As it is non-resistant, it is always victorious. Those who have a warped mind, a mind of discord, have been defeated from the beginning. There is no conflict in love. A mind of conflict, thinking of the existence of an enemy, is not consistent with the spirit of the universe. Those who do not agree with this cannot be in harmony with the universe.

A mind to serve for the peace of all human beings in the world is needed in Aikido, and not the mind of one who wishes to be strong or who practices only to defeat an opponent. I am calm, however and whenever, I am attacked. Aikido is love. You make this great love of the universe your heart, and then you must make your own mission the protection and love of all things.

Morihei Ueshiba, O'Sensei, founder of Aikido,
http://www.aikidosantacruz.org/sayings_osensei.html

If you substitute the word "counseling" for Aikido in the above passage, you can sense the power this attitude could have in your counseling. It would develop your potential for incredible success with your clients.

...

One of the programs I supervise works with high-risk children in their homes. Sixty to seventy percent of the children are diagnosed with Oppositional Defiant Disorder. The key word in this diagnosis is "oppositional." Children become "oppositional" when they feel unfairly challenged, dismissed, or perceive someone is against them. If a child believes a person is on his side, then he will not be oppositional. So, to gain their trust and respect we must show them we are on their side. Does this mean you should agree with everything they say or do, especially if you think they are in the wrong or saying or doing things that are detrimental to their own well-being? Of course, not. The key is not to overpower them with demands or arguments, nor to even stand your ground no matter what. Rather one joins with them in a caring attitude, understanding their point of view and acknowledging its validity for them in the moment saying, "It is understandable why you think and feel that way right now." That often takes the fire out of their argument.

If possible, the next step would be to find out how such an idea might be potentially unrealistic or infeasible, or why their parents have concerns by taking the logic of their thinking to a conclusion. For example, if the client feels like his mother should buy him certain shoes, which are way beyond the parent's means, you can side with him by acknowledging his desire to have the shoes and how important they are to him. If you challenge him that he does not need expensive shoes, or that he is being unrealistic and selfish, this will only infuriate him more and stiffen his will to get his way. However, if you can acknowledge his want in a positive way and get him to see what the family would have to go without to pay for his shoes, there is a greater likelihood that he will back down and agree to forgo it or accept a less-expensive pair. Obviously, not all situations are so easily resolved, but the amazing thing is that if this approach is done strategically, many situations get defused.

Bart, a 20-year-old, presented as having Asperger's. He was stuck at home, and his father could not encourage him to reach out find a job, or look for additional resources to help him. He was content to watch the Cartoon Channel all day and spend much of our sessions talking about episodes in minute detail. When I could get him off topic, one of the other subjects he seemed obsessed with was a girl who went with him to prom his junior year. He professed to be in love with her, even though he had not seen her in 4 years. Convinced that she loved him too. and if he could only contact her, she would instantly want to be back with him. He had a letter she had written him in high school that he claims proved that she wanted to be with him. (Mind you the only time they were "together" was that prom night.) I knew almost instantly that my trying to dissuade him from the idea she was still in love with him would be a lost cause.

So, I took a leap of faith and said, "Let me see if we can find her. I will help you." My thought was if we do find her and he contacted her, she could tell him how she really felt, and we would deal with those issues. As fate would have it, we Googled her, looked on Facebook, and on Snapchat. None of those avenues produced any results. We looked in the phonebook, and still she was not to be found. With each blocked avenue, he became more disappointed, but it became obvious he was starting to accept she would not probably be part of his life. I tried to share in his disappointment. I made statements like, "I can't believe we can't find her," or "I really thought this would pan out." In this way, he did not feel alone in his disappointment.

In a way, I was glad we could not find her since, although this fruitless search had an impact on him emotionally, I think it was a gentler way to accept reality, rather than an outright rejection from her. The most positive outcome of this was that he truly began to trust me, and it deepened our therapeutic relationship, so that I could motivate him to get hired by a sheltered workshop.

Go with It

If a dog bites your hand, the best response is not to pull your hand out, but to push it further into the dog's mouth. I have not tried this, and hope that I never have a chance to, but it makes sense. So, it is with Aikido and with counseling. I never cease to be amazed at what going with something, instead of combatting it, will achieve. A nurse friend shared with me this story.

There was a lady, Mrs. Younger, in the nursing home who was constantly trying to leave the facility, especially in the morning around breakfast time. While it was easy to block her, she would become very agitated, and at times belligerent. No amount of coaxing or dissuasion seemed to faze her. Finally, one of the nurses thought to ask her why she wanted to leave each morning, and she replied she had to catch the bus. She had done this every day for 30 years going to work, and she wasn't about to stop now. The staff again tried to convince her that there was no bus, and that she was in a nursing home, but she refused to believe it. Again, each time they tried to block her or convince her otherwise, she would get agitated all over again.

Finally, one of the orderlies had an idea. He got a bench and put it in the hall and told her to wait there for the bus. Mrs. Younger seemed very pleased with this, since she would not have to wait in the rain or heat. The first morning she sat on the bench quite content to wait for the bus. After about an hour idly sitting there, she got up saying, "I guess they're not coming today," and went quietly back to her room. After several days of waiting for the bus, she gave up saying, "I guess that damn bus isn't coming anymore."

There is a belief that the Chinese character for crisis is composed of two symbols—one for danger and the other for opportunity. While some Sinologists disagree with this, the idea is a helpful one. We all have clever ways to defend ourselves such as building walls that prevent others from knowing who we truly are and what we truly feel. These walls often come down in times of crisis, sometimes fueled by consumption of alcohol or drugs or triggered by acute stress. For therapists, crises can be prime times to get to deeper feelings. The natural inclination for most is to try to calm the person down, which can backfire and add fuel to the fire. "Don't tell me it'll be okay; you don't know that!" might be a typical response. From a therapeutic point of view, it is prime time to go with the feelings to discover the deeper meaning. While one would not want to provoke such a situation, it is wise to utilize this opportunity to discover what is behind the person's wall, i.e., what is at the core of the anger, hurt, fear, anxiety, etc.

Jake completed a 28-day drug treatment residential program. He did relatively well, was very cooperative and compliant, but always seemed guarded and dismissive of any attempts to get him to express any deeper feelings or issues; he always insisted that basically drinking was his only problem. Three months later he showed up back at the center, obviously very drunk. Within about five minutes, he was crying and sobbing about how his family had deserted him, and his children no longer wanted anything to do with him. We discovered that this had happened many months before he came to treatment, and he never mentioned it. In my mind, I was thinking, "Well, why didn't you talk about all that stuff when you were in treatment?"

There is a saying in Latin "*in vino veritas*," (in wine there is truth), meaning that when people are drunk, their true feelings will come out. So, my fantasy was always to set up a bar in the back of the group therapy room, get everybody drunk and then do group therapy. Wouldn't that make for some interesting dynamics? The only problem with that—besides being totally unethical and irresponsible—is that all the feelings would come out drug-affected.

When defenses are down, the greatest opportunity exists to discover the core issues. Taking advantage of a crisis is one way to do this.

The point is, however, that when defenses are down, the greatest opportunity exists to discover the core issues. Taking advantage of a crisis is one way to do this. The hope is by revealing the true source of the pain, you can create a catharsis, or at least start the healing process. Of course, you have to be very strategic about this. You would not want to do this, for example, with someone who was psychotic, histrionic, or manic.

Also, "going with it" does not always mean creating or exploiting a crisis. Here are several ways that "going with it" worked.

- Kids are constantly getting suspended from school for dropping the F bomb. It would be interesting to learn how many suspensions occurred in one year in the US for this offense. Here is one way to deal with this: get the child in a private place and have him say it as many times as he wants with as many different inflections or combinations with other words to discharge his anger. You can even challenge him by saying, "Come on you can do better than that," or say, "Let's see how many cuss words you can say in a minute. I'll time you." The goal is to defuse the situation and decrease the shock impact of using such words.

- People who are psychotic are not easily talked out of their delusions. It is better to go with them. A lady diagnosed with schizophrenia was very isolated and her only contact with the outside world was a weekly phone call from her daughter. This became problematic, however, since she thought her phone was bugged—not with electronic bugs, but real bugs. She was fearful they would come out of the receiver and crawl into her ear. No amount of logic or persuasion would convince her otherwise. When the situation was explained to her therapist, the therapist said that she had a solution. She had just recently learned of a home-made bug spray that would not only kill bugs, but was a deterrent for future bugs. All the client would have to do is spray it on a cloth and wipe down the phone before she spoke. She promised the client the recipe and to make her some. When the client came back the next week, the therapist gave her a bottle she had specially made. The client went home, wiped down the phone, and called to report she thought it might just do the job. After about a month of doing this she reported had no further concerns about bugs in the phone.

The above is what we call "useful fiction," a therapeutic intervention designed to neutralize a false belief with a more constructive idea that would not bear up to scrutiny. For example, you might tell a client that the technique you are about to teach them has a very high success rate with people having similar symptoms. It is a cognitive placebo.

Another client was in foster care getting ready to enter college. She had a long history of cutting herself when experiencing anxiety. Her main worry about going to college was that if the school found out she was cutting, they would try to hospitalize her and perhaps expel her. She had been hospitalized numerous times for cutting but was never found to be suicidal. Personally, she did not think of her cutting as being self-destructive, but more as a self-soothing mechanism. It was only if she didn't have that as an option that she would escalate. I asked her what about the cutting was soothing. She said that just the sight of her blood was enough to calm her down. Since I only would be seeing her for a few more sessions, I told her we would develop a plan such as me calling the college counselor, telling her of the situation, and asking for her cooperation.

Upon hearing this, the foster mom, a diabetic, came up with an idea: perhaps if the girl just pricked her finger, it would draw blood but be harmless. For a short-term solution, it seemed to be a win-win situation; the client could have cutting as an option (which lowered her anxiety), until she could work with the college counselor on a more constructive plan.

Silence

In one of my college counseling classes, the professor began the class by asking everyone to take all their books and papers off the desk and not pick them up. He said we were going to sit in silence for a little bit. Everyone seemed to go along with this for about five minutes, and then some of the students began to get restless. They began fidgeting and looking around the room to see others' reactions. After about ten minutes there were lots of sighs, and it was obvious some were becoming quite disturbed. Soon several students picked up one of their books off the floor and began reading in defiance of the professor's request. After about 15 minutes one of them blurted out, "This is stupid. I pay good money for this course and just sitting here is a waste of time and money." The professor did not immediately respond and within a couple more minutes, others chimed in similar sentiments. Soon there was a whole cacophony of complaints. They were so uncomfortable and threatened by the silence. The professor then processed with the class what that experience was like for them. I was amazed at how much frustration and anger it generated or unleashed. For me, it was one of the most memorable learning experiences of my college education, allowing me to see the power of silence and learning to be ok with it.

Counselors are often uncomfortable with silence. Sometimes this is due to not knowing what to say, and other times, feeling like they should immediately respond to every statement or question, i.e., lead the dance. However, silence is one of the best responses to use on many occasions. The saying, "Silence is golden," can certainly be true for counseling. Offering no response can create space for clients to self-reflect, or take the topic to the next step. This is often referred to as "pregnant pause," meaning that it can often give birth to new ideas or unexpressed feelings. In such spaces, emotional responses can bubble to the surface (as in the college classroom situation above). It is easy to talk away feelings, but in silence we end up having to be with our feelings. For the counselor to talk during such times can actually be counterproductive to the therapeutic dance. Ill-timed or forced responses can be seen as superficial, irrelevant, non-sequitur, or even patronizing.

Not only is silence productive for the client, if counselors can surrender to the silence, their intuition may kick in, and creative answers or ideas may come to them.

Sally was a 13-year-old girl who had been raped numerous times by an uncle. She presented as being very withdrawn and timid. Answering questions seemed almost painful for her. She was slow in responding, and I felt as though I had to proceed gingerly with her. I finally got enough courage to ask her what happened because of the abuse, and she fell silent. I worried I had gone too fast too soon, so I just let the moment take her wherever it led. Her non-verbals indicated that she was struggling to get an answer. We ended up sitting for 20 minutes in silence. I did not prompt her. She began looking at her hands and rubbing her fingers which indicated that she was searching for an answer. During the pause, I mentioned a couple of times that she may have a hard time putting a finger on what happened. Finally, she responded, "I never allow myself to think about it, but I think I lost all trust in people." I was amazed at her conclusion and thanked her for trusting me enough to share that insight. I also realized that my mind works relatively fast, and I cognitively process information at a much different rate than Sally. My "firing questions" at her would only have served to overwhelm her. Though her mind worked much slower, it was no less intense or deliberate. It was only in those 20 minutes of silence that these realizations were possible for her…and me.

Silence is neutral in that it does not lead clients in directions they may not want to go, nor does it inject the counselor's agenda into the conversation. In terms of "clean language" (a phrase coined by David Grove meaning language that is neutral and general, not leading the client in any one direction), silence is the cleanest. It is non-directive and often the best response to a situation in which the client is anticipating some negative reaction. If an adolescent refuses to talk, sitting in silence can easily erode his resistance, if done in a patient and understanding way. It doesn't need to turn into a power struggle; rather it is an acknowledgement that the client does not want to talk. A kind or understanding look and silence can put the client at ease. Clients are more open to feedback when they have to ask for it, rather than when it is freely given. Being silent allows them the space to take the lead and ask for feedback. Silence can be a generous response and the wisest response.

Falling in the Hole

One of the dilemmas that arises in therapy is how much to get involved in the process. There are two ways of thinking about this. One is if clients are not motivated to actively participate in the therapy, they should be terminated. The idea is that a counselor cannot do the work, only the clients, and if they are not motivated or engaged enough then counseling cannot be effective. The other is that the therapist must be willing to go the extra mile to make a difference, to show the client how much the counselor is committed. Making this extra effort on behalf of the client can be the turning-point in therapy. Some think this is what differentiates a great counselor from a regular one.

Both ways have their merits and drawbacks, and trying to understand what level of involvement is needed in any situation can be challenging. There is a balanced way to think about it. Here is one analogy:

Burt goes for a walk in the woods. He is near the end of his jaunt when he hears a voice yelling, "Help! Help me!" He follows the voice and finds a man in a large pit.

"What happened?" Burt asks.

The man responds that he got too close to the edge and the ground collapsed under him. "Help me get out of here!"

Burt reaches in and tries to grab hold of him, but they are not able to make contact, and Burt notices the man is not reaching out his hand very far.

"Please get me out of here," the man pleads again.

Burt reaches in a little further and still was not able to reach the man, who did not seem to be stretching much at all to meet him. Finally, Burt reached in just a little further and suddenly started sliding into the pit. In a split second he fell into the pit.

Now both men are in the pit, and neither can get out.

Thus, balance is needed. When first seeing the client, it is fitting and necessary to give a little more effort for encouragement and to win trust. Later, if you see the client is making effort, but needs a bigger boost or encouragement, you can give more time and energy. However, as time goes by, if the client does not meet you halfway, then you can end up doing all the work and feeling burnt out, while the client has not learned how to help himself.

Walking the Dog

Again, in the dance of therapy sometimes the therapist leads sometimes follows. This can also be explained as walking the dog. There are two ways to walk the dog. One is to take the dog on a leash and make him go where you want him to go. The other way is to let the dog go wherever he wants to go and just follow—as though you have a camcorder on him and are curious as to what he is drawn to and what his world is like. It takes patience and willingness to just follow.

It is easy to lead clients down a path that they may not want to traverse. Often, counselors are not even aware they are doing this. They may think that clients are passive recipients blindly willing to go wherever counselors take them, and because there is no opposition, assume that they are on the right path. Occasionally, they may feel clients "tugging at the leash" and assume that the client is being resistant or in denial. That counselor-led jaunt often is not successful. It leads nowhere, because it is not based on what clients perceive they need.

The corrective for this is to allow the client to go in whatever direction he is willing to go, or to just be curious as to where this leads the process.

Jennifer came to counseling three years after her baby died having only survived less than 24 hours. Though she had received grief counseling at the time of the death, Jennifer began having more and more memories, dreams, and even flashbacks to that time period. She seemed indecisive about what she wanted to achieve in therapy. All she knew was that her grief seemed to be getting greater, not less. We discussed several possible directions to go, but she was very confused, because she did not want to forget her baby, even though most of the memories were painful.

I felt that she needed to resolve her grief in her own way, and so in our third session I asked her to tell me whatever she wanted to tell the about that time. She began by sharing some of her expectations of what it would be like to be a mother. She was excited and fearful at the same time. She loved children and having grown up as an only child wanted a large family. However, her husband was demanding and insensitive, and she was very unsure about the future of their marriage. At this point I could have chosen to take her down that "rabbit trail", but instead I just said, "Tell me more about the situation." This gave her the choice to talk about her husband or continue telling me about the baby. She chose to talk about all the preparations that she had made for the baby's birth including how her room was decorated, the kinds of clothes she had purchased, and the support she had from an excited family.

As she was telling me this she began to choke up. I asked her what she was experiencing. She said that on some level she felt as though having a child would complete her as a person, but that losing the child meant that she was a failure. She had failed to produce a viable child; therefore, she was a failure. A sense of deep shame came along with her grief that she had not realized or allowed herself to feel. Several sessions later she related that by my allowing her to fully explore her feelings, she was able to uncover this added burden, which had complicated the grieving process. Only after we worked through that issue did she feel she could come to terms with what had happened.

I was surprised by the direction the session took. Had I been in charge of which road she went down, I might have focused on the difficulties she was having with her husband, and she might never have arrived at the insight she gained.

There is a time to lead in the dance and equally a time to follow. If someone is *in a hole* and wants help, then you need to lead and give direction, but if they are *on the trail,* it is best to see where it leads before interjecting your own thoughts or perceptions.

So, as you can see the dance can take many forms. It also takes practice both by the therapist and the client. The dance is different for each person. It may be a slow dance, rap, rocking and rolling, jazz, country, hip-hop, or free-form. It is in the synergistic approach that the rhythm of therapy is set.

Stop the Music

Well, the dance is a useful metaphor, but it falls short during times when the therapist must take full control. The therapist must step in if the client is suicidal, is having an abreaction or meltdown, is raging and ramping up, or just wants to talk about the same issues over and over. There is always a risk of provoking the client by doing this, but more often than not, clients are grateful for setting limits and hanging in there with them. Again, their willingness to do so is dependent upon the depth of the relationship we have created with them.

Clients have their own way of dealing with or processing problems. As therapists, we have many more tools with clients such as hypnosis, art therapy, energy therapies, mindfulness, narrative therapy, etc. To introduce such activities, we may have to stop the dance and interject our own approach. Obviously, this is done in agreement with the client, after it has been explained.

CHAPTER 6

Enhancing the Relationship

Where can we go to find God if we cannot see him in our hearts and every living being?

—Swami Vivekananda

The client is the hero in the "drama" of therapy. There are no great therapists, only great clients and therapists working together. *(Miller, 1997)*

ONE OF THE VALUES OF COUNSELING as a profession is that counselors get to develop meaningful, rewarding relationships in which people share their inner-most thoughts and secrets. Where else in life do you can develop this kind of intimate relations with such an amazing variety and depth? This is a privilege that we earn by our sincerity, dedication, and ability to enhance the relationship.

Given this significant fact, the question becomes how can we enhance the therapeutic relationship?

The Uniqueness of the Therapeutic Relationship

There is no other kind of relationship like the therapist-client relationship. In therapy the client meets someone for the first time and is expected to talk about feelings he may never have shared before, perhaps divulging his deepest, darkest secrets. During sessions, the therapist may have the client close his eyes, (which in and of itself is unusual in the presence of a stranger), relax his body, visualize past experiences, or raise and lower his arm. She may have him talk to a chair, or have him re-experience past traumatic events while visually following her finger back and forth. She may have him tapping certain parts of his body or playing with toy figures in a sand box. Where else might someone allow a perfect stranger to take to think we are the crazy ones?

Part of the mystique of therapy and the key to its effectiveness is the unique approach to problem solving. Jeffery Zeig observed the stranger the therapy, the better. Look at where psychotherapy originated—with Freud. A patient was asked to lie on a couch, while Freud sat behind her making no eye contact. The patient would talk about whatever came to her mind, while Freud made few responses revealing nothing about himself. What a strange beginning to a profession...and yet it works.

Many skeptical clients, especially adolescents and men, ask me, "How is talking about my problems going to help? I talk about things all the time, and it has not helped any." My general reply is, "I am not exactly sure why it works; I only know that it works." Come to think about it, it is pretty remarkable.

So, what makes the therapeutic relationship so successful in helping others? The main factors are: acceptance, confidentiality, and non-judgement. These key components create a safe environment, which encourages a deeper level of conversation and exploration. There are other factors as well. The therapeutic relationship:

- provides different perspectives
- creates new solutions
- employs techniques that are not a part of everyday interactions
- provides a safe place to express emotions
- educates about the nature of difficulties
- provides objective feedback.
- teaches coping and social skills

Again, if you think about "normal" relationships, they rarely do all the above. It is not that they can't. In fact, true friendship may include almost all the above.

But it is the ability of the therapist to take the client to more profound levels that distinguishes the therapeutic relationship from average day-to-day interactions.

Scientists have begun to believe that the best therapy is non-verbal—right brain to right brain. In other words, there is an unspoken synchronization of two people's minds. Therefore, the real effectiveness of the therapeutic relationship may not necessarily be driven by data or facts, but rather a meeting of spirits—a connection in the universal mind.

Cheerleading and Coaching

Clients come to therapy usually after all other efforts have failed. They are often despondent, discouraged, enervated, and hopeless. One of the goals of therapy is to embolden them and work to identify and increase their strengths. The first step is to give them hope by looking for any positive quality and fan it as one would a glowing ember. While finding anything positive may seem difficult, just the fact clients are sitting in your office means they have not given up hope and are actively seeking to improve their lives.

Therapists should be cheerleaders finding the positive, consistently pointing it out, and reinforcing it. Comments such as, "You are amazing," or "I love your determination," feed clients' weakened spirits. The stronger their spirit, the deeper they can go, and the more progress they can make. It takes a strong spirit to process past trauma and current crises. The more energy you can sincerely generate for them and yourself, the more capable they will become at coping with their situations. Timing is critical however. If you come on too strong, too early, they may be overwhelmed by your positivity and shut down (especially clients with chronic depression). It may take several weeks of slowly going over the details of their story, before they are ready to hear and accept such positive comments.

Ron Taffel talked about, how when working with children, therapists need to change their tactics to match the developmental age of the child. What works for one age will not work with another. For example, children who are in their pre-teens may listen and cooperate when told what to do, how, and when; whereas, adolescents often rebel or ignore anything they are being told. They feel disrespected and resentful. Ron suggests a better tactic for teens is to coach them. Since parents cannot be with them all the time, the best way to guide and interact with teens is to be like a coach, one who explains several possible scenarios, gives the team strategies on how to handle them, and sends them in to enact them. After the game the coach reviews with them how things went, what worked and didn't work, and what they could do differently.

This same strategy is an effective one that parents and counselors can use. Since adolescents lack experience in many areas of their lives, coaching them is one way to help them navigate the stormy rivers of life such as dealing with peer pressure, handling sexual feelings, negotiating drug situations, or avoiding or resisting risky "I-dare-you" situations. There is no guarantee they will respond to the coaching, but they definitely won't, if they are not given the guidance and opportunity.

For example, parents often struggle about what to tell their teenage children about drinking alcohol. Some believe that if their children are going to drink, it is better to have them do it at home, while others are not tolerant of any such experimentation. Still others fear alienating their children by taking a stand. My advice to parents is to take the toughest stand possible without damaging the relationship and alienating their adolescent. Taking too hard a stance may cause children to rebel, or at least defy, what the parent is saying and block or ignore whatever is being told. The alternative is to coach them by presenting alternative ways to handle the various scenarios with drinking they may face and provide backup plans, if needed. This approach conveys respect and allows input from the teen, rather than lecturing them on the evils of alcohol.

One of the best methods for coaching any client is role play. By creating situations where clients have to put into words their actual responses, they are forced to go beyond glib responses such as, "I can do that, no problem," or "I'll try," or "I'll think about it." The therapist can coach by commenting on the content, the tone of voice, eye contact, and posture and suggest alternative ways of stating things. Taking the situation to this next step is often critical to the success of the interaction.

Operating Out of Love Rather Than Fear

A perfect love casts out fear.

—John 4:18

I believe that every single event in life happens as an opportunity to choose love over fear.

—Oprah Winfrey

There are two basic emotions, love and fear. We either operate out of fear, or we operate out of love. Love and fear cannot occupy the same space at the same time. So, the best way to manage fear is to supplant it with love. Bryan Post says that love is the space that occurs naturally between every human being, but fear stops it from being expressed. The challenge is to inspire everyone to operate out of love. This might sound idealistic, but if you think of love being these qualities: compassion, understanding, tolerance, forgiveness, empowerment, and cooperation, then a love-based approach to therapy seems realistic and desirable.

Love means you are focused on the other person, you are giving to them, and the best love is unconditional. You love them, not because they did anything to earn it … you love them just for being. Likewise, you do not withhold love because of something they said or did to offend you. Does that mean you should love all your clients? No, but it does mean to adopt a loving, accepting, and supportive attitude, even during some significant pathology. To the extent you are unable or unwilling to do this, you compromise your potential effectiveness.

On Christmas I was called to the Emergency Room to interview a person who had just murdered his neighbor and was now suicidal. My immediate reaction was to be repulsed by, and even fearful, of such a person. However, as I interviewed him, it became apparent that he was appalled by what he had done. He and his neighbor had been drinking and had become quite intoxicated. While playing cards, an argument ensued after one accused the other of cheating. Tempers flared, a blow was struck, the neighbor fell, hit his head on the corner of the wood stove and died as a result. The man barely remembered what had happened, and as he sobered up and realized the tragic consequences of his actions, he was overwhelmed with guilt, grief, and despair. While the sheriff and some of the ER staff treated him with disdain, it quickly became apparent that this poor chap needed someone to understand and console him. My goal was to help him come to terms with what had happened and not to judge him or punish him with my attitude. While there was obviously little I could do to help him in his predicament, he was very grateful that I had been so understanding and concerned for his well-being.

If you operate out of fear, you are thinking only of yourself. This is not effective, because your purpose is to benefit the client, not promote your own ego or sense of accomplishment. It's normal for some judgmental thoughts about certain people to creep into your mind, but don't focus on them. Be aware of how you are in a session. This is metacognition. It is like you are watching a movie in which you are playing the role of a therapist. How are you coming across? What is your demeanor? How concerned and sincere do you appear? *How loving are you?*

It is sometimes difficult to maintain the perspective that a client is operating out of fear, because there are several other emotions that seem basic. Take anger, for example, which seems like a basic emotion, but in reality, it is a secondary emotion. Upon closer inspection, we see that fear is fueling the anger. For example, a mother is angry at her son for coming home late, but under the anger is the fear that something had happened to him. A boss is angry, because the project is not proceeding on schedule; he is afraid he will look bad to his superiors. A child is mad because he has to do his homework, but underlying the anger is the fear he won't have time to play his video game. Given this perspective, one can easily see other emotions like jealousy, resentment, and hate are also based in fear.

Fear begets fear. If you are in fear mode, the client will sense that, and it will influence his trust and belief in you. Since the most effective therapy is right-brain to right-brain, if the client learns emotional regulation from the responses or lack of reaction mirrored by the therapist, this may be the true value of the therapy. If the client learns how to ask salient questions to process situations, this may be the true value of therapy. If the client learns the pathway out of painful memories, this may be the true value of therapy.

While conducting a group with ex-offender drug addicts, I was explaining the concept of a Higher Power and how it could help people stay clean. One of the group members, Sam, said he didn't believe in that "Higher Power bullshit." I told him that was ok, that I was not trying to sell him on anything.

I then said to him, "How long have you been clean?"

He said, "Almost five months."

I congratulated him and asked how he was able to stay clean.

He then told the group, "I have a four-year-old son. His mother is a crack whore, and I am the only person he has in his life to take care of him. He doesn't need me coming home all drugged up."

"So you could say that a major reason that you are not getting high is because of your love for your son?"

"Well, yea, you could say that."

"Would it be fair to say that love you have for your son is a Higher Power, because it is keeping you clean?

"Yes, I never thought of it in that way. You might be right."

We cannot underestimate the power of love in healing:

Barry, a 14-year-old, had what I call a love affair with every drug he encountered. He loved pot, and he loved acid, and he loved cocaine. While he was quite open about his drug use with me, and I appreciated his trust, nevertheless he scared me with his tales of drug bravado. I felt like I had little impact on changing his attitude. I did tell him that if he continued to do drugs in a dangerous way, I would have to tell his parents.

Meanwhile, I was a co-facilitator of a domestic violence group and unbeknownst to me, Barry's father had been referred to group. He told of a situation in which he had a son who was into drugs, and how grounding or enforcing other consequences was not having the desired effect. The father had even gone so far as to nail Barry's window shut, so that he could not sneak out at night. One day his son was getting ready to go out, and the father told him he could not leave. His son challenged him saying he could not stop him. They got into a pushing match, and the boy fell down some stairs. Totally exasperated, the mom called the police, and the father was arrested for assaulting his son. By the end of the group, I began to figure out the boy was my client. (I had always dealt with his mom and never the dad.)

In the next group the father expressed fear for his son and an inability to communicate with him. He also disclosed that he had a drinking problem, which his son would throw that up in his face anytime he tried to talk to him about drug use. The group advised him that he was losing his son and his credibility, and he needed to decide what battles he wanted to fight.

He came back the next week saying things had calmed down some. He had told his son that obviously he had no power to stop him from getting high, and that if his son decided to continue to use, it was all on him. He told his son he would not give him money, nor bail him out if he got arrested, and would not come to see him if he was hospitalized. And he disclosed to the group that he was making a serious attempt to stop drinking realizing he was asking his son to do something he himself was not willing to do.

Several weeks later he indicated that the situation at home had improved dramatically. His son had gotten arrested with some buddies smoking pot at a concert. Barry had cut back on his drug use as a result and was also staying at home more. He was very concerned that he would be drug tested when he went to court. His attendance at school and his grades had improved significantly.

While this trend continued, there was an incident that seemed like a major setback. The mother received a call from the school saying that Barry had skipped out of school after first period seemingly to get high with his best friend. This had been his old pattern. The father said that when his wife told him what had happened that evening, he responded differently that he would have normally when Barry came home. In the past he would have been irate and "tore into him." Barry came home around 7:00 and zipped through the living room saying, "Hi, I'm home," and immediately went to his room. The father went to his room and knocked on the door. Barry responded very nastily, "What do ya want?" The father told him in a calm voice that he wanted to talk to him.

"What about?" Barry asked.

"I just want to talk to you about today," the father replied. Finally, Barry opened the door and let him in.

They sat on the bed together and the father shared that the school had called and told his mother that he had skipped out after first period. "What happened?" the father asked. "You were doing so well. I was so proud of you and now I am so disappointed," As he said that, tears started rolling down the father's cheek.

Barry, seeing this, said "I'm sorry, dad. I screwed up," and then <u>he</u> started crying.

They ended up hugging each other, and the father told the group, "That hug had more influence on him than months and months of yelling, cussing, and fighting him." There was not a dry eye in the group either.

And that is an example of the power of love to change people.

Massage Therapy and Counseling

What do massage therapy and counseling have in common? One answer is the metaphor of semi-permeable membranes.

Remember when you learned about semi-permeable membranes in biology class? Certain cells have a semi-permeable membrane, which allows certain chemicals to pass into the cell wall but not to flow out. Massage therapy is like that, and so is doing therapy.

I received training as a massage therapist. The instructor stressed the importance of members of the class taking care of ourselves. He warned us about taking on the negative energy of the client who was in pain. Pain is blocked energy, and the goal of massage is to unblock that energy, in order to promote healing. He told us that we could use our hands to transmit positive energy into the client, but warned against absorbing negative energy. He described the process as being like semi-permeable membranes giving out positive, healing energy, but not absorbing the negative. Massage therapists break up negative energy with a conscious intention to utilize the energy in their hands to promote healing by flowing positive energy to the clients.

So, in counseling clients, you can give positive energy to their problem: attention, compassion, concern, advice, caring, and love, without taking on the burden of their problem: their negativity, fear, depression, or whatever feeling they may emit. We can be compassionate without allowing negative energy to pull us down or stymie us. Taking on their negativity does not help them and compromises our effectiveness. This does not mean we are not empathetic. We may very well accurately sense their dilemma and suffering. The difference is that we do not take it on as our pain. We can detach from it and don't take it home with us. This does not diminish the therapeutic interaction, but rather enhances it. It requires being conscious of our interactions and how the interactions affect us. Maintaining a sense of detachment does not lessen our capacity for understanding or ability to be compassionate. If you find yourself sinking down as clients talk, or you take clients' problems home with you, then that is a sign you have crossed over the line. If you are pulled down by a client's energy or problems, you should stop, sit up straight, and tell yourself, "I care, but I do not need to be pulled down by this situation." To do this the therapist must be mindful. Pay attention to your body: your breathing, posture, and muscle tension. Stay in a relaxed peaceful, accepting, non-reactive mode. You can express compassion without becoming distraught; you can express sadness without becoming overwhelmed; you can express anger without taking it personally. All of this involves a consciousness of self without being self-conscious.

The following exemplifies this and is not only helpful for therapists but a great handout for co-dependents or overly involved parents:

LETTING GO

To let go does not mean to stop caring
it means I can't do it for someone else.
To let go is not to cut myself off,
but to realize I can't control another.
To let go is not to enable,
but to allow learning from natural consequences.
To let go is to admit powerlessness,
which means the outcome is not in my hands.
To let go is not to try to change or blame another,
it is to make the most of myself.
To let go is not to care for,
but to care about.
To let go is not to fix,
but to be supportive.
To let go is not to judge,
but to allow another to be a human being.
To let go is not to be in the middle arranging all the outcomes,
but to allow others to affect their destinies.
To let go is not to be protective,

but to permit another to face reality.
To let go is not to deny,
but to accept.
To let go is not to nag, scold, or argue,
but instead search out my own shortcomings and correct them.
To let go is not to adjust everything to my desires,
but to take each day as it comes and cherish myself in it.
To let go is not to criticize and regulate anybody,
but to become what I dream I can be.
To let go is not to regret the past,
but to grow and live for the future.
To let go is not to control,
but to pray and turn it over.
To let go is to fear less
and love more.

—*Unknown Author*

Massage therapy training is also helpful in learning how to deal with physical trauma. If the client has a very sore place, which may have been traumatized, the first step is to massage around the area and thereby desensitize the surrounding muscles. Next, is go to over the afflicted area quite lightly and continue to gently increase the pressure. If you go too fast too soon, you can end up re-traumatizing the muscle. The key is *to go in gently, win the trust of the muscle, allow it to relax, and exit gently.*

This procedure is a great metaphor for processing emotional trauma. The first step is to find out about the situation surrounding the trauma (how old the client was, what was going on in her life, what she thought was happening, what effect it is having on her now). Once she is comfortable talking about that, then you can begin to ask more specific questions like, "What do you remember about it? Where did it happen? and How did you respond?" And then finally get into the detail of actual events if necessary. The details are only necessary to get to the emotional pain and may even not need to be expressed verbally. Some therapists may want to know out of curiosity or even a kind of voyeurism, but there must be a strong therapeutic reason to pursue the details and only to the extent the client is ready and willing to go there. With certain techniques, such as EMDR (Eye Movement Desensitization and Reprocessing) or brainspotting (See Chapter 10), the material may be accessed and healed with no verbal component or explanation to the therapist of what happened. Once that happens, the therapist needs to reassure the clients they will be fine and to congratulated them for their courage and perseverance. The whole process is designed to diminish and desensitize the impact of the trauma, win the client's trust, build the client's confidence, and to discharge the emotional pain, so healing can take place.

Listen, Listen, Listen

One of the best ways to enhance a therapeutic relationship is to listen intently to the clients. This is so obvious that you may be tempted to skip this section, since we assume we know how to listen. However, too often, effective listening is sabotaged by talking: needing or wanting to interject our own ideas or questions, doing some special technique with the client, or having the impulse to give our professional opinion, i.e., to tell or instruct instead of listen. Some of the best "aha" moments in therapy come when a client truly feels heard, maybe for the first time in his life. One of my clients told me, "I used to think no one would ever really understand me, because no one would take the time or interest to hear me out, but there was something different about what you did. When you were listening to me, I didn't feel like you were judging me; I felt like you really cared, and at times, I felt like you knew me better than I know myself."

We were all taught active listening in our training, so what is so difficult about listening? The question is how active? There is lazy active listening, which is just being able to parrot back to the client what they have just said. We hear the words and ask them to tell how that made them feel. But there is much more to listening than this:

- We can listen for details.
- We can listen for the meaning and deeper meaning.
- We can listen for patterns.
- We listen for clues.
- We listen for strengths.
- We listen for what is not being said.

- We listen for special phrases.
- We listen for specific dates.

We listen with an intention that can include some or all the following:

- We listen to show we are interested.
- We listen because we care.
- We listen so they can be heard.
- We listen to understand.
- We listen so the client can share.
- We listen so the client can discover.
- We listen to build relationship.
- We listen to develop intimacy.
- We listen with awareness of ourselves.

One can learn more about this by reading *The Third Ear* by Theodore Reik described in a *Psychology Today* blog by one writer:

> One of the most illuminating writers on therapeutic listening is Theodor Reik, who studied how the skill of listening to another is intertwined with the ability to listen to yourself. According to Reik, the mind has a natural ability to decipher the deeper emotional meanings conveyed by the speaker, even when these meanings are unstated or unclear. He famously called this natural deep listening ability, The Third Ear, and recommended that therapeutic listeners attend to our internal responses. From Reik's point of view, bad listeners are those who do not slow down and pay attention to how they feel when listening, and quickly respond before letting anything sink in. Our dimly felt inner responses to the other person's words provide the most penetrating understanding of what they mean.
>
> The Third Ear is a rich source of emotional information that can be fruitfully drawn upon in everyday relationships. The next time you are confused or concerned by an interaction, don't respond immediately. Take a momentary pause, and try listening to your inner feelings. You may find that doing so is initially uncomfortable. Awkward memories, unexpected emotions, or strange associations may emerge. However, when patiently pursued, these unbidden inner experiences can awaken a deep understanding and make relationships freer and fuller.

www.psychologytoday.com/blog/meaningful-you, Psychology Today, *Aug 17, 2012*

In today's world of psychotherapy, another way of characterizing this kind of listening is "mindful listening." Reik would have been very comfortable with this movement. By allowing yourself to totally be in the here and now, consciously aware externally and internally, you can be the catalyst for the client's self-discovery and disclosure. It is perhaps the therapist's most effective tool.

The Greatest Therapeutic Tool

While there is a lot of debate over which therapeutic methodology works best for a specific problem, there is one therapeutic tool that trumps all the others. What is that tool? Aren't you curious? Well, that is the tool—curiosity. While on the one hand, it may have killed a cat, on the other hand it has led to some great therapeutic breakthroughs both on an individual level and within the field of counseling itself. If you can nurture this habit by becoming genuinely curious about every client, you will be able to work through most any situation in which you are stuck.

Curiosity by the therapist communicates a desire to understand, maintains a freshness to the counseling and discovers solutions in co-operation with the client. By being curious the therapist sparks the curiosity of the client, too. Instead of seeing their situation the old, tired, overwhelming way, they now see it in a new light, a kind of new adventure. This is especially true if the counselor is enthusiastic and upbeat about the process. It creates a new kind of hope.

Sometimes curiosity means taking therapy to a deeper level and not being satisfied with the status quo.

Raymond, a three-and-a-half-year-old, diagnosed with autism spectrum disorder, had a preoccupation with fans, wheels, and all rotary objects. During intake, the first thing he noticed was the ceiling fan and pointed to it. He wanted it turned on, so he could watch it. He had no interest in playing with blocks, Legos or puppets, only objects with wheels such as cars and trucks and anything that spun. One of his presenting problems was difficulty with potty training. No matter what approach was used, Raymond just became more and more recalcitrant, almost to the point that sitting on the toilet was traumatizing. As a result, he had problems with constipation.

One day the in-home counselor realized that he occasionally had "accidents." She was curious about how and when this happened. She discovered it was usually when he was sitting on his bed. She also observed that it tended to happen when the ceiling fan was on, and Raymond was looking up at it. What she realized was that the fan was relaxing for him, and thus caused him to relax his bowels. Taking it one step further, she got him a little portable battery-powered fan to take with him when he went to the bathroom. Not only did it reduce the trauma, but he started having regular bowel movements and within a few weeks he could regulate himself.

Not content to just know that the fan worked, the counselor was curious to know why. She began to probe into his past, and she discovered through questioning adult family members that his fascinations with circular objects began when he was an infant. His mother tended to neglect him leaving him lying in his crib for hours at a time. He would be hungry or wet with no response. Above him he had a mobile that turned, and he would lull himself to sleep looking at the mobile. She also noticed there were pinwheels on the crib which he would spin when he had no one to occupy him. So, at an early age these spinning objects became imprinted on him as objects of self-soothing.

It was the counselor's curiosity and willingness to pursue the situation that unlocked the origin of the problem and therefore dictated the solution.

One-Downmanship

Generally, the therapist-client relationship is seen as the therapist being co-creator with the client, or the therapist is the expert and the client is seeking help. However, another effective approach is to reverse roles and the power differential so that the therapist takes a one-down position. There are several variations of this theme:

Columbo – A technique for questioning was coined based on the 1970's TV series, Columbo, in which a detective named Columbo played by Peter Falk was known for "playing dumb," so to speak. Seemingly bumbling and disheveled, he would often ask questions for which he either pretended not to know the answer or at least exhibited a kind of cluelessness. This often threw the interviewees off target, because they were expecting someone to come on as demanding, authoritative and intimidating. What they got was just the opposite— someone who was humble and even incompetent. But there was "a method to his madness." He was actually sly and calculating. His questions were along the line of "I can't figure this out. Help me understand what's going on here" or "This doesn't make any sense to me." This kind of questioning helped to put the person at ease. He was also famous for winding up a set of questions and getting ready to leave, only to turn around and ask, "One last question…" People at this point tended to have their guard down thinking the pressure of the interview was over and often blurted out some highly significant fact about who committed the murder.

This approach can be used in counseling, though in a much more benign way. It often helps to put nervous clients at ease. For instance, there are clients who are fearful that therapists or psychologists have some special extra-sensory power to be mind-readers and can uncover their most guarded secrets by tripping them up or seeing through their pretense. The "Columbo approach" puts them at ease. It is also use useful when the clients are being contradictory. For example, a client says he never gets mad, and yet at the same time absolutely refused speak to his wife for three days. The counselor could say, "Help me figure this out. One part of you says one thing, and yet it seems another part is saying the opposite. What's that about?" By taking this approach, the therapist levels the playing field and creates an attitude of accessibility and humility.

You Know Uno – In the spirit of Columbo, it is often critical when working with children to change the power differential. Children are typically in the position looking up to tall adults, who most often are looking down on them. These interactions convey to children that someone who knows much more than they do is telling them what to do. This can be intimidating for the child. I often sit on the floor when working with children while they are seated on the sofa. Making this small move changes the interpersonal dynamics, so that I am looking up to them, rather than forcing them to look up to me.

I also try to find some topic or game with which they are familiar and have them teach it to me. Even though I basically know how to play Uno, I ask them to teach me. It puts them in the role of expert. I also see how clear they are in their instructions, how well they can express themselves on neutral subjects, and to whether or not they change the rules in their favor. I may or may not let them beat me… and sometimes they honestly do. In this way, I can model a graceful way to lose or reinforce some positive aspect of the child.

"Wow, you are pretty good at this. What else are you good at?"

Mahatma Gandhi — Mahatma Gandhi's grandson tells a story about a time when he was young and was charged with picking up his famous grandfather from the airport. However, on this particular day he was running late. When he arrived late to the airport to pick up his famous grandfather, he was asked by Gandhi, "Why were you late?" Gandhi had called and knew already that his grandson was running late, so he was not reprimanding him, but merely inquiring as to the cause. Nevertheless, the grandson lied.

In relating this story, he says, "I lied to Gandhi!" He says that his grandfather, obviously realizing the lie, turned to look at him and tears began to well up in his grandfather's eyes. He spoke these words as tears streamed down his face, "I must give repentance for whatever it was that I did to you that would cause you to be so afraid of me that you would have to lie. So… I will walk home these fifteen miles."

The grandson states that he still remembers following his famous grandfather, five miles per hour in the dark, as he walked the fifteen miles because his grandson had lied to him.

—Bryan Post in *Why Kids Lie*

In the spirit of Mahatma Gandhi, another way to change the power differential is to take on the burden of whatever difficulty there may be in the relationship. If someone lies, and it becomes obvious, take on the burden by apologizing that you had not come across as someone to whom they could tell the truth, that somewhere along the line you had given them the impression you could not be trusted. So, instead of confronting the person about their lying, the therapist assumes the responsibility, which takes the burden off the person and places it on the therapist. The point is that the relationship is more important than the lying. Ironically, this often has more of an impact on the client than confronting them about the lying.

One day I got a call from the receptionist that the mother of one of my adolescent client had called and said her son refused to come to the session. She wanted me to "talk some sense into him," and get him to come for therapy. They had been arguing, and he said he was through with therapy. On top of that, he said at his last appointment, he had to wait in the lobby for 15 minutes until I came down to get him. So I was anticipating a hassle with a kid who is going to be a pain.

Before I answered the phone, I paused and asked myself, "Am I operating out of love or fear?" The answer was obviously fear—fear that I wouldn't be able to get him to change his mind, fear that he would stop coming, fear that I had somehow failed or offended him, fear that this phone call would take up time that I had scheduled for another client. However, I decided to change my attitude to be open to whatever was happening in a loving and calm way. Mother was obviously very upset and complaining. I listened patiently and understandingly. Finally, I said I would be glad to talk to him.

"Hey, buddy, what's happening?"

"My mom and I are fighting, and I don't want to come to counseling."

"I'm sorry to hear that, but I respect your decision. Your mom said you were upset that you had to sit in the lobby for 15 minutes last time. I apologize for that; I thought I explained I had an emergency call."

"You did. I wasn't that upset," he said, "I just said that because I didn't want to come to a session today."

I thanked him for being honest. "It is totally okay with me if you don't want to come today, but sometimes when arguments arise and people are at a stalemate, it is a good time to come for a session. It might help to talk it over.

He started to calm down and said, "I don't know. Maybe I will, maybe I won't.

I said "Okay, see you in a half hour. Thanks for being open," ignoring the "maybe I won't" part.

He did come to the session, and we had a productive time during which he gained some balance in his perspective and his emotions. Also, I could validate his concerns about his mother, and yet get him to be open about more constructive ways of responding to her. It was by changing my attitude that he changed his attitude. The session was effective due to sincerely connecting with him and being genuine.

This approach can be used not just with lying, but other situations such as apologizing to the client for having given them the wrong homework, since they did not do it. This may also be used when clients are avoiding subjects by saying that you may have introduced them too soon, or that you are going too fast in therapy, and that you must have misread the signals. Some may object to this approach for it seems to "let the client off the hook." However, it is a way to discuss the problem without automatically putting the client on the defensive.

Being Present

One of the characteristics of the great masters of psychotherapy is the ability to be fully present with the clients. This means being totally attentive to the client's every nuance, verbal and non-verbal. Perhaps no one did this better than the famous psychiatrist, Milton Erickson. Having had polio as a young child, he was limited in what he could do physically. So, he mainly observed others. He was later able to take this power of observation into the therapy room with him.

> He (Erickson) emphasized the use of all the therapist's sensory modalities, especially watching and listening, in the search for clues to effective therapy and to how therapy was working. The patient's language changes, changes in vocal dynamics, alternations in muscle tonus and gestures were some of the things he mentioned as important to observe.
>
> Erickson once told me about a psychiatrist who came to him and was talking about his ex-wife. The man claimed that for professional reasons he did not want to tell Erickson his ex-wife's name, but he kept dropping hints to the contrary. During the session, Erickson got a nagging sense of wanting to call an acquaintance of his. He interrupted the session to call this woman and told her than even though her name was Kathy, he had the strongest urge to call her Nancy. As he said this, he looked meaningfully at the psychiatrist, who was listening as Erickson talked on the phone. When Erickson said the name Nancy, the psychiatrist exclaimed that that was his ex-wife's name. The man opened up more after Erickson's discovery of his ex-wife's name. When I asked Erickson how he knew the name, he replied that his unconscious mind must have picked it up. The man had probably stressed the syllables "nan" and "see" as he was talking to Erickson. His unconscious, through association with his friend Kathy, had put the clients together.
>
> —O'Hanlon, William, Taproots, pp.15-16

When I was a resident-in-counseling, I asked my supervisor (who had the most thriving private practice in town), what the key was to his success. He said something I will never forget. "Whenever a client is in my office, there is no person, no phone call, no situation that is more important than the client right in front of me."

Also, in the process of building a practice I developed several marketing strategies and listened to lectures about building a successful practice. But one day it dawned on me that the best way to build a successful practice was to make each session a success by switching my focus from some grand entrepreneurial scheme to fully focusing on building success with each client in each session.

What did that mean? How do I do that? I had to give each client my fullest attention and be totally committed to helping them, i.e., to be totally present with them. Sometimes this called for breathing with them at the same rate, posturing myself to match their posture (I almost always slouch down in my chair when working with adolescents), to listen for repeated phrases that may indicate a pattern, or pick up and follow through on unusual words or metaphors, which often can lead to opening an emotional doorway. On a subconscious level, clients sense the degree of intensity of your involvement with them. They may never recognize it, or acknowledge it, but you can see it in the increase in ease with which they express themselves.

Jeremiah was 14 and reticent to talk. He told his mother that no one could get him to talk. He slumped down on the sofa, crossed his arms, said, "I don't have anything to say," and fell silent. I mirrored his position and posture and told him I totally understood why he might feel that way. I told him that I would probably feel the same way if I were in his shoes.

Then I began to muse, "...and if I felt that way, I wonder how I could get myself to open up and talk?" I then did something unpredictable: I sat on the floor. This automatically had me below him looking up at him and he was above me looking down at me. Most adults in authority had towered over him.

"Help me understand what it would take to get someone to open up?" I was taking a one-down position by asking for his help.

He said, "I don't know. You're the counselor."

I said, "Ah, yes, but you're the client." I saw him start to back down a little bit; his arms were not so tightly held.

"Why do you think people don't want to talk?"

He said, "They don't think it will do them any good."

Now he is talking. I began to appeal to his sense of wanting to validate his position. "I understand that; logically talking about a problem doesn't make it go away. I often think about that myself. What is it about talking that works? In a way, I don't know how it does, but my experience is that it does. My experience is just that it works."

"Well, it won't work for me," he replied.

"Maybe," I said, "I like your determination. How did you become that way?" I asked.

"I think I inherited from my dad." Then he promptly said, "You're getting me to talk."

"I won't tell anyone," I said, "it will just be between you and me."

Being fully present means going wherever the client wants to go, joining in their concerns, emotions, thinking patterns and behavior. This is called pacing. But then if you have the right kind of rapport you can begin to challenge, encourage, or re-direct them, and see if they will follow, always being aware of how they are responding to your direction. This is called leading. Pacing helps you join with the client, and leading is intervening in a way to move clients, sometimes out of their comfort zone. They can do this if they know you will support them and they can trust you to understand and provide safety for them.

Be a Student of the Client

As mentioned earlier every client has something to teach us. Each client presents a unique situation that we have never handled before. There are many things clients can teach us.

They can teach us about their disorder. The best way to learn about a disorder is to work with it in each client who can demonstrate his or her version of what it is about. Obviously, what depression is for one person is not what depression is for another. The best source for learning about disorders is the people who have them. Each time you work with a client diagnosed with schizophrenic, you learn more about schizophrenia. Each time you work with someone who with selective mutism, you learn more about selective mutism.

They can teach us about what works for them and what doesn't. When you try a technique or hypothesis with a client and it is effective, it validates that technique or hypothesis for that client. Likewise, if it does not work, you may or may not discard it for that client. It may be that you did not adequately explain it or its purpose, or that the timing was wrong, or that the client did not see its relevance. In any case, it is valuable to ask what they thought about the technique and what fit for them or what they did not like about it. If this can be negotiated and better understood by you or the client, then give it another try; otherwise move on to other approaches.

They can teach us about their medications. A great opportunity to learn about different psychotropic medications is to explore the effects they are having on each client. Take the opportunity to study each one, explore how they are benefiting the client, or not, and what the side effects are. In this way over time you will have learned about a large variety of drugs and their impact.

They can teach us about their culture. Talking to a client gives you some sense of the kind of culture from which they come, whether it is a distinct culture or subculture. The best approach is to ask clients about their traditions and beliefs rather than automatically assuming you know what works for them.

They can teach us about faith, perseverance, and survival. Each client has his own struggle. Some clients show great bravery and strength in coping with their problems. They can inspire us, both in our personal life and our professional life by affirming the goodness of the human spirit and the value of the counseling we're doing

They can teach us about little known facts. As mentioned previously, I had a client who was obsessed with the Cartoon Channel. He taught me about many different cartoon programs— their characters and plots—much more than I ever wanted to know!

They can teach us about their interests. While being a counselor I have learned about race car driving, organic gardening, flying airplanes, the best kinds of marijuana, Japanese Anime, dinosaurs, pickup trucks, Norse Shamanism, pseudo-seizures, fireworks, rap music, sex techniques, raising poodles, Egyptian paganism, running a bakery, hunting, and Civil War battles, just to name a few. Most of this was unsolicited information from clients, but valuable in terms of establishing rapport.

They can teach us about ourselves. I ask supervisees after we have processed a difficult case, what they have learned about themselves from working with this client. This question usually surprises them as they have neither taken the time nor had the inclination to think about the client in this way. When they do ask themselves, most often they will start out listing the negative aspects of what they did such as how they gave up too easily, how much they invested their ego into having successful outcomes, or how prejudiced they were toward a certain diagnosis. However, they can also learn about their positive characteristics such as their creativity, clinical insight, or their ability to navigate through rough situations. Most therapists I supervise have humility and rarely give themselves credit for playing a role in any client success. While this is laudable on the one hand, on the other hand, they are missing an opportunity to learn about their clinical strengths.

They can teach us about how we don't want to be. Sometimes it is difficult to see what we can learn from certain clients. They are not particularly interesting, or they have some personality trait that offends us, or they may be involved in mean or immoral acts, which run counter to our values. In a round-about way, they may reaffirm for us that we never want to be that way, because we see how damaging it can be.

They can teach us how to help them. I never cease to be amazed at how honest teenagers can be if you have the right rapport with them and ask them the right questions. One of my favorite questions to ask teenagers is, "If you were your parent, what would you do with you?" Often they will say, "I would be a lot stricter on me. They let me get away with too much." In this statement, they are saying they need more guidance and interventions from their parents. In effect, they are telling me how to help them. Many clients know what they need to do to get better, but they have certain roadblocks that prevent them from achieving their goal. By asking what they need to do to get better and then coming forth to help motivate or strategize with them, our job becomes easier.

They teach us how to be better counselors. I start nearly every group supervision group by asking therapists to talk about their successes. There are many reasons for this: It starts the group off on a positive note, it forces counselors to search out their successes (which often is difficult for them to uncover), it gives the other therapists ideas they can try and most importantly, I follow up with asking what made their success work?

I also do a similar process with clients as we review their week. Was there any gain or progress? What worked for you? I want to know how did you do that? What changed? What have you or did you learn? What does this say about you? How can you use this for further change? Client feedback can be our most important learning tool to help us grow as counselors.

Contract for Therapy

If therapy seems to be going nowhere, it may be because there is no *contract* for therapy. Things can go amiss because the therapist thinks one thing is happening and the client another, or the client is lost in the process and has no idea how to proceed.

Sarah, a 30-year-old divorced, white female presented for therapy with depression and stated that she felt like her life was going nowhere. Her husband had been abusive to her, and she came to believe she had deserved this treatment. She had thoughts of being with other men, and though she never acted on them, she felt guilty nonetheless.

She also had recently been in a car wreck, which was her fault, and she was devastated that she had caused some harm to others, i.e., dented their car. Each session she covered the same story repeatedly. While the counselor was sympathetic, after several weeks of her repeating this story, it appeared that the sessions were going nowhere. Sarah seemed restless, and the counselor was bored. Finally, the counselor said, "I'm not sure what the purpose of our getting together is. I want to help you, but I'm not sure how it is you want me to help you." Sarah said she had no idea, but that her idea of doing therapy was to come in and talk about problems, so she thought she was doing the right thing. She immediately started apologizing, and then started crying saying, "I can't even do therapy right." The counselor immediately said she was supportive of the effort that Sarah was making, but pointed out that there is more to therapy than just talking about problems—the goal was to define and achieve what she would like to have different in her life.

The problem was there was no contract. The counselor had not set out the goals and structure of therapy. The counselor worked hard to create motivation and direction, but the counselor felt like she was doing it all alone. There were major areas to focus on: the client's depression, her history of abuse, low self-esteem, and the effects of her car accident, but Sarah was unclear about what she wanted; she just knew that she was miserable. Because of the above interaction, the therapist developed a contract with Sarah that helped her outline the problems, set priorities, and develop solutions. Having this contract helped Sarah to better understand the therapy process and what was expected of her, and for the counselor to better understand Sarah's needs and goals.

The contract seals the therapeutic bond and identifies each person's responsibilities. It provides a clear guideline for how to proceed. It is mostly done informally. Just a question like, "Let's review again what you would like to get out of therapy and what you would like to achieve," can clarify the contract.

The Risky Business of Confrontation

While we have been talking about many ways to build a strong relationship with the client, there is a therapeutic intervention that many therapists are hesitant to take for fear of damaging the relationship, and that is . We can easily build a relationship with someone who is agreeable, understanding, and accepting; it is another matter to build a relationship in which you are challenging the other person. You run the risk of alienating the client by challenging them at an inappropriate time in the therapeutic process. The relationship should be strong for clients to hear and accept the therapeutic challenge, but once that bond has been created, you can confront clients with the harshest of truths, and they will accept it.

Early in my career, it was suggested that I as a clinical supervisor of a drug-treatment program, visit a therapeutic community. Therapeutic communities in the late 70s and early 80s were unique in their treatment approach. Based on philosophies generated by programs such as Synanon, they often took the most confrontational approach to therapy, which from the outside may appear abusive. In the current days of Human Rights, most of these programs would no longer be permitted to provide the kind of treatment they did. The basic idea was almost like a therapeutic boot camp. Clients were confronted and challenged from the very beginning of treatment. Sometimes they were forced to cut their hair, carry signs, do menial tasks, and endure being yelled at for not doing a chore or homework. At the program I visited, there was even a monitor sitting in the lobby to whom participants had to report their every move. ("Sir, I am going upstairs; Sir, I am going to the bathroom; Sir, I am going across the street").

This was the kind of program in which the staff would come in the middle of the night, and if there was ketchup on the top of the ketchup bottles, they would take a five-pound bag of flour and throw it all over the house, wake up all the clients, and make them clean it up. Obviously, under these kinds of conditions many feelings rose to the surface. Amid all this pressure and sometimes chaos, there was group therapy, which a client could call for at any time with permission from staff. The group therapy sessions were incredibly intense with people breaking down, screaming, and crying; while others gathered around that person offering support and understanding. This level of intensity of group therapy often created feelings in other clients, and they too would be crying and have a group supporting them. So, there was a method to the madness, and it was effective for helping this targeted population to go beyond their hard-core defenses to more meaningful feelings and issues.

My first day there, it was decided that I would go through the different levels of the 18-month program, so that I could experience them. My first task was to sit in a chair in the corner facing the wall and think about why I was there and what I wanted to achieve. I only had to sit there for an hour, but other participants had to sit there all day on their first day. I went through all four levels in three days ending up in a staff meeting—probably the fastest anyone had ever done that.

One of the nights I was there, some of the residents were doing a variety of tasks at 3:00 a.m. Some were cleaning the tops of the windowsills, and these windows were 10 to 12 feet high. Some of the senior members were working feverishly to decide how to hang a sign from the front porch. I asked one of the members why they were awake at this time trying to decide how to hang a sign. He told me that Henry, the director, had requested it before he left for home earlier that day. I asked him why he it was so important to do what Henty requested. He said that the director informed him that he had spilled more dope than the client had shot. He then told me that Henry knew him better than any other person in the world, and he knew there was nothing this director would not do for him, even risking his life for him. "Therefore," he said, "I will do anything I can for this man."

Right there and then I realized that once you have the respect and trust of clients, you can say or do just about anything to them, and they will respond, but if you do not have that kind of relationship and you challenge or demand something from them, they will balk. So, the best confrontation exists in the context of a trusting relationship.

Another important factor in confrontation is to soften the blow. This involves pairing the subject of the confrontation with good intentions. This often takes some creative thinking. One could do the stroke-kick method cited in Chapter 4, where a client is complimented followed by a sometimes stinging observation:

- I know you love your children, Mrs. Jones, but I wonder why you are so tough on them.
- I think I know you pretty well, and I would bet the last thing you would want people to think about you is that you are cheating on your wife.
- I am amazed at how much you care about others, and yet you continue to play the victim role.

> This principle can be extended to even longer interactions. John Gottman, the famous marriage researcher, wrote: "The research shows that if your discussion begins with a harsh startup, it will inevitably end up on a negative note, even if there are lots of attempts to "make nice." Statistics tell the story: 96% of the time, you can predict the outcome of the conversation based on the first 3 minutes of the fifteen-minute interaction. A harsh startup dooms you to fail."
>
> —*Gottman, Silver, 1999*

He was talking about marriage, but the same principle applies to counseling. By harsh, he means criticism, sarcasm, blaming, and shaming.

A shorter version of this could be called the "soft-hard-soft" approach. Soft means that you use a soft voice and "soften" the message by being complimentary or inquisitive. So, you start off softly and say something positive, then confront with the truth, and then exit with a soft follow-up, which makes what clients did more understandable. This is kind of an extension of the stroke-kick method.

- You seem like such a caring person, and yet the way you neglect your family must make you lie awake at night. I can't imagine it doesn't bother you, given how sensitive you are.

- The majority of men look at pornography, and while you doing it tremendously hurts your wife, I imagine you thought it was not affecting her.
- It seems that your drinking was a great way to make friends and progress at your job, and you never thought that it would end up costing you your job.

The soft-hard-soft approach confronts but places the feedback in a positive light, generally assuming there was a positive intention for what they did. The goal is not to minimize the effect of or to excuse the action, but rather to encourage clients to come to terms with their short-comings without raising their defenses or damaging the relationship.

Another approach to confrontation is the two-way mirror described in Chapter 4. A way to confront someone with sensitive feedback can say, "I am conflicted. Part of me believes that you really care, and another part of me believes you are being self-centered. I don't know which part to believe. Help me figure this out." In this way, you can present the opposites and let the client sort them out.

Well-planned interventions can be extremely powerful and helpful, but poorly timed or harshly stated confrontation can easily dilute the therapeutic good-will built up over time.

Most therapists have to work too hard to build a trusting relationship to see it crumble, if the client perceives that the therapist is being unfair or too hard on him.

CHAPTER 7

Empowering the Client

You must be the change you wish to see in the world.

—Mahatma Gandhi

WHAT IS THE GREATEST RESOURCE FOR ANY COUNSELOR? It is the client. The counselor is only the catalyst to activate clients by giving them the support, direction, and encouragement to make whatever changes they need to overcome their distress.

The story is told that in the 1900's when circuses started popping up in America, most of them were centered in large cities. Realizing that there was a vast market in the "hinterlands," the circuses decided to take the show on the road. One of the biggest attractions for most people then was the exotic animals, including elephants. Most people had never seen such a large animal in person. The problem became how to transport them, and how to keep them from wandering once they arrived, since there were no transportable structures large enough to hold them. What the circus people knew, however, was that if a baby elephant's leg was tethered to a large stake with a large rope, it soon would quit struggling to roam and accept its "limitations." So, the management thought maybe they would just take baby elephants. But what they discovered was that as the baby elephants grew, they could still be tethered by just a stake and a rope, even though a grown elephant could free itself with one large tug on the rope. The elephants just accepted they were bound by the stake and never tried to free themselves.

And so it is with clients. They have often lost sight of their strengths and potential, but it is amazing the resources clients have of which they are not aware. Sometimes these resources lie just below the surface or in their successes of the past. Often they may know what to do, but lack the confidence to try, or they have tried a solution once that did not work, but might work now. Simply asking the question, "What do **you** think you need to do?" will often reveal the solution. And then follow that question with, "What keeps you from doing that?"

Clients are empowered by giving them support and helping them to identify their strengths. If they have grown up in an environment in which all their observations, ideas, or feelings were criticized, belittled or ignored, then they come to believe that what they think and feel is not valid, no matter what. Helping them break through that belief can be critical. This requires trust in the therapist and ultimately in themselves to overcome the fear that blocks them from unlocking the answers conscious or unconscious.

Client's Model of the World

One of the greatest ways to work with clients is to explore their model of the world, i.e., the world from their perspective and, more specifically, their perspective of their problems. This seems like common sense, and it is, but there is a depth and timing to it that is very critical. This is the heart of client-centered therapy.

There are two aspects of exploring a client's model of the world. One is to get a general idea of their world—what are their beliefs, values, strengths, weaknesses, concerns, inspirations, or their relationships, jobs, hobbies, or pastimes? By looking through these lenses, you minimize resistance to therapy and can begin to understand the context of the problem. With more reticent clients, this can take many sessions; with more seasoned or cooperative clients, this can be done in one or two sessions.

The second aspect is exploring a client's view of the problems and what Scott Miller identifies as the client's theory of change. This includes *"… the client's ideas, attitudes, and speculation about change."* He further states, *"Honoring the client's theory occurs when you follow, encourage, and implement the client's ideas for change or when you select a technique or procedure that fits client's beliefs about their problem(s) and the change process."*

He explained how best to do this. *"Exploring the client's theory of change requires a therapist to adopt a view of him- or herself as an alien from another planet. The 'alien' therapist seeks a pristine understanding of an encounter with the client's idiosyncratic interpretations and experiences, having no other database from which to draw conclusions.*

The therapist patiently listens, permitting the client complete freedom to tell the whole story without interruption. Clients not only provide their views regarding the problem, but also their orientations about life, their goals and ambitions, and the pressures and events surrounding their complaints. In short, clients unfold their philosophies of life.

The therapist learns and converses in the client's language and allows as much room as possible for the client's words and interpretations to emerge. Conversing in the client's language is respectful, demonstrates understanding, and prevents the imposition of different connotations not intended by the client." (Duncan, Hubble, Miller 1997)

Why is this so important? One reason is that realizations and solutions generated by clients are much more powerful than those imposed by the counselor. There is an immediate ownership and hopefully an "aha moment" that accompanies their realizations. Their solutions make sense to them within the context of their world, while imposed solutions by the therapist run the risk of being idiosyncratic or impractical. This is a mistake often made by rookie therapists who feel compelled to jump in with their perspectives or answers.

Solutions are developed out of the client's resources, whether they are internal or external. Again, the best way to identify the resources is to ask the client. These are some of the questions that can help identify the resources:

- What has worked in the past?
- What ideas do they have?
- What are their strengths?
- What do they know from other areas of their lives that work?
- Whom do they have for support?

It is important to identify the resources they had when they were functioning optimally.

- When did they feel the most empowered?
- When did they like themselves best?
- When was the period of greatest achievement?
- What was their greatest achievement?
- Have they had a "peak experience"?
- How did that come about?

These questions constitute a base line of competency for the client as opposed to the base line of problems on which most counselors focus. Once this time of excellence and resourcefulness has been identified, then the following questions are helpful:

- How did you do that?
- What was different in your life that helped to bring that about?
- How did it make you feel?
- What did you learn from that?

With answers to these questions, the therapist has an idea of the client's significant resources. The key is to help them re-contact and connect with that "self" and bring it forward into the now. Look for that spark or ember of potential that can be fanned and re-ignited into full-blown competency. Then the question becomes: **"How would that younger effective part deal with this problem you brought me?"** Amazingly, when people can tap into their "higher self," they come up with incredibly effective solutions that can be applied to their present situation.

Becky was the director of a group home for adolescent males. She said that one of the house activities was to have weekly community meetings, in which all the residents would discuss their issues among themselves, and then invite Becky and other staff members to join them. While she thought the meetings were generally productive, she had grown to dread participating in them. Often the residents would confront her about trivial issues or about situations beyond her control. She was concerned that she often had no good explanations for certain situations, and more often, the residents rejected the explanation offered. Frequently the residents challenged her with exchanges becoming heated and unmanageable. She knew this was not good for her or the boys.

I asked her what inner resources she needed to be successful in the meetings. She said strength, courage and perseverance, but she was not able to think of a specific situation in the past where she had exhibited these qualities. She thought and thought but could not come up with one. I then asked if she had an image of how she would like to be, and if there was anyone she knew who could serve as a model for her. She immediately said, "Rocky." Rocky was a boxer in the movie by the same name played by Sylvester Stallone. After being beaten down, he became inspired and began to train with a vengeance. In the most memorable scene he was running through the streets of Philadelphia with by-standers cheering him on and then running up the hundred-plus steps of the Philadelphia Art Museum. With stirring music in the background and his arrival at the top of the steps, the excitement reached a crescendo with bystanders chanting, "Rocky, Rocky," while Rocky jumped up and down with arms stretched high in the air. So, we practiced what she would feel like if she were Rocky. I had her jump up and down waving her arms, and she immediately became empowered and emboldened declaring, "I will be Rocky when I go in there (to the meetings)." She later reported that psyching herself up before the meetings worked wonders, and she felt totally in control and able to cope with whatever they threw at her.

Not only was she able to conjure up a model for how she wanted to be, she was able to manifest the qualities she sensed she needed. In other words, had she not had those qualities of strength, courage, and perseverance, she could not have been effective even though she had chosen a powerful image of how she wanted to be.

•••

There may be some hesitancy to plug into a client's model of the world, if counseling involves children or clients who are severely mentally ill or delusional. The assumption is that they do not have the experience or mental capacity to address their own needs. It is reasonable to expect children need training and lectures, and that people with psychosis need grounding in reality and rational thinking. With this expectation, however, you may block a valuable resource. The underlying message is, "I have the right way of thinking to help you, and if you want to get well, you need to do what I tell you." This is patronizing rather than empowering. If you want someone to join you, seek to join them first. Join with them, connect with them, and then invite them out.

Carrie, a little 4-year-old girl with major medical problems from birth, needed intensive daily medical care from her parents and from professionals who would come to the home. In addition, she averaged a stay in the hospital about a week in every month. Early on she became traumatized from continual medical procedures such as changing dressings, taking oxygen, and even more invasive procedures such as catheterization. She got to the point that she refused to cooperate with any attempts to treat her. She would have to be held down by one adult, while the other performed the procedure. She would scream and cry and refuse to let anyone near her. Her parents were desperate for help.

The counselor started by doing play therapy with her, focusing on playing doctors, nurses, and patients in a hospital setting. Carrie was able to show how the health professionals treated her and why that was so upsetting. Next, they role-played how she thought little girls in the hospital should be treated. For example, she described certain things that professionals said that were not helpful. "Don't tell me things like it won't hurt, but it does hurt. Be honest." Another was, "This will not take long; we will be quick." That was not reassuring to her because, as she explained, quick meant the procedure would be more painful and that doing the procedures slowly was much better. The counselor gave this feedback to the parents and other care providers who implemented changes.

Additionally, the therapist realized that the little girl was responsive to calming music and that she had a fascination with the iPad. The therapist could utilize the iPad and the music to help change Carrie's focus during procedures. She observed that by placing the iPad on the child's chest, it blocked her vision of the procedures. These modifications helped calm and eventually eliminate the girl's resistant behaviors. Carrie drastically changed her reaction to the point that she did not complain at all and worked cooperatively with the parents and medical personnel, while they provided the necessary treatment. When she had to be re-hospitalized the doctors and nurses could not believe that she was the same child because of her tremendous improvement in attitude and behavior.

This all came about because the therapist took the time to consult with her and get her feedback as to what would help, which no one had done previously.

With delusional clients, you can often work with them within their delusional system.

There is a legendary story about Milton Erickson, who was working as a psychiatrist in a mental hospital in Arizona. There was a schizophrenic client who was very withdrawn and isolated and who insisted he was Jesus Christ. The more staff tried to prove logically that he could not be Jesus Christ, the more entrenched he became in his position. Erickson upon meeting him for the first time said, "I hear that you are Jesus Christ."

The man said, "Of course."

"What do you do for a living? I heard you were a carpenter."

"Yes," said the man.

"That's wonderful," Erickson said, "We need someone with your experience and talent in the woodworking shop."

The man agreed to give it a try and soon, instead of isolating and being idle, he began to be productive and interact with others.

Erickson worked with this man's model of the world and utilized the man's delusional thinking to work for him. Later as the man engaged in the work and interacted with others, he became more lucid and productive.

Affirmations

One of the questions that I perpetually ask myself is, "Why don't I always do the things that are good for me?" I know what they are: eat the right foods, meditate, be kind to everyone, take my vitamins, think positively, get a good night's sleep, be mindful, exercise daily, etc. Affirmations fall into this category. I have experienced the power of affirmations, but rarely do them.

Affirmations are powerful. Not only do they counter negative thinking, they help to create new realities for people. Suze Orman, a popular financial guru, conducted a workshop during which she was teaching affirmations. In her book, *The Twelve Steps to Wealth,* she tells the story about how though she didn't come from a wealthy family, she became a millionaire. When she was growing up, the message was always "We don't have any money."

She was working as a waitress, and the most money she ever made was $400 a month. She decided that she could do better than that. So, every morning before she went to work, she would write repeatedly: "I am young, powerful, successful, and earning at least $10,000 a month." She said she wrote this statement at least 25 times a day. She would also sing it, scream it, and say it silently. She was shocked when in 1980 Merrill Lynch hired her as a stockbroker. Even after getting this job, she still felt she was less than everyone else. She kept remembering her mother saying, "Don't tell your friends, Suze, that you have money, because they won't like you." In a few months, she reached her goal: $10,000 in a month. When she showed her mother the first $10,000 check, her mother said, "Suze, nobody makes money like this," but Suze never believed that and definitely proved her mother wrong.

During the workshop she was conducting on wealth management, she said "I am young, powerful, successful, and earning $10,000 a **week**. Then she said, "Why do I deserve this, and you don't? The answer is you do. Why am I able to do this, and you aren't? The answer is that I made my affirmation and I believed it."

She then instructed people in the audience to write their own affirmations. One lady wrote, "I want to be able to get out of debt." Suze said that was a horrible affirmation. When the lady asked what was wrong with wanting to get out of debt, Suze replied, "There is nothing wrong at all about wanting to be out of debt, but first of all your affirmation of *wanting to be able* to get out of debt is two steps from being out of debt. Secondly, you should make your affirmation as though it is already happening. Wanting to be able is not doing it. Also, why just out of debt? Why not have an abundance of money beyond what you need to pay off your debt?" Suze asked her what she would do with an abundance of money, and she said that she would like to have enough to take care of herself and family. "Anything else?" Suze asked. The lady replied, "I would like to help support the church and the homeless." "Okay," said Suze, "I think we've got it."

Here is the progression she took her through:

> I want to be able to get out of debt.
> I want to get out of debt.
> I am debt free.
> I am debt free and have extra money.
> I am debt free and have an abundance of money to take care of myself and family.

I am debt free and have an abundance of money for myself, my family, and others.

While the power of affirmations can be described as "fake it until you make it" or more succinctly, "you talk the talk, eventually you walk the walk," there is a more scientific explanation for their effectiveness. One of the recent discoveries of neuro-science and the study of the brain's neuro-plasticity is that "what fires together, wires together." Prior to this was the belief was that once a person turned 25, his brain was fully developed, and it was all downhill from there. Now science is discovering that the brain is amazingly versatile and that certain exercises, both physical and mental, can replenish nerve cells and build new neural pathways. For example, research has shown that someone who is learning piano can practice either on the piano or in his mind, or a basketball player can practice making free throw shots either mentally or actually shoot the basketball. Both ways affect the brain in the same way and learning takes place equally between the two methods.

So, the idea of making an affirmation and saying it or writing it 25 times a day can create new neural networks. The more it is done, the more it becomes part of who we are. Scott Adams, creator of the cartoon series, *Dilbert*, when he was graduating from college created an affirmation that he would be a nationally-syndicated cartoonist. He made this affirmation religiously for several years, and today *Dilbert* is in more newspapers than *Doonesbury*.

Another aspect of doing affirmations is that by writing them 25 times or more a day you are integrating a motor activity (writing) with a mental process, which deepens their impact. Each time you write the affirmation, the brain contemplates "How will that happen?" "What will that be like?" and" What changes do I need to make?" thus paving the way for the reality to take shape.

When working with clients on affirmations, just the process of developing the affirmations to reflect what clients want in their lives is a huge step. It forces them to review what their priorities are and to start actualizing them. Clients often have difficulty seeing beyond their own reality. Thinking about what is positive in their life is often antithetical to them. Ironically, some are really creative at thinking about all of the bad things that could happen. It can be quite a stretch to think about their potential or to begin to think positively and dream again. The process of constructing affirmations is a hope-builder.

> # Perhaps an affirmation for those reading this book is, "I effectively and lovingly manage any situation with clients when I do not know what to do."

Of course, doing affirmations is not just for clients. It can be tremendously effective for therapists. It helps to understand the process, but even more importantly is the power of affirmation. Perhaps an affirmation for those reading this book is, *"I effectively and lovingly manage any situation with clients when I do not know what to do."*

You Are Not Alone

Despite social media and all the ways for human beings to connect with each other, it seems people are more and more isolated. Many efforts are being made however, to educate and link people together. Witness the amazing growth of 12-step groups, on-line chat rooms around specific disorders, and the more widely accepted use of psychotherapy and group therapy. These groups tend to counteract the growing tendency towards isolation. Still many clients who come for therapy believe they are unique, and that no one can understand what they are going through. In addition, they feel shame because of their mental illness, uncontrollable emotions, or uncontrollable behaviors.

There is a saying, "Don't compare your insides to others' outsides." It is easy to look at others' outward appearances and think they have it all together, but rarely are we able to see what inner struggles they are going through, the demons they have to tackle, or the unresolved trauma with which they are wrestling. It is not uncommon to hear, about a couple getting a divorce, "They were such an ideal couple, the last ones you would think would get a divorce." So behind closed doors, what looks good on the outside could well be a different story.

The point of this is to normalize, but not discount, clients' pain and suffering. Realizing they are not alone in their suffering, and that there are others who have the same problems, helps them feel less abnormal and stigmatized. Clients experience hope and relief when they learn of others' success in overcoming similar problems.

The following beautifully describes the common dilemma... and ultimate bond we all feel:

Please Hear What I'm Not Saying

Don't be fooled by me.
Don't be fooled by the face I wear for I wear a mask, a thousand masks,
masks that I'm afraid to take off,
and none of them is me.
Pretending is an art that's second nature with me but don't be fooled,
    for God's sake don't be fooled
I give you the impression that I'm secure,
that all is sunny and unruffled with me,
within as well as without,
that confidence is my name and coolness my game,
that the water's calm and I'm in command
and that I need no one, but don't believe me.

My surface may seem smooth but my surface is my mask,
  ever-varying and ever-concealing mask.
Beneath lies no complacence.
Beneath lies confusion, and fear, and aloneness.
But I hide this. I don't want anybody to know it.
I panic at the thought of my weakness exposed.
That's why I frantically create a mask to hide behind,
  a nonchalant sophisticated facade to help me pretend,
  to shield me from the glance that knows.

But such a glance is precisely my salvation, my only hope,
  and I know it.
That is, if it's followed by acceptance, if it's followed by love.
It's the only thing that can liberate me from myself,
from my own self-built prison walls,
from the barriers I so painstakingly erect.
It's the only thing that will assure me of what I can't assure myself, that
    I'm really worth something.
But I don't tell you this.
I don't dare to, I'm afraid to.
I'm afraid your glance will not be followed by acceptance, will not be
    followed by love.

I'm afraid you'll think less of me,
that you'll laugh, and your laugh would kill me.
I'm afraid that deep-down I'm nothing and that you will see this and
   reject me.

So I play my game, my desperate pretending game,
with a facade of assurance without and a trembling child within.
So begins the glittering but empty parade of masks, and my life
   becomes a front.

I idly chatter to you in the suave tones of surface talk.
I tell you everything that's really nothing,and nothing of what's
   everything, of what's crying within me.
So when I'm going through my routine do not be fooled by what I'm
   saying.
Please listen carefully and try to hear what I'm not saying,
what I'd like to be able to say, what for survival I need to say,
but what I can't say.
I don't like hiding. I don't like playing superficial phony games.
I want to stop playing them.
I want to be genuine and spontaneous and me
but you've got to help me.
You've got to hold out your hand
even when that's the last thing I seem to want.
Only you can wipe away from my eyes
the blank stare of the breathing dead.
Only you can call me into aliveness.
Each time you're kind, and gentle, and encouraging,
each time you try to understand because you really care,
my heart begins to grow wings—
very small wings, very feeble wings, but wings!

With your power to touch me into feeling
you can breathe life into me.
I want you to know that.
I want you to know how important you are to me,
how you can be a creator—an honest-to-God creator—
of the person that is me
if you choose to.

You alone can break down the wall behind which I tremble,
you alone can remove my mask,
you alone can release me from my shadow-world of panic,
from my lonely prison,
if you choose to. Please choose to.

Do not pass me by.
It will not be easy for you.
A long conviction of worthlessness builds strong walls.
The nearer you approach to me
the blinder I may strike back.
It's irrational, but despite what the books say about man I am irrational.
I fight against the very thing I cry out for.
But I am told that love is stronger than strong walls
and in this lies my hope.
Please try to beat down those walls
with firm hands but with gentle hands
for a child is very sensitive.
Who am I, you may wonder?
For I am every man you meet and I am every woman you meet.

—*Charles C. Finn September 1966*

Reframing

They say a cat always lands on its feet when it falls. Helping clients land on their feet in the process of doing therapy is called reframing. Reframing is a process of creating new perspectives and new meanings for difficult situations. This happens by broadening the client's frame of reference of negative behaviors or emotional states into more positive or resourceful ones. For example, a parent might see the child as being argumentative and defiant. This can be reframed as the child sticks up for himself and has a strong sense of fair play. Another example: a client who is "confused" may be reframed as "being open to several options," instead of always being sure he is right. Such a reframe is valuable for clients who are stuck and tend to see no way out.

Reframing means looking at a situation that has one frame around it (a belief or perception), and giving it an entirely new look with a different frame. For example, telling clients that their "hopeless situation" is an opportunity for change, and that others have successfully recovered from similar situations is amazingly helpful. The power of this simple reframing is tremendous, especially when the client has faith in you. *"My therapist said I can overcome this."* Conversely, therapists' proclamations that there are no real solutions for a problem (a negative reframe) can seal the client's fate.

Another benefit of reframing is based on the idea that every symptom has a reason for being, so that one can look to its beneficial aspects or its *raison d'etre*. Take suicidal thinking for example; how can that be beneficial? In a way, it is like a relief valve. The unacknowledged thought may be, "If all else fails, I can end this suffering by killing myself." It is important to acknowledge the client's suicidal part and explore what it has to say. Ignoring or avoiding it, allows it to stay underground and strengthen its hold. By acknowledging that it exists and has a purpose, the energy related to it is dissipated. Then the goal is to find other ways to achieve the stated purpose without giving in to the suicidal thoughts.

There are two basic kinds of reframing: content reframing and context reframing. In content reframing the focus is on changing the meaning of a specific situation. The question to ask is, "Is there some other meaning you could place on this?" With context reframing, the focus is on finding where a behavior might be desirable or constructive. The question to ask is "In what situation would this be acceptable?"

Content Reframing

Annie, a counselor, told me about an experience she had with a seven-year-old boy who had been very defiant and disruptive. In fact, he had tried to strangle his mother with an electric cord from the backseat of the car while she was driving him to the store. Annie had been trying to get him to calm down and read a book with her. He was restless, wandering around the room totally distracted. She grabbed him and put him on her lap.

He became defiant and spit in her face. She held him closer saying, "I love you," which required great restraint on her part. He spat in her face several more times. Each time she held him tightly saying she loved him. He did it one more time, and she said more intently, "I still love you very much." He looked at her in disbelief and said, "How can you love me when I am such a bad boy? I hate myself; you can't love me." And he started crying profusely and melted into her arms.

Annie said afterwards when she went to the bathroom to wash her face, she looked in the mirror, and saw what he had done. You know what she told me? "Jon, it was only spit, and compared to what this boy had been through, it was nothing."

This is not only an incredible reframe, it reflects the quality of a deeply committed and conscientious counselor who is trauma-sensitive. She could take an experience most of us would find repugnant and find its inner value.

Here are some more examples of situations and possible reframes:

Original	Reframe
Stubbornness	Determination
Controlling	Caring, protecting
Chaotic	Interesting way to gain attention
Manipulative	Very bright and insightful
Misbehavior	Asking for help
Overwhelmed	Very caring, caring too much
Rebellious	Very much own individual
Enmeshed	Loyal
Passive and guarded	Protecting others feelings
Angry	Feels passionately
Guilt	Self-correcting mechanism
Anxiety	Body's warning of stress
Bizarre dress, tattoos, etc.	Trying on different costumes
Destructive behaviors	Testing limits
Lazy	Conserving energy
Shame	Innate sense of right and wrong
Flip-flopping	Flexible, responsive to new ideas
Social isolation	One friend at a time

Context Reframing

A situation that might be wrong in one setting might be quite appropriate in another. For example, cutting someone down in public could be seen as cruel, but if done in a comedy club it may seem quite appropriate. Victor Frankl, a Nazi concentration camp survivor, wrote in *Man's Search for Meaning* the following example of context reframing:

> Once, an elderly general practitioner consulted me because of his severe depression. He could not overcome the loss of his wife, who had died two years before and whom he had loved above all else. Now how could I help him? What should I tell him? I refrained from telling him anything, but instead confronted him with a question, "What would have happened, Doctor, if you had died first, and your wife would have had to survive you?" "Oh," he said, "for her this would have been terrible; how she would have suffered!" Whereupon I replied, "You see, Doctor, such a suffering has been spared her, and it is you who have spared her this suffering—to be sure—at the price that you have now to survive and mourn her." He said no word but shook my hand and calmly left the office. In some way, suffering ceases to be suffering at the moment it finds a meaning, such as the meaning of a sacrifice.
>
> *(Frankl, V. 1985)*

One summer I had the opportunity to train some summer staff from Legacy International, an organization committed to world peace. Each summer children from many nations come to Virginia for a program called Global Youth Village, a program which Legacy sponsors. This particular summer a contingent of about 15-20 youths was coming from Iraq. This was a most difficult time for the people of Iraq. The U.S. military had invaded and occupied the country. There was fighting between the Shiites and Sunnis. Most of the children had been exposed not only to the invasion of US troops, but in some cases, destruction of homes and neighborhoods by one sect fighting another. Some of the children were under the threat, that if discovered to be in the United States, their families could be killed.

I was asked to train the staff on how to recognize and respond to the signs and symptoms of trauma, if they occurred. During one of the trainings, a staff member sincerely asked if we were doing these children a disservice by bringing them to America and exposing them to a way of life and culture so radically different from their own, and then sending them back to a war-torn nation. I thought about this long and hard, and then responded that I believed what we were doing would be tremendously valuable to these children, because they would realize that people can live together in peace, that the reality of their home life was not the only possibility, and that in times of dark despair, they would have memories to hold on to and cherish even when things around them seemed to crumble. So, by changing the context from one of a disservice to the children to one of an example of hope, I was able to turn the staff member's perspective around.

To a lesser degree, we face the same dilemma working with at-risk youth and their families in the intensive in-home program. We go into their homes, try to win their hearts and trust, and then in six months to a year, we have to leave. In some cases, conditions have not significantly changed— dad has not stopped drinking, grandma still has cancer, or there is still no income, but the children have an experience where someone believed in them, supported them, and even loved them. That experience will stay with them on some level and have the potential to nurture them in times of deepest need.

•••

Not all reframing serves clients well. Sometimes clients reframe the situations that get them into trouble to excuse their behavior. People naturally try to find ways to make what gets them into trouble acceptable. Therapeutic reframing is not about making excuses for irresponsible behaviors, but about creating new perspectives and insights that help the client experience and perceive behaviors or situations in a more understandable way. Then the behaviors can be shaped into something positive, rather than be eliminated.

The therapist should find a more constructive reframe by addressing the beneficial effects and the purpose of the behavior, not to validate or condone it, but rather to validate the reason why the client might have such difficulty.

Situation: Client is physically abusing his children

> **Client reframe**: I am only trying to teach them right from wrong.
> **Good reframe**: You are parenting the way you were raised, but times have changed.

Better reframe: I think this may be the only way you know how to deal with misbehavior. However, there are other ways to correct behavior.

Situation: Client is gambling and has run the family into debt

Client reframe: I just want to make some money on the side to help the family.

Good reframe: You care about your family, but your gambling is harming them rather than helping them.

Better reframe: It seems like you are determined to get out of debt, but in desperation you continue to gamble, yet rather than bringing relief, it is creating more stress for everyone.

Situation: Child is aggressive and frequently gets into fights

Client reframe: I'm not going to let anyone push me around.

Good reframe: In your effort to protect yourself, you end up being the bully instead of the bullied.

Better reframe: You've been taught that to avoid being picked on, you need to be tough, but walking away from a situation takes more courage and creates more respect.

The client is better able to face the reality of the behavior and lessen the stigma when the therapist reframes the behavior as an understandable logical process.

Reframing is also useful in numerous other situations. For example, having a panic attack for the first time can be the most fearful experience of clients' lives. They feel like they are having a heart attack and rush to the emergency room. A friend of mine used to race motorcycles, and he said, "You never know how fast you can take a curve until you spill. If you go 70 miles per hour and spill, then that is the limit for taking that curve." Likewise, with stress, we often do not know how much we can take on until we crash. Our brain tells us we should be able to take on more responsibilities, but when we have a panic attack, our body is telling us we have gone too far. So, in a way, instead of a panic attack being our enemy, it is our friend telling us to cut back and reduce our stress.

Another situation: Often clients do well at the beginning of therapy (kind of a honeymoon phase) and make great progress. Then they seem to hit a wall or experience a deeper level of symptoms they didn't know even existed. This is especially true for trauma victims. However, there is another way to view this supposed downturn. I suggest that what they are experiencing are the "fruits of their efforts," at which point they look at me like I am totally crazy, thinking and sometimes saying, "How can this be positive, when it feels so negative?" I explain that at a certain point as clients gain more strength, there is a mind/body wisdom that takes over and says, "I think I can handle this painful memory now that I am stronger." It is like a little capsule of blocked, repressed trauma-energy gets released when the person is strong enough to handle it. I tell them that while what they are experiencing feels bad now, but if they had had these memories or realizations when they first started therapy, they would not have been able to handle them at all. Now, at least, they have some tools, an experience of success, and a better sense of who they are. These are all new resources to help them get through the difficulties. This is a very powerful reframe that helps clients gain a more empowered perspective on what they are experiencing.

Reframing is useful not only for the client but also for the therapist, especially if he views clients or their problems as difficult. Learning to reframe clients' difficult situations as "grist for the mill" helps to lessen the burden and normalize what might be seen as problematic, as "this is just what I do as a counselor."

One final thought: When is a problem not a problem? I attended a conference many years ago where they were selling "AFLE" buttons. AFLE? I asked the clerk what AFLE stood for. She whispered to me, "Another F**king Learning Experience." So, when is a problem not a problem? When it is an AFLE! Clients love this, when the timing is right. It can bring laughter, sometimes to the point of tears to neutralize a previously heavy burden. This is a good example of a reframe.

Reframing is an art and requires practice. Having an optimistic and supportive attitude is crucial to developing this skill.

Empowered by Trials and Tribulations
In the desert of Arizona, the Bass brothers, of shoe fame, financed Biosphere

2, an enclosed ecosystem designed to test the possibility of colonizing other planets. The biosphere was created to maintain a natural balance necessary to sustain life. The site included gardens to grow food, trees to produce oxygen, and animals to provide food and materials for the clothing. A year later the trees in the biosphere had become thin and weak and many large branches were breaking off, despite the idea that this seemed like a perfect environment for them (no insects, regular watering, no threat of fire from lightening, etc.). Botanists and other scientists were recruited to study the problem. After much research, they discovered that collagen (the substance that holds all the cells together) was not being produced in the trees, because there was no wind in the biosphere. With no resistance, the collagen did not develop. Wind creates resistance for the tree, and trees grow strong and hardy as result. Trees with the hardest wood are those by the ocean where the wind is the strongest and most consistent.

In the same way, adversity has the potential to make people strong. When people can understand this, it helps them to deal with their struggle. And so it is that when clients feel defeated and overwhelmed, it is helpful to point out that they can grow from this struggle; they can emerge stronger and wiser. This is often not an easy sell, especially when they are in the throes of their difficulty, but it can generate an attitude of hope and optimism, perhaps not immediately but in the future.

I was asked to do a mental-health consult on a lady on the diabetic unit at the hospital. Upon interviewing her I learned that over the course of the progression of her disease, she had to have both feet amputated due to gangrene setting in, and now had to have one of her hands removed. I was shocked and speechless. I think I even had tears in my eyes, because she said, "Don't you fret, young man, I still have one hand, and the Lord has blessed me to play the piano. I can still play even with one hand, and that's all I need."

Here was a lady who did not let adversity get the best of her. I went in to help her out, and she gave me a greater gift than I could possibly have given her.

The beauty of empowering clients is that as they get strong and more resourceful, they can solve their own problems making our job easier. It is a win-win process.

CHAPTER 8

Client or Therapist?

Knowing your darkness is the best method for dealing with the darkness of other people.

—Carl Jung

WHEN DEALING WITH SITUATIONS in which you are stuck and don't know what to do is ask yourself how you fit into the therapeutic equation. Usually most of our energy and effort are focused on clients or finding solutions to their problems. Rarely do we look at ourselves. We are, however, a major part of the equation—our presence, demeanor, input, and responses are all factors in the success or lack thereof in our work.

At first, this may seem insignificant, but as stated before, research has shown that how the client and therapist connect is the *most important factor* in successful therapy. Ideally, if changing ourselves is a key component, it should be the place where we can focus the least effort for the best outcome. The fallacy is that we tend to think the locus of trouble is external to us, and therefore we don't attempt to change ourselves.

In a survey by Kenneth Pope and Barbara Tabachnick, 84% of psychologists reported having had psychotherapy themselves (*http://kspope.com/therapistas/research9.php*).

Most have entered the field of counseling after having been through some major crisis or trauma in their own lives. Having somehow navigated through the morass of their own troubled history, they arrive at a place of solace, understanding, and integration. This process is often the impetus that propels counselors to enter the field with a sincere desire to propagate the dynamics of healing they experienced. While this has the potential to enhance their practice, it is also possible that unresolved aspects of past events could be triggering or undermining the quality of therapy. This is possible because, even for therapists, it is rare that every situation has been fully resolved or healed.

This is where counselors are the most vulnerable. To the extent they have not resolved their issues, conflicts, and difficulties, the more likely they may become stuck in sessions. Unknowingly, they may mirror uncertainty, confusion, and hopelessness. There may be a tendency to lose focus on the client and become entrenched in self—even if for fleeting moments. This chapter offers ways to understand how to overcome personal difficulties that emerge in sessions and stop us in our tracks. Counselors are not blank slates. We have many blind spots because of our histories, which include a unique set of experiences, beliefs, and perspectives. All these factors affect what happens in therapy.

When Is the Problem Me?

It takes courage and sincerity to examine one's self in the role of a counselor. When therapists were asked to rate their skills and effectiveness, 80% see themselves as above average. Think about that. How can everyone be above average unless they are from Lake Wobegon? Ironically, those counselors who are the most adept and willing or able to evaluate themselves objectively were in the 20 percent who rated themselves below average.

The question becomes, "What is the yardstick to measure your abilities?" First, there are many aspects of counseling, subtle and not so subtle. There is the physical aspect. What is your presentation i.e., the way you dress, the appearance of your office, pictures, and decorations? What is the message clients get from your physical presentation?

Next what is your knowledge? What are your areas of expertise? What is your education—formal and self-education? How much do you seek to improve your knowledge and abilities to find new skills and answers for your clients?

Next is your personality and presence. How much interest and curiosity do you show towards your clients? Do they feel like you are with them in a caring nonjudgmental way? Are you able to match their emotional state and feel and acknowledge the intensity of their pain? Do you model healthy ways of responding, problem-solving, or relating, including courtesy and respect?

Next is your emotional state. How comfortable are you with your feelings and those of others? What is the limit of your emotional understanding and your tolerance? At what point does the client's emotional distress cause you to back off because of your own discomfort? What emotional coping skills do you have? What are your emotional vulnerabilities?

Finally, there's spirituality. This is not necessarily a religious perspective (though this can be a vital source), but rather your capacity for compassion, love, understanding, forgiveness, and consciousness. What do you have to give? Are you easily judgmental, withdrawing, intolerant, impatient, or critical? Will you turn the tables if you perceive you are being attacked? How quickly can you bounce back from discouragement, frustration, or confusion? How strong is your spirit?

Can you honestly admit your shortcomings, and more importantly, are you willing to do anything about them? Help is available for all these aspects through counseling, taking courses, reading books, getting reliable clinical supervision, and consulting with other professionals.

It takes humility, integrity, and a desire to excel to go down this path. As I said before, "You are only as good a therapist as you are a person." The converse is true: the better counselor you are, the better person you are.

Energy Consciousness

On a very practical level, we need to be aware of our energy. We say that we have high energy today, or that we feel drained and have no energy, yet most people are not conscious of their energy input and output on a minute-by-minute basis or even daily. Many things sap our energy, especially listening to people's problems all day. Clients often draw upon the energy of the therapist to supplant what is lacking in them. It is easy to expend our energy to the point that we give out. Some clients, through no fault of their own, are like energy black holes—no matter how much thought, love, and guidance we give them, there is no change, and we end up depleted.

How can we keep our energy from being depleted by our clients? One example is Mother Theresa and her giving to the poor. She never seemed to give out. Her secret was that her compassion and love were continually replenished by her faith. She could tap into an endless and fulfilling energy source. When we are conscious, there's an infinite source of compassion available to us. Most of us don't have that depth of consciousness, but we can train ourselves through mindfulness and meditation to open ourselves up to the Infinite.

If you are conscious of your energy and the flow of it, you cannot experience compassion fatigue. Compassion is not limited. For example, we may feel as if we have no more to give, but should our child get sick or injured, we immediately feel a resurgence of compassion. It comes from deep inside our soul. It is not that stress cannot take a toll on us, but we all have a reserve that goes untapped, until a real crisis happens.

Here are some questions to ask yourself to determine how your energy is being affected:

- What do you do that works?
- What do you do that doesn't work?
- Which clients take energy? Why?
- Which clients give energy? Why?
- What is the client's buy-in for therapy?
- What do I want to change?
- Where does my energy go?

The goal is to be able to access a sense of peacefulness, no matter what is going on around us. It is like being in the eye of a hurricane and venturing out into the storm knowing that we can always return to the center and seek refuge in a peaceful state of mind. This allows us to gain our bearings and let go of the chaos in the world. This state is attainable for all of us through meditation, deep relaxation, or guided imagery, which I will address later in this chapter.

Your Trauma History

One of the goals of competent therapists is to be present and open to anything or any problem clients present. The process can be complicated either by our lack of experience in dealing with such matters or by unresolved feelings within. We can only take clients as deeply as we have been or are willing and able to go. When dealing with clients' traumas, the nature, intensity, and depth of the trauma may catch us off guard, triggering feelings from unresolved events from our past. We need to be as clear a vessel as possible to absorb and reflect on the clients' most disturbing events and thoughts.

The therapist is asked to stay in the right brain and fully experience the client's feelings, no matter what comes up for them or what raw emotion is triggered from their own history. In other words, the therapist isn't just an observer of the client's emotional journey or even a disinterested guide, but a fellow traveler, resonating with the client's sadness, anger, and anxiety.

Rather than recoiling from the intensity of the client's experience, the therapist is providing the stability (the ballast, so to speak) to keep the client feeling not only understood, but safely held and supported, through tone of voice, eye contact, exp

Obviously, this kind of demanding work requires therapists to have their own inner act together. A critical way to manage these situations is to do our own trauma history/inventory to uncover those feelings that interfere with our being able to go deeper into the emotional content of the client's history.

Even the most seasoned therapists sometimes get triggered and have automatic emotional reactions that may take them by surprise. If these reactions become so overwhelming that they are no longer able to focus on what the client says, this should immediately be noted to ferret out vulnerabilities and to consciously work on them either alone or in therapy.

A more deliberate and strategic approach is to identify any weakness beforehand by doing a formal trauma history. It includes the following:

- What traumas have you experienced?
  - Prenatal
  - Early childhood
  - Medical problems/illnesses
  - Accidents
  - Verbal abuse
  - Physical abuse
  - Sexual abuse
  - School – bullying, being shamed

- Work situations
- Frightening events
- Losses
- Victim of crimes
- General disaster
- Forced sexual experience
- How did they affect you?
- What lasting harm or input did they create?
- What unresolved issues or feelings do you have?
- In what ways have they handicapped you?
- What might be some topics difficult to address with clients?
- How did the traumatic events shape your behavior or emotional responses?
- What have you learned from such experiences?

Minimally, the goal is to acknowledge unresolved feelings related to previous traumas, which if triggered, could compromise your effectiveness in a session. Ideally, you need to resolve and heal from these emotional wounds. This process not only includes cognitive-processing to understand the impact of what happened to you, but also to work from the bottom-up to identify and release any physical impact stored in the body because of these issues. If any overpowering or threatening feelings still exist, seek out help.

Part of the process of becoming an effective counselor is learning, knowing, and working through your own vulnerabilities. One of the advantages of doing this, is that as you work through your own trauma, you discover facets that may be helpful to your clients. This can increase your understanding and feeling for the difficulty and frustrations clients may have participating in therapy. It also helps you to recognize and overcome stumbling blocks, which prevent clients from going forward and also to join in and celebrate the benefits and joy of healing.

> **Part of the process of becoming an effective counselor is learning, knowing, and working through your own vulnerabilities.**

Countertransference

As much as therapists try to have *unconditional positive regard* for all clients, sometimes this is difficult or even seemingly impossible. We all have limitations as to whom and what we are drawn or can even tolerate. Any time these negative feelings start to creep into our relationship with the client, we are experiencing countertransference. Not being able to get beyond these feelings can cause us to be stuck, and possibly even apathetic.

> Sigmund Freud originally developed the concept of countertransference. He described it as a largely unconscious phenomenon in which the psychologist's emotions are influenced by a client and the psychologist reacts with countertransference. Classical psychoanalysts, such as Carl Jung, who faced his own struggle with countertransference, characterize it as a potentially problematic phenomenon that can inhibit psychological treatment when left unchecked. In other words, therapists must master their tendency to participate in unconscious countertransference by developing healthy boundaries and remaining mindful that the issue can pose a threat to the therapeutic relationship and their work with clients.
>
> In contemporary psychology, clinicians typically make a distinction between helpful and unhelpful countertransference. Many contemporary psychologists openly share their own feelings with clients and may use countertransference, in a conscious manner, to understand differences between their own experiences and the client's experiences. Unhelpful countertransference, or even harmful countertransference, can occur when the therapist transfers feelings to the client that are misplaced or uses the client to meet his or her own psychological needs.

> *brettnewcomb.com/countertransference-and-the-skill-set-of-the-therapist/* Feb 24, 2012

Countertransference, therefore, can be either an overt or covert attraction to or dislike of the client that compromises the effectiveness of the therapy. Simply put, it is difficult to maintain objectivity working with someone we don't like, for whatever reason, or to whom we become overly attached. If we are to be helpful, we should change the lens of our involvement with that person. For example, we can look through the following lenses, just to name a few:

- the lens of identifying the good in the person

- the lens of understanding and compassion
- the lens of clinical curiosity
- the lens of detachment
- the lens of tolerance
- the lens of personal challenge

Margie, a middle-aged mother, referred her son, Blade, age 5, for in-home counseling. He and she were constantly battling, and he was having numerous problems such as encopresis, major temper tantrums, and expulsion from school for using foul language. The boy was suspected to be on the autism spectrum.

Margie grew up in a family with much conflict. Her mother was hypercritical, and her father was emotionally absent and would often berate her by cussing her out. She seemed to have little interest in participating in counseling, and it seemed she just wanted a baby sitter, while she went out with her boyfriend. It was also soon discovered that she would leave Blade alone in his room for hours to entertain himself however he could. This was symptomatic of an even bigger problem, when it became apparent that Margie had very little interest in raising a child. Many of the ideas and suggestions to help Blade went unheeded, and it seemed that once the counselor turned attention away from Blade and towards her, she began canceling sessions or being absent when the counselor came.

The counselor found it easy to work with Blade. He was a bright boy with a good sense of humor and a real desire to connect and be loved by someone. When he was away from home, he was a different child. He engaged with the counselor, made jokes, and showed curiosity about everything. When told what to do and what not to do, he quickly picked up on it. He would even take the counselor's hand whenever he felt uncomfortable or unsafe. However, when he came home, he immediately withdrew and his whole demeanor changed. The counselor was surprised by the sudden change in behavior. When Margie was informed about this, she broke down and cried saying she hated special-needs children and wished that she had never had him. She was not sure she could ever love him.

This was a show-stopper for the counselor. How could a mother say she hated her child and did not think she could love him? The counselor's first reaction was shock and then antipathy towards the mother. He confessed in supervision that he did not think he could work with a person like that, or at least he did not know how to help her. When he sought supervision on this issue, I asked him which lens he planned to use to deal with this situation. Was he going to continue to see Margie as mean and unloving towards her child, or see her as a victim of her own upbringing, who never experienced the kind of love and acceptance he was expecting her to give to Blade? While his reaction was understandable, the reality was he needed to overcome his counter-transference in order to fulfill his responsibility and provide the help this family needed.

The big question was could he set aside his feelings about Margie enough to proceed. He said he would try, but her reluctance to participate made it even harder. We decided that he would continue to work with Blake to reduce the boy's stress level with the hopes that mother would not only see that Blake could change, but more importantly the counselor would model how to handle Blake when he started his meltdowns. He was able to get Margie to commit to a month of special effort, after which, if there was no change, we would terminate therapy. She agreed.

A breakthrough came when the counselor decided to set aside his personal feelings and focus on Margie's childhood and what had been missing. A parallel was made between her experience as a child and Blade's. She admitted that she did not know how to love, and she felt guilty about not loving her son. She had felt cursed by having a child with special needs, and she just wanted him out of her life. Though she knew it was not his fault, she admitted that is how she sometimes thought of him and treated him. Once this level of honesty was achieved, she opened up to seeing Blade in a new light. By the end of the month, she could tell the counselor that she was learning to love her son, and that while she still doubted her abilities, she no longer blamed him for her difficulties. This was a huge step for her.

In supervision, the counselor saw the irony in the parallels of the situation. He was critical of Margie for whom he did not think he could have positive regard. Likewise, Margie was critical of her son for whom she did not think she could have positive regard. It was only after the therapist changed his attitude that Margie changed hers.

Countertransference also occurs when you feel like you should solve the client's problem for them or resolve their conflict. Solutions you provide may not address the issue that the client feels is important; rather these solutions may reflect your own bias or set of values, or they may reflect your own need to overcome feelings of incompetence. Acknowledging and understanding these feelings can improve your effectiveness and increase your personal growth.

Countertransference is also a problem, if the client is having problems similar to the therapist's. For example, if a client comes in for marriage counseling and the therapist is in the process of getting a divorce, it would be easy to think, "I have no business seeing this person to help their marriage, since I could not save my own. What if my client finds out I am getting a divorce? Will they lose confidence in me? Am I a phony pretending to know about successful relationships, when I obviously failed at mine?" While there may be some legitimacy to these questions, they should not undermine your basic competency. In these situations, you need to learn to compartmentalize, which requires you to set aside your own doubts and use your therapeutic skills. Obviously, every situation is different, and the nature of your problems in your marriage is probably totally different than the ones in the client's marriage. Also, you may have some critical insight into the client's problem having been through the process yourself. In any case, you can always depend on using the basic techniques of listening, supporting, co-exploration of solutions and strengthening the positives.

Countertransference can also arise if clients are deliberately hostile, demeaning or even abusive. It is easy to get personally offended and to defend oneself. There is no need to quibble about the facts or try to disprove their assertions. This reactiveness may possibly drive clients deeper into their negative assertions about you. It is important not to take what is being said personally, but realize that this is a learned pattern that they possibly had to develop to survive in the environment in which they grew up. Taking a clinical, curious approach will be much more effective than arguing with clients. It is important, however, once a *therapeutic* reason has been established, to say to them, that though you understand and are concerned about their thoughts and feelings about you, expressing them in an abusive way is not acceptable. You can offer to teach them new ways to express or explore what is behind those feelings.

One of the ways to help cut through countertransference is to say that you understand clients' feelings or thoughts, but this does not mean you agree with them. Given their nature, background, and temperament, it may be easy to understand why they feel the way they do. When I was a director of a substance abuse treatment center, clients would often come to me with complaints about the staff, some of which were justified and some were not. No matter how irrational their concerns, I soon learned that if I just empathized with them and said that I understood their feelings, they would thank me and leave my office. I was surprised they did not want me to do anything about the situation; they just wanted to be heard and understood.

Overall, countertransference should be an opportunity to check out your limitations and prejudices. We are all human and we all have our limitations, which is to say that there may be clients with whom we cannot work. If, after having thoroughly examined our own attitudes and weaknesses and worked to overcome them, the difficulty still exists, the main option is to refer the person.

Ethical Dilemmas: I Can't Treat That!

Therapists are often confronted with clients' points of view with which they disagree. Sometimes clients strongly hold these points of view and state them powerfully. What do you do when you are in this position? There are many ethical stumbling blocks involving counseling, but this is one area that is rarely discussed: the ethics of dealing with the issues where your point of view, values, or beliefs are diametrically opposed to the client's. An example of this is the dilemma Dr. Melfi, the psychiatrist in the HBO series, *Sopranos,* had in dealing with Tony Soprano, who was a mobster and a Mafia Don. She gently sidestepped some of the major issues such as his murdering or ordering the murder of others. On some level, I'm sure she felt conflicted about helping him to feel comfortable whenever his conscience bothered him, though it rarely did. Being able to put aside what she knew about him to genuinely help him must have been a source of conflict for her.

Consider this situation. While doing group with recovering addicts, one of the clients admits to shooting and killing a man in a drug deal gone bad. What would you do with this information?

- Should it be reported to the police?
- Should the client turn himself in?
- Should he be assuaged?
- Should he be shamed to make him realize the significance of what he did?

- Do we refuse to engage with him on the issue in order to avoid the appearance of complicity?

Because of confidentiality, it cannot be reported. The client should be encouraged to turn himself in. He also needs to identify and express his feelings about what happened and clarify those feelings in the individual sessions.

Consider this in terms of a more prevalent phenomenon, i.e., the lawyer defending criminals who commit crimes that are morally repugnant to the lawyer. Lawyers may have many strong personal feelings against the defendant and his alleged crime, but professionally they do whatever is needed to insure the client is represented fairly within the judicial system. Their commitment is to the deliverance of justice for all individuals.

Likewise, with the counselor, the client is to be dealt with in a nonjudgmental way. If for some reason, the act is so morally repugnant or goes against your own belief to the extent that you lose your objectivity, then you need to get supervision. You cannot discharge clients just because you do not agree with their moral stance (ACA Code of Ethics, 2014). The professional responsibility is to help clients with whatever aspects of the problem that bother them, and we need to set aside our judgment and address the person behind the act who is hurting.

Bart was sent to me having been court–ordered for sexual abuse of a minor. He began to tell the story of his attraction to the 13-year-old daughter of his girlfriend. While he was discussing this, there was an inner struggle going on within me. Part of me was incredulous at his apparent naïveté and/or the way he deceived himself or others.

He claimed the child was the one who initiated it. "She would follow me to the bathroom and come on to me. I tried to discourage her, but she insisted. I was not mean to her; we had a good relationship. I think she enjoyed it. She was not upset with me, so I don't think there was any harm done."

What is your reaction to this? What are the possible lenses through which we can view this? Here are some possibilities:

Critical/judgmental – I think he is totally trying to deceive me and must think I'm a fool.

Anger – How dare he even think this way?

Indignity – How can anybody think that what he did is not harmful?

Prosecutorial – You need to be locked up, and the key thrown away.

Confrontational – You can't actually believe what you just told me; you are so full of it.

Generalization – Sex offenders are notorious liars and will say anything to defend themselves.

Skeptic – I'm not sure I believe anything he just said.

Clinical curiosity – How did he ever get himself into this situation, and what are the dynamics that caused him to behave in this way?

Credibility – There is a possibility that he believes what he just told me.

Fairness — He deserves to be at least heard without judging him.

Compassionate understanding – This person is very misguided, but he needs help.

Advocating for the victim – You have no idea what harm you did to that child.

Goal orientation – What do you want me to do to help you?

How do you decide which lens to use? What criteria should you use to decide about how to proceed? Are you able to put your feelings aside? Should you even put your feelings aside? Do you even want to continue with this person? The answers to these questions can easily be influenced by the therapist's experience, bias, personal history, culture and religious values, clinical training, and commitment to professionalism.

While there is no one answer that will totally address the issue, let me suggest two things: One, the client is coming for help, even though it may be only to get an evaluation and/or a report for the court. You owe it to him to help him to the extent that he is willing and/or to the extent that you can help motivate him to change.

The second idea is to provide therapy that will do the greatest good for all. To do this, I needed to put aside my personal feelings about the subject and the client. I decided to hear him out while trying to understand his perspective. I also felt it was my responsibility to educate him on the effects of sexual abuse on children in general. I consciously assumed that he did not know how damaging such actions can be. I was neither unkind, nor did I sugarcoat what I told him.

I felt we had an honest exchange, and it seemed to impact him more than I had expected.

William Doherty proposes a somewhat different perspective in his book, *Soul Searching: Why Psychotherapy Must Promote Moral Responsibility*. He posits that psychotherapy should go beyond being morally neutral, and that it is imperative that psychotherapy be part of the moral dialogue that is needed in our society. He believes that we, as therapists should engage clients in moral discourse and exploration. He writes, "The exploration of moral issues in therapy does not occur mainly inside the head of the therapist playing moral philosopher or moral judge. It occurs in the heart of the therapeutic dialogue, in conversations in which the therapist listens, reflects, acknowledges, questions, probes, and challenges – and in which the client is free to do the same and to develop a more integrated sense of moral responsibilities." He even goes so far as to suggest that "...therapists at times should consciously influence clients to change their behavior in light of the moral issues involved."

Knowing when to invoke this dialogue is a big challenge for therapists. Do you bring up moral considerations if a client is being unfaithful in his marriage, a client dodges paying child support, an adolescent admits to selling drugs at school, a client is racially prejudiced, or you find out a client has consistently lied to you? These are just a few of the many situations involving moral issues with which you may be confronted. Bringing up the issue of morality can be done easily by just asking if they have considered the moral implications of their actions. The process of getting them to change their position is much more delicate. You can ask for further clarification about the basis for their moral values, and then begin a dialogue as to how their actions fit their criteria.

The key to these issues is to engage in dialogue and to curiously explore the nature and ramifications of the client's beliefs and behaviors. We are not to be the moral judge, rather we must exhibit fairness and open-mindedness to explore the underlying issues including the client's sense of morality. We can also present alternative ways of viewing the situation to see if the client is willing to change his point of view given this new perspective.

Turn Off Your BS Detector

While doing group at a drug-rehab center, one of the more astute clients said,

"I used to think all you had to do to be a counselor was to say, 'How does that make you feel?' Now I realize to be a counselor here all you have to do is say, 'Bullshit' to everything we say."

Beginning counselors seem to be on high alert for lies and subterfuge. Many clients, especially addicts and sex offenders, are very experienced and talented deceivers. It is part of their knowledge base and even a survival mechanism.

The challenge is for the therapist to remove his ego from the equation. So what, if your clients mislead you? They are the ones who will suffer from their dishonesty. At the beginning of Chapter Five of the *Big Book of Alcoholics Anonymous*, it states that, "Rarely have we seen a person fail who has thoroughly followed our path. Those who do not recover are people who cannot or will not completely give themselves to this simple program, *usually men and women who are constitutionally incapable of being honest with themselves.*" This can be applied to all clients. This does not mean they cannot make progress, but if they are more intent on protecting themselves or continuing their façade, they miss the full benefit of being in therapy. I don't care how seasoned a therapist you are, there is always a client who will get over on you.

So, you don't always have to have your guard up. Many times, clients are sent by the courts and want to present the best picture or minimize their difficulty. I try to be upfront about the situation and tell them I have no way of telling if they are telling the truth or not. However, I make a point that my report looks best, if I can show the efforts they have made to change. To do this, they need to tell me the reality of their situation, so I can contrast it to where they are now. Generally, stating this at the beginning tends to minimize the game playing.

If you're searching for BS, that is what you will find. It is much more effective to look for the good and the strengths of the client; that's what you will be more likely to find. This is not to say that we should overlook this tendency for deceit, but to be aware of it, accept it, and confront it in a kind and caring way when the time is right. The goal is to build the kind of relationship in which the client feels safe to be totally honest. Anything short of that is the therapist's responsibility, i.e., the fault is with the counselor.

But you might say, "Some people will just be dishonest no matter how accepting, trusting and kind you are." Maybe, but having that attitude blocks the opportunity to help the client. You may be the first person who was accepting and did not react. You never know how effective kindness, respect, and trust can be in eliciting the truth unless you exercise them.

Recharging Ourselves

One of the unwritten benefits of being a conscientious counselor is that **one can never have a bad day.** By that, it is meant that we should be up for all our clients; we need to set aside any of our personal problems, negative emotional states, and thinking. Each client is an opportunity to set aside our self-preoccupation and occupy ourselves with another's concerns. Most the time, our problems pale in comparison to those of our clients. I may come to work feeling down or discouraged, but usually within ten minutes of engaging with a client, my personal concerns disappear or at least are significantly diminished.

When I think about all the major blessings I enjoy in comparison to all the other people on earth, I realize I have nothing to complain about. Of all the people on the earth, I am probably a "1-percenter."

> *I have a car, home, clothing, and electronic gadgets.*
> *I have a good education.*
> *I have a safe environment free from poverty, violence, war, and disease.*
> *I live in a reasonably clean environment.*
> *I have people who love me.*
> *I live in a democratic country.*
> *I am relatively healthy and have access to the most nutritious foods.*
> *I am even grateful for having the consciousness to be grateful.*
> *I have a strong spiritual belief which sustains me.*
> So what do I have to complain about?

Amid turmoil, you can retreat into a state of gratitude. It is like pain management where we teach clients they can't make the pain go away, but they can go away from the pain. It is like changing the channel on the television—you can switch from the "poor-me channel" to the "gratitude channel," or the "count-my-blessings channel" or even the "compared-to- everyone-else channel." Does that solve the problem? No. **But there's no rule that says that constantly being occupied with your misery is a prerequisite for overcoming it.** In fact, the more you learn to change the channels, the lower your stress level, and the more likely you can find a creative solution.

Back in the 1980s, there was a lot of attention being given to the subject of codependency. Based on the book by Melody Beattie, *Codependent No More,* codependency became a social phenomenon with codependency therapy groups and Codependency Anonymous groups springing up everywhere. Codependency is defined as people who were addicted to taking care of others to the point of their own detriment. One of the participants in a codependency group challenged me: "Aren't you codependent? You help people all day long." I quickly responded, "The difference is that I bring my okayness into the relationship, whereas codependents get their okayness out of the relationship. I am not dependent on helping others to feel good about myself." Having said that, I need to check myself to make sure that I am okay. Part of my job as a therapist is to keep my batteries charged—to have okayness to give others. What this means is I must keep my stress level low, maintain emotional stability, and keep a clear mind. How do you maintain this wellness?

> Give yourself a good talk.
> Surround yourself with people who support you.
> Make and practice affirmations.
> Set emotional boundaries.
> Eat nutritious food and exercise.
> Don't take things personally.
> Maintain an attitude of gratitude.
> Practice what you preach.
> Learn from others' struggles.
> Learn from your own struggles.
> Set a positive intention for each session.
> Be willing to make mistakes.

Learn to surrender and not think you are in control or responsible for everything.

I am sure every reader could easily add to this list. The most important thing is the Nike phrase, "Do it."

Mindfulness

Everywhere you turn today (articles, blogs, workshops, books, webinars, etc.) there is the topic of Mindfulness. It was popularized by Jon Kabat Zinn, who translated mindfulness from the realm of religion to the realm of psychotherapy in a way that made it acceptable and even highly worthy as a therapeutic tool. While not designated as so, mindfulness was probably the first form of mental health care ever developed. Its origins go back centuries to the beginnings of most major religions. Buddhists, Christian ascetics, Hindu yogis, Sufi dervishes—all developed and practiced some form on mindfulness. Simply defined, it is a state of consciousness in which a person is fully present in the here and now, which creates a peaceful, receptive sense of being.

There are two aspects of mindfulness: one is to be fully present and aware of your physicality and inner processes. The other is meditation, in which you release all thoughts and allow yourself just to be. Many times, these words (mindfulness and meditation) are interchangeable, and while they have many commonalities, they are two distinct processes. The first helps to focus the mind on details in the here and now, while meditation clears the mind to be free of thoughts, yet be conscious and open.

Both can be helpful personally for a therapist. One can de-stress on a regular basis using meditation. This not only helps to provide an alternative to worry and perseveration, it creates a refuge that becomes a core from which to function Meditation is a way of nurturing and expanding this sense of calmness, as well as to more fully understand oneself in a way not reachable by cognitive processes.

Mindfulness, on the other hand, can be most effective when doing therapy to overcome confusion and loss of direction. You start by noticing when you are starting to react, losing control, or becoming emotionally overwhelmed by what the client is saying. The goal is to shift away from the chaos and confusion of the client's mental and emotional machinations to center oneself with a calm presence, which maximizes your potential for most effective ways to respond. You are making yourself more available to the client by expanding your conscious awareness of yourself. This is a non-linear, right-brain process based on using the power of your being as opposed to the power of your knowing or doing. It requires a certain faith in the power of being and connecting, rather than having a verbal, cognitive interaction or solution. This state may give rise to a cognitive solution, but it is not the explicit goal of the exchange.

Clients sense your assuredness, patience, and balance that arise from that state, and this gives validity to your interactions and role as a therapist. As described earlier, it is like being in the flow with the client—a special connectedness that is not easily recognized by the client nor easily described. There is an implicit power in this that can override uncertainty, insecurity, and doubt about the therapist, the therapy, and the client's own ability to participate and benefit from the therapy.

One way to train therapists to do this is through videotaping sessions. The supervisor can point out the therapist's verbals and non-verbals by inquiring, "What was going on with you when you said that? What were you sensing? What were you feeling? Where in your body did you experience that? What about that made you uncomfortable?" The supervisor can then help the counselor to relax and view his interactions from a calmer state of mind. With practice, this process can become internalized and automatic.

Jon Kabat-Zinn states that, "… mindfulness as a practice provides endless opportunities to develop greater intimacy with your own mind and to tap into and develop your deep interior resources for learning, growth, healing and potentially transforming your understanding of who you are and how you might live more wisely and with greater well-being, meaning and happiness in this world" (Kabat-Zinn, 2012).

That is quite a tall order, but achievable if one is willing to commit the time and effort to do it on a regular basis. A student asked a guru, "What is the best kind of meditation?" His reply was, "The kind you do every day." It can even lead to deep spiritual awareness and deeper self-understanding through meditation. We learn to know oneself, our true nature, without having to meet anyone's expectations or judgments. It frees us to be our true self.

Having mindfulness in your back pocket, so to speak, gives you a strong calm base from which to work and allows you to smooth over rough spots in the counseling process. It is a means and an end in that, as we shall learn in Chapter 10, is an invaluable tool for the client as well.

Give Out and Give Up

One of the ramifications of doing therapy for long periods of time dealing with high-stress traumatic situations is compassion fatigue. This has been defined as "...*the natural consequent behaviors and emotions resulting from knowledge about a traumatizing event experienced by a significant other or from helping or wanting to help a traumatized person*" (Figley, 1995). It is similar to post-traumatic stress disorder, except it is a reaction to experiencing others' trauma. It has been referred to as secondary-stress disorder. Compassion fatigue is more likely to happen to therapists who have a history of personal trauma, are highly empathic, work with a client population with severe histories of abuse, or large numbers of people such as those therapists who worked with 9/11 survivors or their families. One can experience vicarious traumatization, whereby the therapist becomes stressed from hearing the stories of victims of trauma.

Compassion-fatigue takes a toll on counselors. It can cause burnout and psychological distress including apathy, irritability, somatic problems, and feelings of horror, dread, and nightmares. It may cause counselors to distance themselves from others, or overly commit to helping others, including family members. It is also common for the counselor to feel guilty about the good things in life (a kind of survivor's guilt), or feel ineffective in doing therapy and in other areas of their life

Compassion fatigue can also happen to clients who are caretakers of others. An analogy is a friend who wants to borrow money. You reach into your pocket and freely give the change you have. Then he insists he needs more than that, so you reach into your wallet and empty it. Then he comes back for more, and so you write him a check and keep writing checks until you deplete your bank account. Still, he convinces you he needs more. And so you use your credit card. Finally, he comes back one more time for more, and you have no more to give: you are bankrupt. This is true in reality and metaphorically. For instance, there are parents who go deeply into debt to help their addicted child and also become emotionally spent.

What can be done about this? One first should acknowledge compassion fatigue is possible even with experienced therapists. It is the natural outcome of working with a traumatized population, not an indication of the therapist's worth. The next thing is to vary your caseload, so that you don't have a steady diet of these clients. Also, you can help the client take "therapeutic vacations" by not focusing on the trauma every session. You can intersperse intense sessions with more neutral sessions depending on the client's needs. It is important to maintain emotional boundaries. (See *Massage Therapy and Counseling*, Chapter 8.) Supervision and staff support groups are necessary to maintain perspective and address possible countertransference. It is important also to focus on the positive and how hope and renewal can come out of crises. Finally, it is important to balance the rest of your life with fun, rest, good nutrition, exercise, and hobbies or work totally unrelated to counseling.

Compassion fatigue can contribute to feeling that you don't know what to do, or that therapy is not working. No one likes to admit defeat, especially counselors working with their clients, but there are counselors who give up too soon. The main reasons counselors do, but probably shouldn't are:

- Not recognizing that the client's lack of progress is part of their psychopathology
- Feeling offended by the client who gets angry or abusive towards the therapist
- Becoming discouraged by the client's lack of motivation
- Experiencing compassion fatigue.

There are many suggestions in this book on how to overcome malaise.

Believe it or not, there are times when you may want or need to call it quits. How does one objectively decide? Here are a few ideas:

- Therapy is not a panacea for all ills.
- Some people are determined not to change.
- There are extra-therapeutic factors that have a much greater impact and are beyond our control.
- Clients may need more or less intense therapy.
- Clients can be completely immersed in their dysfunction and yet have no thoughts of trying to change.
- Not everyone can benefit from counseling due to capabilities, intellect or attitude.
- You have a finite focus and ability that may not be the right fit for what is needed, and you are dealing with problems

outside your area of expertise.

- Clients cross certain boundaries such as stalking or becoming physically or sexually attracted to the therapist.
- You lose your objectivity to the extent that you become critical and judgmental towards the client.
- You know of other approaches, which are more effective, but in which you are not trained.
- You gave it your best.

It may be difficult to believe that giving up may be more productive than continuing, especially if so many issues are unresolved, but it takes a certain amount of courage and humbleness to admit that you may not be or have what the client needs at that time. A well-placed referral or consent with client to take a therapeutic break from therapy may be the best approach.

Therapy is not magic, and therapists are not magicians. Life happens to us just as it happens to our clients. We have limitations, hidden prejudices, and unsolved problems in our own lives. The key is to admit this upfront, search out our own shortcomings, and get help with them. There is no shame in this. In fact, the benefits can substantial. Not only do you learn about yourself and how you overcome difficulties, but you will be "practicing what you preach" and growing personally.

CHAPTER 9

What to Do with What You've Got

It's always too early to quit.

—Norman Vincent Peale

SOMETIMES WE GET STUCK, not because we don't have enough information or facts, but because we have too much or it is too confusing, and we don't know what to do with what we've got. Getting through and over the bombardment of problems and emotions can seem a daunting task for both the clients and the therapist. Therapy often takes time and sustained effort. Several years ago in a codependency group, members, who had been struggling with a plethora of issues and felt overwhelmed, learned to repeat and remind each other, "Therapy is a process. Therapy is a process. Therapy is a process." We need to keep reminding ourselves this and help clients to understand that as well.

Process vs. Content

There are two aspects of information-gathering, content and process. Content is "what" is being communicated, and process is "how" it is being communicated. Too often in therapy, content gets in the way of progress. What happens is we get bogged down with information and neglect to pay attention to the process. Process includes recurrent patterns of behavior, non-verbals, linguistic anomalies, narrow perspectives, clients' reactions to therapeutic interventions, and recurring themes. There is a tendency to focus on clearing up the content and not dealing with the underlying dynamics. Often the solution lies not in the content, but rather the process.

One of the ways we get lost while doing therapy is to get caught up in the details of the client's narrative or story. When confused or distraught, some people try to explain or give more details to the situation thinking more is better attempting to be helpful. However, often more details are irrelevant. This is especially true with the ramblings of clients with disorders such as dementia, mania or schizophrenia; talking is how they discharge their energy or stress. Some clients love to tell long stories with many details, sometimes rambling, or just not knowing what else to say. It is often difficult to keep up with all the details with your mind trying to sort through what is relevant.

Clients are often unaware of what they are doing, or whether or not it is helpful. When we get to this stage in the session, our mind may begin to shut down, wander, or get confused. This obviously can be overwhelming. When we start thinking, "I have no idea what they're talking about," the best thing to do is to stop focusing on content and look at the process, which is to see the patterns of interaction by asking ourselves the following questions:

- "What is going on here?"
- "What is the client trying to do?"
- "What is the pattern I am seeing?"
- "How is what is happening related to the client's overall problems?"
- "What is the client not talking about?"
- Why is the person talking about this now?
- What is the person trying to say?

These are all process questions looking at the dynamics behind the content. Part of the role of the therapist is to discover these patterns and make clients aware of them. This is an art that is often overlooked, and the lack of it can often cause the therapist to be stuck for many sessions sorting through a morass of meaningless information. Being able to point out to the person the pattern we are seeing is a way of refocusing from the details to the larger perspective. For example, "I notice that every time I bring up the question of your mother's death, you immediately begin talking about your siblings' quarrels over her estate, rather than talk about how her death affected you."

The skill of making the process conscious is dependent on a feedback loop that goes something like this:

> Therapist: I would like to give you some feedback about what I am observing in the sessions as you talk. Would you be okay with me telling you what I am seeing?
>
> Client: Yes, sure.
>
> Therapist: I notice that every time this issue is brought up, you tend to deflect it. Are you aware of that? You may not have thought about it in that way, but is it true?
>
> Client: I'm not sure. Why do you think that?
>
> Therapist: People tend to avoid talking about painful issues. Is there some pain associated with this?
>
> Client: Part of me feels threatened by what you are saying, so maybe it's true.
>
> Therapist: Can you tell why talking about that threatens you?
>
> Client: I don't know. I feel lot of shame.
>
> Therapist: Perhaps that's it. Tell me more about that.

The therapist should always ask permission to give feedback. Doing this engages clients, sparks their curiosity, and increases the likelihood they will be receptive to what you have to say. It is also important to ask for their validation by asking, for example, "Does that sound right to you?" "Have you ever seen it that way?" "Does that make sense to you?" or "Am I on target or not?"

The feedback we give can be in terms of how clients coming across, or how they are relating the information. These are some sample areas to be on the lookout for:

- Are they guarded or defensive?
- Are there certain emotional blocks, such as a sense of discouragement or fear of failure, they are hiding?
- Are they self-conscious and worried about how the therapist will see them and fear being seen as uncaring, unlovable, and unworthy?
- Are they overly sensitive?
- Are they responding with what they think the therapist

wants to hear?
- Are they blocking all suggestions?
- Are they challenging everything the counselor says?

Many times, the process they are engaged in goes back to patterns learned in early childhood. These patterns that pay off in early childhood become the basis for that person's personality, behavior patterns, and source of self-esteem. Often these patterns are counter-productive and even destructive, especially when the children grow older, and yet are so ingrained that the person is either unaware of what they are doing, or so used to them they believe that is the only way they can be.

Teaching them more productive approaches can often free the person to be more genuine and less manipulative enabling them to have deeper, more meaningful feelings and relations. This can best be done if it is re-enacted during the therapy session. If the client gets upset or over-reacts to something going on in the session, this may be a learned pattern from many years ago. For instance, if a client is constantly asking for reassurance, the therapist can comment on it and ask when did the client stop trusting his own judgment. Many childhood patterns may be re-enacted in the therapy session. The therapist should be aware of this possibility and explore it with the client.

Effective processing involves always looking for underlying feelings or meanings. It is a challenge to go deeper into what is being communicated. Ordinary conversations rarely take on this task. Words are used to cover up deeper feelings. One way to break through this is to just observe and allow the client to sit with a thought or statement without further intervention from the therapist. The silence can be an exclamation point. For example, "Isn't it amazing the power you have that you never realized?" (prolonged silence).

Another approach is, if it seems the clients are blocking their feelings, you can use your own thoughts or feelings to approach or highlight the situation. Some examples include:

> "I am aware that as you are telling what is bothering you,
> there is more to the story than what you are telling me or
> even aware of yourself."

"I am confused when you say it doesn't bother you, and yet
when I think about what that must have been like for you, I
feel upset and concerned. Could it be that you have not really
let yourself feel the impact of what happened?"

"I notice that every time this subject is brought up, you appear
more anxious than the situation calls for. It makes me think
that it might not be just that situation that caused you to feel
that way. What do you think?"

By approaching clients this way, it avoids our getting into an accusatory mindset such as thinking, "He is not telling me the truth. How could he possibly think I buy what he is telling me? I wasn't born yesterday." It also allows for the acknowledgement that the therapist may be wrong about his conclusions. For example, I observed a female client who every time I mentioned losing her job she would tear up. I said, "I guess that really makes you sad." "Hell no!" she exclaimed, "It makes me angry." It was then and there I learned to ask what people are experiencing and not assuming I know. And the other lesson was that some women cry when they are angry.

Another interesting phenomenon is that some clients will talk about everything but the problem—like ignoring the proverbial elephant in the room. There are several reasons for this. One, is that they are fearful of even stating the obvious, thinking that by not identifying or addressing the real problem, it will magically go away. Another reason is that clients unconsciously feel that their situation is hopeless, and that if they don't play their last card, so to speak, they still hold onto hope. If they implement it (and it is sometimes an obvious solution) and it doesn't work, then they are defeated. There is always hope if they procrastinate and don't attempt the *final solution*.

Michael was in his early 20's and had developed a drinking problem. Once an honor student and star athlete, he had been in a terrible car accident in which he sustained a concussion that left him with traumatic brain injury. This caused him to have headaches, loss of coordination, slurred speech and confusion. He walked with a limp and even when sober could appear to be drunk. He would easily become combative especially with his mother who was at her wit's end as to how to manage him. On one hand, he seemed hell-bent on destroying himself getting more and more out of control with his drinking. On the other hand, he was a very sensitive, struggling person who was witty, intelligent and conscientious. An obvious battle was raging within him.

Much of our beginning time together consisted of him railing about his mother, bragging about and defending his drinking, and fantasizing about "getting laid." Anytime I tried to address his illness, he would minimize and deflect it, even to the point of refusing to discuss it at all. I struggled to give him free reign to talk about whatever he needed to talk about and to win his trust that I was not going to "make" him do anything. To me it was obvious that his illness was at the core of all his concerns. I sensed that he felt helpless to do anything about it, and that was the major reason he did not want to discuss it.

As fate would have it, he began a relationship with a woman he had known in high school. Once that happened, he began to open up—first by being willing to look at his drinking, and how it might affect his relationship and sex life. Then I shared with him that I often tell females if they want to know how they will be treated in a relationship, look at how the guy treats his mother. I asked him what he thought about that. At first, he was very defensive, but then he acknowledged that he had treated his mother poorly, and that deep down he knew she was only trying to help him, even though her tactics infuriated him.

Finally, I could approach his illness, how he thought his girlfriend viewed it, and what he wished she could understand about it. At this point his whole demeanor changed. It was as though the person he previously had been with me was just a persona he had adopted to face the world. Now there was this scared person, deeply-frustrated and disappointed, who broke down crying saying that his life fell apart when he had the accident. He felt like no one could ever love him, and that he had lived his life believing that it was better to hurt and reject people rather than let them hurt him. Now he sincerely asked for help, saying he was in a situation where he did not want to hurt his girlfriend, and for the first time, believed that someone could love him.

I would like to believe that I brought him to this realization, and perhaps I did to some extent, but it was another person believing and validating him that was the main catalyst for his change. We ended up taking a very circuitous route to get to the core issue. I just had to be patient, always focusing on uncovering his true self that lay buried under all the hurt and frustration. Once he had his breakthrough, he started making major changes in his life. He cut back his drinking significantly, began exploring moving out from his mother's house, and even signing up for Vocational Rehabilitation to begin a career. While I am sure he will suffer setbacks from time to time, the fact that he could break through his wall and be himself was an invaluable accomplishment.

Learning to process situations takes a kind of mindfulness and great objectivity. We often have to set our own values aside and be willing to go where the client takes us, while at the same time not getting caught up in the details, but searching for underlying causes and dynamics.

Chunking Up or Chunking Down

Clients get easily overwhelmed by their problems. Their lives may seem too complex to straighten out. One way to process these situations is to chunk them. This is a concept developed from Neuro-Linguistic Programming (NLP). You can either chunk up a situation or chunk it down. To chunk up a situation means to look at it from a higher level, i.e. seeing patterns to the problems, similarities, or cause-and-effects. This "meta-level" of the problem often reveals secondary benefits. Once a person is conscious of the pattern from this level, she can consciously decide whether to change the pattern or not. The saying, "A rising tide lifts all boats," addresses this phenomenon. As over-arching aspects are discovered, modified, and improved, many of the problems can take care of themselves.

Marie was in the middle of a divorce, which was adversarial and, at times, even vicious. She and her husband would have daily arguments on the phone for a half-hour to an hour, during which she would get upset and scream at her husband. Her two children would often overhear these vituperous remarks, and she was worried about how this was affecting them. Her health was also suffering since the stress was compromising her immune system. This was causing her to miss work, and she had been suspended for losing her temper with a customer.

I suggested we do the Miracle Question, and she got quite involved in realizing, among other things, that she did not need to engage in this type of daily conversation, and that she could turn her focus towards more productive concerns. I asked her to pick a day and pretend as though the miracle had happened. She did, and when she came back the next week, she said that things had gotten much better, she was feeling more positive, and therefore, did not feel the need for further counseling. Marie was able to "chunk up" her situation and see the destructive pattern into which she had fallen. Once she made the decision to refocus her life, many of her problems began to disappear. I congratulated her on her success after just one session. We left it open for her to come back, but she never did.

Chunking down, on the other hand, means to break down the problems and establish mini-goals that can be easily achieved. This is exemplified by the statement, "The journey of 1,000 miles begins with the first step." Small successes build larger successes.

When I first began my private practice, I was concerned about how I was going to get new clients. I developed an elaborate marketing plan including brochures, business cards, presentations, volunteering to be on committees, and taking people to lunch. Then after much consternation and a sense of helplessness—since I had no control over who called for an appointment— I realized the best way to build success was one hour at a time, meaning that more important than striving to carry out the elaborate marketing plan, I had to chunk down my attempts to attract clients to one-hour increments focusing on making each session a success for the client.

Dealing with a small change can easily set up a ripple effect that can have many payoffs.

Marty, a 31-year-old male, came to therapy trying to manage the demands on his time between his wife, a new baby, and his mother, who was dying of cancer. As a result, he was having chronic headaches, anxiety attacks, and even occasional thoughts of suicide. His comments often were things like "My life is a mess," or "Everywhere I turn someone wants me and my time," or "I can't go on like this. I'm of no use to anyone." He saw his problems as a huge burden weighing him down, suppressing his energy and motivation.

In many ways, his situation was like dealing with a tangle of yarn. One has to take one end and slowly unravel it, and that dictates how to proceed. We decided first to focus on what he could do that was the most manageable. I suggested that he start with himself reminding him that if he had no energy and was frazzled, he did not have much to give others. Therefore, taking time to get himself together was critical. He agreed he needed to focus his energy on becoming more stable. His diet was very poor, he was not taking any time for himself, and he was physically and emotionally drained. Once he saw the rationale and began to discover possibilities beginning with himself, he grew encouraged. In other words, we had to chunk down his problems to more manageable units.

Another form of chunking down is establishing criteria for success. It is said that if you put a frog in a pot of water and slowly turn up the heat, the frog will not notice the change. However, if you put a frog in a pot of boiling water, it will immediately jump out. (I think whoever came up with this must have been the same one that tried to kill two birds with one stone and explored ways to skin a cat. Where was PETA?) Anyway, the point is that subtle change is often unnoticed, whether it be negative or positive. Often clients improve but are not even aware of it—they are less tense, their mood has lifted, they have reduced their negative thinking and they are better able to make constructive decisions and set boundaries for themselves. By setting small goals at the outset, they can more consciously monitor their progress.

Useful Fiction

Sometimes the therapist can create and tell a story. The purpose of doing this may be seen as a process of manipulation. Manipulation often has a negative connotation in that it can imply that one uses another for one's own benefit. However, there is a more benign definition—*the act of using or changing (numbers, information, etc.) in a skillful way or for a particular purpose.* (Merriam Webster Dictionary).

Manipulation in psychotherapy can be a major way to create change. One form of manipulation is called "useful fiction." You may tell clients stories in an attempt to educate them about a subject or to motivate them to change. For example, you may tell them you worked with a client who had a problem like theirs, and how he successfully overcame it. While this may not have happened, per se, it gives the client a sense of hope that because others have done it, they may also have a chance of being successful. The *fiction* is that it may have been a composite of clients or a different demographic to help them relate to it more readily e.g., you changed the story to match the gender or age of the client. Anyway, giving them exact data borders on breaking confidentiality.

Another way useful fiction is used is to say, "I have a client like you and I need your help. I wonder what you think would help them?" This useful fiction is helpful to deal with clients who deny they have a problem or are so defensive they cannot extract themselves enough from the situation to objectively assess their role. By taking the focus off themselves, they often come up with solutions. These solutions can then be applied to them by asking, "Do you think that could help you?"

Another technique is to say, "Research has shown that people who do (whatever intervention you want the client to do) has been very effective in bringing about a positive result." This will tend to give more validity to whatever approach you are trying to introduce.

There may be some ethical concerns about such tactics. It seems like you are lying to the client, but the intention behind it is important. If the intention is to prove you are right or to boost your ego or to impress or deceive others, then it is faulty. However, if you are doing it for the benefit of the client, then it can be considered acceptable, if it is based on sound facts or data.

Barry, a 21-year-old college student, was a participant in a men's group. He was referred by his fiancée, a social worker, who was worried about his lack of assertiveness and poor self-esteem. When she referred Barry, she told me on the phone that he was very kind-hearted and a good person, but he would routinely put himself down. She was most concerned about his drinking, since he would often get drunk to the point of not remembering what he had done the night before. One night he stumbled and fell into a ditch and passed out not being able to make it into the house.

In group, he was withdrawn and guarded and would only respond if directly called upon. He seemed nervous, anxious, and fearful of saying the wrong thing. My attempts to draw him out often failed. One day before group, I pulled him aside and said that I needed his help with another group member, Bud, who was divorced, depressed, and feeling guilty about having had an affair that was now over and was missing his children. Since Barry had been the product of divorce, I suggested that one of the best ways to help someone to get over the guilt of being a divorced father was to talk to someone who had gone through their parent's divorce (useful fiction). I told Barry he was uniquely qualified to help Bud, and I felt like it would be of great benefit to Bud, if Barry shared his experience. He reluctantly agreed to do so and in the process, began to disclose some of the hurt and difficulty his parents' divorce caused. Bud was touched by Barry's disclosure, and they grew to help each other. Barry could tell Bud what he thought his children might need, and Bud could communicate to Barry what a dilemma divorce creates for parents.

Tell the Truth

While "useful fiction" is beneficial, so is telling the truth. It is amazing how tangled and convoluted people's lives can get. This is partly due to false beliefs acquired as a child. If the person has received accurate information growing up, then this can be a blessing and a foundation for a successful life. But if the messages are hurtful, untrue, and negative, they can steer the person in the wrong direction in life. Those who believe the lies build their lives on illusion, all the while thinking the lies are real.

Often these lies become clients' reality. They build stories around these lies, and these stories can determine and define their reality—or at least their perception of reality. Many times, these stories are clouded by false perception, false information, unwillingness to face the truth, fear of expressing the truth, and conditioning to not tell the truth. These patterns become so implicit that clients have no idea there is another way to look at their situation, and sometimes this means that the therapist must be the one to tell the truth.

Marie brought her son for counseling. She was quite upset with him and had a list of complaints that did not seem disconcerting to me: He was not always prompt; he left clothes scattered in his room; once took the car without her permission to go to the store to get something to eat; and he would not do his chores unless prompted. After hearing all of these complaints, I was still unsure what the big problem was, so I asked her what the big problem was, and she said, "I just want him to act his age."

The truth is not a club we use to hit someone over the head. Truth is not our opinion, our theory, or our preferences, so it is a tricky course to navigate, and it must be revealed with an attitude of love.

Before I could stop myself, I blurted out, "He is acting his age! This is what 16-year-olds do." She was not satisfied with that answer and further explained that he just never does anything right. At that point I kinda knew what this boy's problem was.

Ironically, after our meeting we went out into the lobby and found her son doing his homework. Immediately I began to praise him, since truthfully I had never seen a teenager so intently doing his homework in the lobby. I purposefully pointed out in front of his mother how he was doing something right. She was so beat down that she could not see his good points even when they were right in front of her.

One of the counselor's responsibilities is sorting through fiction and falsity to uncover what is truthful and real. It takes a certain level of consciousness, clarity, and presence to be *the bearer of truth*. The truth is not a club we use to hit someone over the head. Truth is not our opinion, our theory, or our preferences, so it is a tricky course to navigate, and it must be revealed with an attitude of love. While the truth is often hard to hear, when revealed correctly, it can be enlightening and exciting. We often hesitate to speak the truth because 1) we think it may be presumptuous to say we know the truth, or 2) we are not certain we know the truth or 3) the truth as we think we see it may reflect our own agenda or biases. Most of the time, it is a matter of stating the facts.

Bruce, one of the therapists I supervise told me of a situation in dealing with Mark, a 14-year-old boy who lived with his mother and sister. Mark would get into almost vicious arguments with his mother insisting that she buys him certain top-of-the-line clothes or shoes. He was very fashion-conscious and felt like he must dress a certain way to be respected and to attract girls. His mother was working two jobs and had barely enough to pay the bills. Mark seemed to have no sense of the sacrifice it took for his mother to provide him with basic necessities, let alone his demands for more. He insisted that she didn't love him, and that if she did, she wouldn't turn him down. Of course, this was the mother's Achilles heel, and when he played that card, she often gave in. However, the more he acted up, the less likely she was to want to make any kind of sacrifice for him, so a pattern was established that kept escalating.

Bruce developed good rapport with Mark rather rapidly, since there were aspects of Mark's life that paralleled his own life. After he had witnessed the arguments between mother and son and saw how unrealistic Mark was being, he confronted

Mark by saying "Mark, I know what the problem is between you and your mother."

"You do? Tell me."

Bruce said, "I see some tendencies you have that I used to have. Mark, you are selfish. You tend to only think about what you want without regard for the impact on your mother or sister. I don't see you putting yourself in their place and understanding what they have to endure. I think you need to back off and be more reasonable and understanding. I was thinking I never saw it in myself, until someone pointed it out, so I felt I had to tell you."

Mark looked like he had been hit with a lightning bolt. He said nothing for almost two minutes. Then he said what most counselors beg to hear, "I never thought of it in that way. I think maybe you're right. How did you change that?"

Telling a client the truth takes a tremendous amount of trust. Sometimes counselors dance around a subject for fear of hurting the client's feelings, but the truth can be told if delivered in the right way and under the right circumstances.

This is sometimes "the elephant in the living room" that no one wants to talk about, which is typical in families with a drug problem or domestic violence. One member of the family will present with major family relationship problems and never mention the hidden secrets. It may be that they are ashamed to admit them or, they take the secrets for granted, since that just seems to be the way things are in that family. In some cases, it is seen as disloyalty to tell about the family problems.

The truth is often blotted out because of family secrets, often thought of as the family's *dirty laundry*. These may be intergenerational, as when there is a child born out of wedlock, an affair, or incest. It can manifest in many ways with certain family members being shunned for no apparent reason. There may be secrets about sexual orientation or gender identification, which some know about and others do not. The television series, *Transparent,* explores the family dynamics of a situation of a transgendered father who comes out to his family as a woman.

These situations can create a large sense of betrayal and distrust. Resentment and anger are common when the secret is not known, and sometimes when the secret is known. Searching for and/or dealing with these kinds of secrets depends on having a solid working relationship with the family or family member. A great deal of trust is needed. At the same time, the therapist may be risking the relationship by taking the family into these well-guarded areas. It is further complicated in that uncovering the secret can bring great relief to everyone, or it can create a wasps' nest of hurt for all involved. A great rift can occur if, instead of dealing with the impact of the uncovered secret, the family creates a diversion by attacking the therapist for shining a light on the subject.

There is a saying in the recovery community: "Our secrets keep us sick." Only by clients getting honest with themselves and others can they truly recover. A therapist who is understanding, non-judgmental, and insightful can be the key to opening these secrets and helping to uncover the truth.

Don't React to Symptoms; Respond to Causes

When clients present us with information or behavior, there are two levels to approach them: react to the symptoms or search out and respond to the underlying causes. This is a very important concept in therapy. The first part is understanding the difference between reacting and responding. I had a friend in college who made me acutely aware of the difference between reacting and responding. She lived in a trailer in the woods with only her cat. One night she awoke sensing a little whishing feeling on her cheek. She opened her eyes and saw that her cat had captured a rat, which was still alive and its tail was rubbing against her face. She said, "I could have reacted, and yelled and screamed bloody murder, which would have freaked the cat possibly causing her to let go of the rat, and they both would end up running around my bedroom. But I responded. I slowly took hold of the cat with the rat in her mouth, and carried them both to the door and tossed them into the yard. Then I screamed and hollered." This has always helped me remember the difference between reacting and responding. Another simple example is if you have a flat tire, you can either react or respond. To react would be to get all upset, kick the tire, and cuss. To respond would be to get out the spare and change the tire.

In a more profound example of responding, Dr. Lori Stevic-Rust, a board certified Clinical Health Psychologist wrote in the *Huffington Post* on November 5, 2015:

> I just finished reading the book, *I Am Malala*. It is the story of a young girl who was shot in the face by the Taliban for speaking

out for the education of girls. While her story of survival after the shooting is nothing short of heartbreaking and miraculous, it is her thinking before the shooting that is truly inspirational and offers us all a great life lesson.

Death threats were frequently made to her and her family for several years. First, the threats were subtle and quiet, and then in the year prior to the shooting they became more overt and frequent. At the age of only 14, Malala began to rehearse how she would keep herself safe and what she would do if confronted with a terrorist.

"I'd imagine that on my way home a terrorist might jump out and shoot me on those steps. I wondered what I would do. Maybe I'd take off my shoe and hit him, but then I'd think if I did that there would be no difference between me and a terrorist. It would be better to plead, "OK, shoot me, but first listen to me. What you are doing is wrong. I'm not against you personally, I just want every girl to go to school—including your daughter. Now do with me what you want."

Her reasoning and insight is profound as it speaks directly to the distinction between reacting and responding. Her young life is marked by the purest definition of living a life of responding to pain, insults, and threats rather than reacting. She is the true definition of somebody living an authentic life.

—*http://www.huffingtonpost.com/lori-stevicrust-phd-abpp/react-respond_b_4252438.html*

Hopefully, we will never have to encounter such a serious situation in our lives, but the thought and spirit with which she met adversity is something we can model.

The second part of "don't react to symptoms, respond to causes" is to differentiate between symptoms and causes. We may easily be confronted or intimidated by a client's attitude, sharp words, and discontent. These are symptoms we may react to, but having an ongoing attitude of acceptance and openness will help to ensure that we won't react in such a way as to shame or dismiss our client. This is the major problem with reacting—people tend to feel threatened, devalued, attacked, or ignored—all of which can happen in a counseling session. By stopping and considering the reasons for the behaviors and seeing the client in a non-judgmental way, the therapist can stop reacting and begin to respond addressing the underlying issues that are causing the behaviors.

Another version of this is, "Don't react to behaviors, but listen to their behaviors." Often younger children and some cognitively-impaired adults do not have the vocabulary or awareness to verbally express their feelings, instead they act out their feelings. We need to seek out the deeper cause of these behaviors, most of which are rooted in fear.

Tayvon, a first grader, was having a difficult time adjusting to school. He was reluctant to come into the classroom, and at times the teacher literally had to drag him in. He would often refuse to participate and would get under a table and not come out. Again the teacher often had to pull him out kicking and screaming. And the biggest irritant was that he would not take off his hoodie. He always wanted it on his head. Being sent to the office, lecturing by the principal, and having the parent come to the school were having no effect. These were all situations in which people were reacting to his behaviors. The school's concern was that if we let one child do it, then everyone will do it.

Luckily, he was assigned a counselor who began responding to him. She discovered that most of his behaviors were the result of a combination of over-stimulation, his lack of sensory integration, and social phobia. Having a hoodie on his head was protection and created a sense of security. It also helped to minimize the sensory overload. The counselor was able to convince the teachers and principal to work with her in helping him.

Her first step was to let Tayvon sit outside the classroom with his hoodie on, until he became de-stressed enough to go into the classroom. Then he was allowed to keep his hoodie on, until he felt comfortable taking it off. Any time he retreated under the desk, the counselor would get down on the floor with him, suggesting in a soothing voice that she imagined that he felt safer under the desk, and when he felt safe again he could join the others. All these responses seemed to pay off, because in less than two weeks he could come directly into the classroom, take off his hoodie, and join the others without going under the desk again.

The counselor responded to him by addressing his need for safety and security, rather than reacting to his symptoms like the school staff had previously done.

Reactions are knee-jerk responses that are often irrational, judgmental, and mean-spirited. By responding instead, the therapist could find the root cause and drastically improve his chances for success.

The Power of the Story

Most of the information clients reveal about themselves comes in the form of stories. The nature of these stories can be an incredible help or an incredible obstacle. The mistake is often made that the narrative is assumed to be true, or that it is insignificant in and of itself as a therapeutic tool. Since the past exists mostly as memories in the brain (there are body memories as well), and those memories are usually experienced as stories, working with stories can alter the effects of the past.

At a conference on multi-cultural sensitivity, the story was told about the Harvard Program in Refugee Trauma working with Cambodian refugees who had been the victims of the Pol Pot regime, during which two million of eight million people died of starvation or murder. These survivors witnessed and experienced torture, rape, and mass killings sometimes daily. Dealing with these refugees using traditional Western psychiatric approaches of was not working. They were diagnosed from a Western perspective as having mental illness. Doing formal intakes, prescribing psychotropic medicines, and looking for underlying causes were not working. Not only were the victims were not improving, they were getting worse.

A team from the television series, *Nova*, asked to interview some of the victims. Reluctantly, the staff agreed, thinking there was no way these severely traumatized people would talk about the atrocities they experienced or witnessed. Many different interviews were held, some of them utilizing a group setting. After the interviews, many participants reported they felt better and somewhat relieved. This was a mystery for the psychiatrists, until they discovered that in the Cambodian culture one of the ways of healing was through storytelling. By being able to tell their stories, they could share their worries, concerns, and trauma, which brought a sense of connection, community, and healing to their lives. The effectiveness of the program increased significantly when the mental health staff began using a bi-cultural approach that included the Cambodians' traditions and healing approaches combined with modern psychotherapeutic practices.

Richard Mollica in his book, *Healing Invisible Wounds: Paths to Hope and Recovery*, tells of the Cambodian survivors' recovery. "Survivors must be allowed to tell their stories their own way. We must not burden them with theories, interpretations, or opinions, especially if we have little knowledge of their cultural and political background."

So, stories are a powerful medium. There are many therapeutic levels and kinds of storytelling:

- Putting feelings into words and words into stories help to discover underlying feelings or events and allow the client to put a *beginning and an end* to situations which seem endless.
- Many clients have deep secrets which they have never told anyone. Sharing can bring great relief in knowing that another person knows the secret and did not react.
- Repeating a story in some cases helps to clarify or desensitizes the person to the impact of it.
- Telling a story from a different perspective or playing it out with a *happy ending* opens possibilities for new solutions.
- Being able to view childhood stories from an adult perspective can empower the person to deal with the events with new resources and understanding.
- In Narrative Therapy one personifies symptoms and creates a story about them. For example, the therapist could ask, "Can you tell me the story about when your eating disorder came into your life, and what it wants for you?"
- One can use therapeutic stories about others to either metaphorically or directly influence how a person perceives their situation.

We all have stories to tell of our past. Each event could be told from many different perspectives depending on our knowledge, level of insight, involvement, and state of mind. The story we end up telling to others may or may not be the story we tell to ourselves. Even the story we tell ourselves may not be the real story.

Jack was 12 when his mother left him. At first he was just surprised, and then he began to wonder why. He began to think that it was because of him. He had been in trouble in school and gotten suspended for hitting another child. He asked others why they thought she left, and they gave varying versions ranging from her having a mental illness to meeting another man and eloping with him. So, there were several ways he could look at what happened and decide which story he would tell about her. He missed her greatly and became very upset, which caused him to lose focus in school, and he began failing. This reinforced his original thesis that he was to blame, and this was the story he told himself. To others he would explain that he had no idea, but he was sure that she must have had a very good reason. To some extent, he carried the guilt of his mother leaving for many years. It was only later in therapy when he reviewed the situation that he realized that he could not have been bad enough to cause his mother to leave the whole family. He then had to change the narrative of the story and to stop blaming himself for her abandonment.

Updating or challenging destructive stories of the past can create healing for the client. Seeing that things were not necessarily the way they were remembered or being able to give new meaning to them can bring great relief.

The Question of Questions

How do you discover the necessary information you need to solve a problem? The most natural way seems to be to ask questions. Some experts believe that counseling is a process of taking clients through a strategic set of questions, and that questions are the key to opening undiscovered territory. They believe that excellent therapy is a process of honing your ability to ask questions to arrive at deeper and more critical underlying issues.

There is another school of thought that believes that the use of questions should be severely limited, because questions set the therapist up as an interrogator, and questions put the client on the spot. In his book, *Effective Techniques for Dealing with Highly Resistant Clients,* Clifton Mitchell posits that "…when dealing with highly resistant client, questions are likely to impede progress and foster resistance…and put people in a one-down defensive position." He further argues that not all questions are alike. Some are more helpful than others. He warns against leading questions, which are often used to lead the client towards a pre-determined outcome. Some examples are:

- Do you think that was a wise thing to do?
- Are you sure that's what you meant?
- Couldn't you have done it another way?
- Why don't you try telling me what that was really all about?
- Are you sure you didn't mean to do that after all?

Mitchell suggests instead of questions, use reflective statements such as, "Tell me more about that," or "Help me to understand what that was like," or "Describe the situation for me." In addition, he cautions not to use more than two questions without a reply.

Obviously, each point of view has its validity. The strategic use of questions can be an invaluable aid if used sparingly with awareness of the effect it may have on the client.

One questioning technique is the use of neutral questions, which are usually the most helpful, since they give clients free-rein to express whatever they are feeling, experiencing or remembering without the influence of the therapist. This is a subtle process. If you ask a question such as, "What are you *feeling* right now?" you have influenced their answer by making them focus on their feelings, but maybe they were having an important thought or memory instead. The same is true with the question, "What do you *think* about that?" which forces the client to focus on thoughts. These are not neutral questions.

Neutral questions are more general:

- What was that like for you?
- How did that go?
- What did you experience when that happened?
- You can also get greater detail with the following:
- Tell me more about that.
- Was there anything else about that?
- Can you give me an example?
- Do you remember any more details?

As you proceed in doing therapy, you may develop some favorite questions, ones that get to the heart of a matter. Some of my favorites are:

- "What part of that is the most difficult for you to deal with?" (This is useful when someone seems overwhelmed with a problem or emotions.)
- "What is missing in your life?" (This is a great diagnostic statement in that it often goes to the heart of a person's existential difficulty.)
- "Who were you before you became who you are?" (This helps a person to get in touch with their more essential self.)
- "What's going on with you right now?" (This is a neutral statement or clean language, which is broad enough to allow the client to choose whether to talk about feelings or thoughts.)
- "What makes you do that (or think that)?" (The client may be so focused on **what** they did, but never explore **why** they do something. A variation of this is useful with parents who have a list of complaints about their child: "Why do you think they do that?" This often takes parents to a level they never explored about their child.)
- "What do you think I would tell you about how to handle this situation? (If they can answer this, it may mean they don't need me anymore, because they have internalized the therapy process and learned what they needed to succeed.)
- "When did you feel most in control of your life or were having the most success?" (This shows the person's potential and changes the focus to a positive basis.)
- "What else?" (This under-used question repeated several times helps the client to move past the first superficial answer to a deeper level.)

What do all the questions above have in common? They almost all begin with the word, "what," which is a much more powerful question than "why." "Why" questions invoke shame (Why did you do that?) and/or may lead to alibis, justifying, lying or asking for an answer that the person is not even conscious of and may not be able to verbalize. ("I don't have any idea why I do that.")

So, learning to develop and ask the right question at the right time can determine the difference between success or failure.

Conflict–The Opportunity for Resolution

While therapists always hope sessions will go smoothly, there is always the possibility of conflict erupting. Conflict is the Scylla and Charybdis for counselors, for it seems that no matter which way we go, the outcome could be disastrous. Whether it is in couples counseling, family therapy, or even in individual therapy, it is a common occurrence. Conflict can occur in three situations: 1. when clients cannot resolve conflict within themselves. 2. when therapists are often placed in the position of feeling they should agree with a client when they don't, or 3. in couples or family therapy when the therapist is faced with having to agree with one person over another. This can undermine neutrality and give the appearance of taking sides. Helping people resolve conflict is a tricky proposition. However, by taking a different perspective of the conflict, the client can come to different conclusions, which can lead to resolution.

With clients who have inner conflict, a helpful technique is to identify each side of the conflict and have a dialogue between these parts. Often each part has valid points, and being able to air these and discuss them brings the issues to light. The level of shame or conflict lessens by validating each part's right to exist within the person. By externalizing and verbalizing the conflict in this way, clients can see their dilemma in a different light.

Betsy was sent by her employer for constant tardiness. She had so many late notices that, if she was late one more time she would be fired. She had been at the job for more than 20 years, and the thought of being fired terrified her, and yet she had no faith that she could stop being tardy. Rather than me further try to convince her not to be late any more, I had her develop a dialogue between the part of her that did not want to get fired and the part that did not think it could change. At first, the part that was scared had a lot to say, and the part that was chronically late had little. As we proceeded, however, the chronically late part began to speak up. Both parts agreed that she should not lose her job, both parts agreed, that on the surface, being on time was not an insurmountable task, and both agreed she needed to change. Her responsible side said that if she got up in plenty of time and did not dally around just as she was getting ready to go (her habit for which she had no explanation), she should be fine.

Her late part admitted at that point she did not care if she was late. "Being on time puts too much stress on me. If I do it, people will expect me to always do it, and I cannot handle that stress. My sister was always on time, and I chose not to compete with her or be like her. She was always the good one, and I was the one blamed for everything, so I figured why try? I think I must still be feeling that way, though I don't even have contact with her anymore."

As the parts interacted, the late part agreed that, here-and-now, the bigger pressure would be getting fired. She agreed to have a talk with herself right before she was getting ready to leave. In fact, the responsible part wrote out what she would tell the late part, if she started to fade on her commitment to leave early enough to be on time. Furthermore, the responsible part acknowledged the late part and her struggle, while reminding her that the situation with her sister no longer was relevant.

As for clients, who are looking for validation of beliefs the therapist does not agree with, the therapist can take the stance, "I understand why you strongly believe that, and given what you have experienced, I can understand why you feel that way." What you are doing, in effect, is agreeing with the person's *right to have that opinion* without agreeing with the opinion.

A way to manage conflict in marital situations is to help the parties first identify what they agree upon in relation to the issue. This, by itself, begins to change the dynamics of the conflict. People in conflict vociferously argue their own point of view and are not in the mode of compromise. Looking for commonality reduces tension and encourages cooperation.

It is not uncommon in conflict to hear one person say, "I totally disagree with you," but in reality, there are probably many points in common. Take parenting, for example. It is not unusual for the father to take a tough stance with the child, and the mother to take a more nurturing approach, so the parents may be very much in conflict over the *right* approach.

Mother: "I think you're too hard on the children. They fear you."

Father: "You baby them and let them get away with everything."

Therapist: "It seems like both of you have very different ideas about raising children. Is that right?"

Couple: "Yes." (They both agree—the beginning of the agreement process).

Therapist: "I'm not so sure you two are that far apart. Let's see if we can find some areas you agree upon.

- Do you both agree you want your children to be well-behaved?
- Do you both agree you want your children to be happy and healthy?
- Do you both agree you want your children to get along with others?
- Do you both agree you want your children to feel good about themselves?
- Do you both agree you want your children to respect you?
- Do you both agree you want your children not to suffer?
- Do you both agree you want your children to love you?
- Do you both agree you want your children to love each other?
- Do you both agree you don't want to do anything to damage them?

I don't think you are so different. Obviously, you have different approaches, but your goals are the same. It may be that since you both do have the same goals for your children, it is okay for each of you to take a different approach, but it is going to the extremes that causes the conflict. Maybe, if you each modified the intensity of your approach and position, you might find that your approaches can become compatible and less conflictual. How do you think you can modify your approach to make it less problematic?"

So, conflict can and should lead to compromise with the proper guidance. When compromise is rejected, then the problem is more one of relationship rather than substance. Until the relationship can be repaired, and each party is willing to work for the benefit of the other, the dynamics of conflict will often remain with each person pursuing the goal of winning and, thereby, have the other losing. It is only when win-win becomes the goal and the norm, can conflict be a building block instead of a stumbling block.

Looking for areas of agreement and creating a win-win situation is equally true in the counselor-client relationship and is crucial for the success of therapy.

Stop. Take a Break

Sometimes the pace of therapy is fast and furious. Events are unfolding, the client is hyper, and there is a lot of confusion about what is happening and which way to go. The situation seems out of control. In these situations, sometimes the best thing is to stop and review what has and is happening. "There is so much happening now in your life; I am wondering of all the things you have brought up, which ones you want to focus on next?" This becomes the time to process where the therapy is going. First, get clients' thoughts or ideas. In this way, you can observe what they are absorbing from the therapy, and/or what is utmost in their minds. You can also invite them to give you feedback about the course of treatment, and how they think it is helping or not helping. Then you can offer to give them your feedback. Clients are usually very intent on what the therapist observes. It is also tremendously helpful to point out the progress clients have made. Often they are so intent on overcoming their difficulties, they lose sight of what they have achieved. The therapist can also change the pace by not responding to everything that is being said and slowing down in his responses. In this way space is created that will allow for the emergence of new thoughts and perspectives. This time pause creates the opportunity for the client to *stop feeding the therapist and to digest what is being offered.*

Other situations may also call for a break. Therapy may have reached a standstill. The same topics are being discussed repeatedly, and each session starts to sound like the session before it. The counselor has imparted all his therapeutic wisdom and insight, and still there seems to be no movement. There may be several reasons for this.

One reason is the client has become dependent on the therapist to have someone with whom to communicate. The client is comfortable with the therapist, and the therapist is comfortable with the client ... or not. In the client's mind, the therapist has morphed into a friend and may be the only source of honest communication. This may also be a time to review where the client is in the process, renew the therapeutic contract, and set some goals. But it may also be a time to say, "I think we have covered a lot of territory, and you have come a long way. I would like to suggest we take a break and see how you can apply what you have learned. We can always get back together if things start to fall apart again."

The second reason is the client has done some very intense work and is not able to handle anything more for now. It is normal after an intense therapy situation to spend the next session on a less-charged topic. This should not be done, however, if the client is unresolved about the previous session or other serious issues have cropped up.

Giving clients the choice to continue by going deeper or taking some time off gives them a better sense of empowerment. It also counteracts the idea they need to keep going, because that is what *good* clients do, or thinking the therapist expects them to continue with that intensity. Clients may take a therapeutic vacation for several weeks or a month to process what they have experienced, while at the same time keeping the door open for emergencies or resumption of therapy. Some people need time to assimilate what they have experienced. Continuing can sometimes create more confusion and distress, and clients can get the idea that therapy is just too stressful, and they were better off before they came to therapy.

The third is the client is holding back on an issue and is too fearful or embarrassed to bring it up. It may lie just below the surface, and the client thinks that the therapist will somehow address it, or the client is in mortal fear that it will be brought out. Again, the Columbo approach may be best. "I sense there is more to the story than you are comfortable telling me right now, but I may be wrong. I don't want to read too much into a situation, yet at the same time, if there is an issue that needs to be discussed, I don't want to avoid it. Feel free to tell me one way or the other which you think it is." In this way, you are addressing the possibility without defining it and giving the client a pass, if they need it.

Prescribing a Reaction

One strategy in dealing with potential problems in the counseling relationship is to predict and prescribe them beforehand. This is a way of normalizing and reducing the impact of a statement about clients or their situation. There are times when you should confront clients with their behaviors or contradictions. One way to soften the blow is to prescribe what you anticipate their reaction will be beforehand. "This may upset you, but...," or "You might not like what

I am about to say…," or "I feel like I need to tell you what I see, and you may disagree." This technique is particularly effective with oppositional clients, since they may be out to prove you wrong. "I'll show you. I won't get angry or upset. I can handle whatever you throw at me."

You can set the stage for this at the beginning of therapy when you explain how you work. "I will try to share with you my thoughts and concerns about your situation. Some of what I say to you may not sit well with you. It is not my purpose to upset you, but to be honest with what I am sensing."

Tyronda, a 27-year-old female, was in a difficult marriage. Her husband, Jeff, was of a much different nature than she. He was spontaneous and free-wheeling. She was much more cautious and organized. In her attempt to rein him in, she was pushing him away. She was oblivious that he was staying away from home on many nights to avoid her and their incessant arguments. She grew suspicious of his absence and surmised he was having an affair. The more she insisted that was the case, the more he avoided her, feeling he could never convince her that this was not true. Unknown to her was that he would hang out with his sister, brother-in-law, and their two children.

After finding out the truth from the husband, the therapist felt she needed to give Tyronda feedback to as to the effect of her actions and suspicions. She said, "What I am about to say to you, you may easily discount or not want to hear it, but I believe that your husband is staying away, not because of an affair, but because he is being driven away by your attempts to control him. He does not want to come home to such a contentious environment."

Sometimes the feedback hits the client like a ton of bricks.

Joey was in the second grade and very sensitive to any negative feedback. He would often cry if he made a B or C on an assignment. Further inquiry into his situation revealed that his grandmother was hyper-critical of him and would yell at him for the slightest offense. When the school counselor discovered this, she felt conflicted. If she confronted the grandmother with this information, the grandmother might become even more forceful and critical of Joey for telling on her at school. However, left unchecked, Joey's meltdowns were becoming more often and more explosive. The counselor decided to tell the grandmother, but preceded by posing all the precautions first. She said, "I know you love your grandson and want him to do his best, but I am about to tell you something that may upset you. My goal is not to criticize, but to give you some feedback about how he views your relationship. He has not said this directly to me, but it is obvious from what he tells me. Your attempts to correct him are having a devastating effect on him. He is super-sensitive and even fearful of you. He screams and cries if he gets into any trouble and begs us not to tell you. I feel for him, when he gets like this. He has not complained about you, but he is deeply affected by your actions, which I doubt is what you want to have happen."

The grandmother was shocked. "Oh my God, I had no idea that I was being so harsh on him, and that he was taking it so hard." She started crying. When he came home from school that day, she apologized to him saying she was sorry she had been so hurtful in her words. She promised to change. He broke down and was finally able to share what he had been feeling but was so afraid to tell her.

This approach helped to minimize her defensiveness and give her feedback in a caring way.

One danger in predicting a reaction is that if you are wrong, they may take offense that you would think that of them. However, if they protest the prediction, you can always praise them for their self-control and even one-down yourself by saying, "I really underestimated the power of your ability to handle unpleasant situations."

If they do react in the way you described, the point is not to gloat, but to sympathize with them about how difficult it is to accept feedback from others. You could even include a situation of your own in which you overreacted in a similar way. The goal is to get them to hear the truth that you observe, so they can internalize it and make changes.

Let It Be. Let the Train Wreck

A boy and his older friend were walking along the railroad tracks near their house. Off in the distance in front of them the heard a train. Only seconds later they heard another train in the distance coming behind them. It did not take long to figure out there might be a train wreck. "Oh my God," said the older boy panicking, "What do you think we should do?"

The younger boy said, "I need to go get my brother."

"What can he do?" asked the older one.

"Nothing," replied the younger one, "but he has never seen a train wreck before."

Therapists may think "letting it be" is a failure, but sometimes letting things take their course and allowing natural consequences to occur can pave the way for change to take place. As much as we want to help people avoid the consequences of their decisions, there are times when there is little we can do to prevent an action from happening, and our goal is to help the person through it with the least impact. At other times, the only thing possible is to let the situation play out and hope the consequences will force a change.

Joey, a 7-year-old, constantly complained about his life at home—the rules, the chores, and the schedule. He repeatedly said that any place would be better than this. His mother was very tired of hearing this, so she conspired with the counselor to play out a scenario. She pretended to call Social Services and spoke with the lady about placing him in a different home. She announced to Joey that through much work, they were able to find him a placement with Mrs. Fitzgerald.

Joey was very excited about being able to go to a new home. When the day came, he told his mother he needed to pack. She told him that would not be necessary, since Mrs. Fitzgerald had everything he would need. He began to be a little disappointed. They got into the car, and the mother took him to the scariest neighborhood in the city and noticed a light on in front of a house. She pulled up to the curb, told Joey this was where Mrs. Fitzgerald lived, and she was expecting him. He was hesitant to get out and asked his mother if she would go with him to the house. "No," she said, she had already worked out the details with Mrs. Fitzgerald, and he just needed to go knock on the door and let her know that he had arrived. He very reluctantly got out of the car, but when he was halfway up the walk, he turned and ran back to the car. "I don't want to go live here. I want to come back home."

"Are you sure?" his mother asked.

"Yes," he said.

"Even with all the rules and chores?"

"Yes," he said even louder.

"Ok, but I know Mrs. Fitzgerald will be very disappointed. I'll see if I can patch things up. You can come back home, but no more complaints, right?"

"Yes, Mom, I promise."

If people with substance-use disorders are not motivated for treatment, they are often told that they have to hit bottom before they will change. This may be true for some. Also, different people have different bottoms. For one person, it may be the threat of divorce or a DUI; for others, it may be they have lost everything and are still in denial. The more fortunate ones are the ones who can see or anticipate the future and not have to hit bottom. The further down the bottom is, the longer it takes to climb back out. One of the reasons staged interventions work is that when confronted with the consequences of their addiction in a way that they cannot deny the negative impact on their lives, they give in. This is true especially if the interventions are done by the family. They are much more powerful since they strike at a deeper emotional level than the therapist can elicit.

With other cases in which you think the person or situation is not going to change, you may just have to coach the person through the process on how to get help and how to minimize the effects. This is common working with at-risk youth, who, through no fault of their own, are stuck in a situation with a parent who is hypercritical, mentally ill, or addicted.

Levi, a 14-year-old, lived with an alcoholic dad and his two younger siblings ages 9 and 4. Dad would often leave the home to go out drinking and tell Levi to watch his brother and sister. This put a lot of pressure on Levi. He often could not manage his siblings, and they grew to resent him. In addition, the father would come home drunk and find some reason to criticize Levi, yelling and cursing at him. Levi expressed that he wanted to kill himself. An attempt to put a counselor in the home did not seem to help. The father continued to deny his drinking problem and convinced himself that the counselor was the problem for stirring things up. Fortunately, Levi was very cooperative in working with the counselor, and the counselor was able to coach Levi on how to avoid confrontations with his dad and provided an outlet for Levi's frustration and anger. It was obvious that under the current conditions the father was not going to change, so it was a matter of increasing Levi's coping skills and support.

We obviously cannot control our clients. They often do not do what we strongly feel they need to do and what would be in their best interests. We make our best efforts to educate them, sometimes confront them, and sometimes coach them. Then we have to surrender. That does not mean to give up; it means to put for our best effort and surrender the outcome, hoping that in the end things will work out for them, and they will come back for counseling when needed. This is the approach used in Motivational Interviewing, which advocates avoiding argumentation, rolling with resistance, and supporting self-sufficiency. Pushing too hard can alienate clients, thereby destroying any chances of our being helpful. Better to keep the relationship strong and go along, or terminate with goodwill, than to force the issue and destroy their connection to counseling, not only with us, but possibly all future counseling.

CHAPTER 10

No Ideas What to Do

While we may have come from different ships, we are in the same boat.

—Martin Luther King, Jr.

NOT KNOWING WHAT TO DO can be quite stressful for a therapist. In this chapter, we'll examine some working strategies for how to proceed when you are at a loss as to how to help a client and share some illustrative stories. It is written to develop the rationale to normalize and hopefully de-stress therapists and the dilemmas in which they find themselves.

Admit It

In keeping with the idea of being genuine, it is permissible to admit that you don't have the answer. Not knowing and admitting it is one of the most genuine interactions a therapist can have with a client. Clients often respect this honesty, rather than some evasive answer that may sound good, but does not address the issues. Of course, you can then follow this frank admission with, "I will do some research on this," or "I will consult with my supervisor." This requires curiosity, developing of resources, and willingness to take the extra time and effort to investigate.

When I was first embarking in private practice, a rather elderly couple wanted help with their 23-year-old son who had cerebral palsy and was diagnosed as mildly mentally retarded. (This was before the time of the new diagnosis, intellectual disability.) They said that I had come highly recommended as the one person who could help their son. Well, I had never, ever worked with a person who was "mentally retarded," and I melted in my seat. Whether it was vanity or curiosity, I agreed to see him. His parents were very concerned that, while he was generally very pleasant to be around, he was more and more prone to severe outbursts of anger, even to the point of striking out at them.

During our second session, I started asking him about his cerebral palsy—what it was, how it affected him, what was challenging about it, etc., because I had little knowledge of it. When I asked these questions, I could see that he either had no idea or did not know how to access this information. He became quite agitated and frustrated at one point, so I told him that I did not know about it either and suggested that maybe we could explore this together. Fortunately, I had a book in my office library that gave a detailed description of the disorder—symptoms, causes, effects and prognosis. (This was pre-Google days, when googol was only a very large number.) We explored the information together. As I mentioned certain features associated with the disorder and asked if he had experienced any of them, his presence and countenance seemed to lighten up, and he enthusiastically answered "Yes," followed by a big smile. He said that now he understood why he had had so many difficulties; they were a result of his disability.

For the third session, I was curious about what it must have been like for his parents to discover their infant child had cerebral palsy. I asked if they would meet with us, to which they readily agreed. I wanted to talk to them about their discovery of his having cerebral palsy, because I thought it would be helpful for their son to get another perspective on his disorder.

They shared with us how and when they had learned of the diagnosis, what their reaction was, how they dealt with it, and what they learned about it as their son grew up. They also shared how they learned to cope with the symptoms and integrate his disability into their lives. In addition, they shared how they respected their son for his accomplishments. Again, their son lit up, and much of the almost constant strain in his face relaxed. He seemed almost joyful as he heard the details, and I think he gained a greater understanding and appreciation of himself for his struggle. By the end of the session, the parents were in tears as they hugged him.

As therapy progressed, he became less stressed and combative. His parents related that he was like a new person. One day he disclosed how angry he would get while at the bus stop waiting for the bus. People would stare at him, and he became ashamed of his disability. I could point out to him in a reframe that perhaps the people were just curious about his condition like we were when he first came to treatment, and that perhaps their stares were not meant to be harmful, but only an indication of their curiosity. He liked that idea, and it helped him to see himself as "interesting," instead of feeling like a freak.

Even though I did not know at the beginning how to proceed, the client and I explored the unknown together. It helped to build a therapeutic relationship between us. I learned several valuable lessons, and I know he benefitted as well. I helped him see more deeply into his reality, and, thus, I learned about his reality; a rewarding experience for both of us.

No Hopeless Situation

I once interviewed for a position to run a therapy group for parolees with a history of alcohol and drug abuse. When it came my turn to ask questions, I asked the interviewer how he would characterize the people with whom I would be working. "They are a very hopeless population," he said. I told him that I don't work with hopeless people. "What do you mean?" he asked. "If I see people as hopeless," I responded, "then I don't have any business working with them. If I can't give them hope, who can?"

It is easy to become hypnotized by our clients by becoming hooked on their hopelessness. We can end up feeling as hopeless as they do. As they are telling us their tales of woe, we can become so entranced by their story that we also begin to feel hopeless. But you have to start out with the belief that there is no hopeless situation.

Declaring there is no hopeless situation does not mean that you always know what the hope is, but just by embracing and declaring the possibility of hope, you can inspire hope. There is such a thing as false hope, otherwise known as hype. The difference between hope and hype is that hype is manipulation that depends on making things up that sound good. Hope is awareness that miracles are possible (the field of psychotherapy and medicine are replete with miracles),

Hope is not the experience of a specific outcome, but, rather the expectations that, as a situation unfolds, the purpose and meaning will be revealed.

but these miracles are based on faith and a commitment to put forth the necessary effort to pursue options and create outcomes.

Hope is not the experience of a specific outcome, but, rather the expectations that, as a situation unfolds, the purpose and meaning will be revealed. In the Alcoholics Anonymous "Big Book" there is this passage: "No matter how far down the scale we have gone, we will see how our experience can benefit others." People who became alcoholics and suffered greatly learned that by sharing their stories of pain and recovery, they could be an inspiration to others. What once seemed hopeless now becomes a source of inspiration for others.

The same is true for others who have experienced hardship or trauma. For example, those who were abused as children find that the lessons they learned can educate others and give them hope. Hope comes from the unknown–it may be just over the horizon. We would have to be very arrogant to presume we know the future and further disavow the possibility of hope. Just as problems arise out of the unknown, so answers do as well. And if you really don't know, isn't it better that the person goes through the situation with a glimmer of hope, rather than none at all?

There is a story about a man and his family who were victims of a flood. To escape the rising water, he and his wife and children were forced to the rooftop of their home. In desperation, he cried out to God to help them. In about a half-hour his neighbor came by in a boat and offered to give them a ride to shelter. But the man refused, thinking that God would take care of him. A little later a helicopter spotted them and offered to pick them up, but again the man refused. An hour later a rescue team from the fire department came by in a dinghy and offered to take them to a shelter. Again, the man refused, thinking God would help them. As it started to get dark and they were getting cold, again the man prayed to God to help him. At that point God spoke to him and said, "I sent you two boats and helicopter, what more do you need?"

Here was a man who felt like he was in a hopeless situation and prayed to God for help. Three times the solution to his problem was right in front of him, but he did not see it, because he expected it to look a certain way and arrive in a certain way.

As therapists, our job is to keep that hope alive, guide the client to an unknown outcome, and to finding meaning in the situation.

Two Heads Are Better Than One

Sometimes I struggle with an issue and think that I have exhausted the possibilities. However, if I present it to my supervisor, and/or my colleagues as a case study, I am always amazed at how many new and different ideas come up. When well-meaning, dedicated people get together, there is an energy generated which sparks new ideas and opportunities for resourcefulness. When contemplating therapeutic situations, the saying, "Two heads are better than one," is true.

Carlos Casteneda wrote several books in the 1970's about his experiences with a Yaqui sorcerer named Don Juan. One of the more memorable realizations Don Juan imparted to Casteneda was the question, "What makes you think reality is only about how you see it?" There are several explanations of this statement. One is that there are alternative realities that the average mind is not trained to see or understand. Another is that we each have a skewed version of reality based on our specific set of experiences. A third is that we only have partial ideas of reality, and there is much that we do not see or know.

Each of these limitations can affect us at any time. For example, there may be metaphysical aspects to the client's problem; some therapists have used past-life regressions to release certain psychic blocks resulting from incidents or trauma in previous lives. Also, we obviously are influenced by our breadth—or lack of breadth–of experience. Since I have never been in combat, I am limited in my ability to know and understand what an Iraqi war vet may be experiencing.

Jack had served two tours of duty in Iraq. He was present during the original invasion. His leg was shattered by an IED, and he was stateside awaiting medical evaluations. Like many veterans, he was experiencing PTSD symptoms. He said that he was having a hard time making the transition back home. He gave one graphic example: His family and friends wanted to welcome him home by having a barbeque. He felt conflicted about this, because on the one hand, he understood that this was their way of celebrating, they had no idea that the smell of meat cooking on the grill reminded him of the smell of burning bodies, victims of the torching or bombing he witnessed in Iraq. He would become nauseated and have to leave, not really wanting to give the real explanation for his sudden departure.

Working with a client and thinking you have all the answers or must have all the answers is egotistical. Consulting with your supervisor, colleagues, and other resources is not only recommended, it is best practice therapy. There is always someone who knows more than you, who has different experiences, and can offer new ideas and solutions. Seek out help for difficult situations.

The Answer is Out There—Google It

I once worked with a couple that had Huntington's disease, something I did not know starting out with them. But I kept noticing something unusual about the way they communicated, and to some extent, their thinking patterns, and how these affected them emotionally. I was curious. What was going on? It wasn't until the third or fourth session they mentioned that they had Huntington's. I immediately wanted to find out about this disease. At that time, before the Internet, information was not so easily available, so my research required a trip to the library and a call to the clinic at the University of Virginia to learn about the treatment and prognosis. Eventually, I got the address for the , Disease Foundation and wrote them to get more detailed information. Once I had expanded my knowledge, I was better able to connect with my clients. Today all I have to do is Google it, and the information is at my fingertips.

I supervised a counselor who had a four-year-old client with mitochondrial disease. The daughter was traumatized by the many daily medical procedures, including changing of dressings, insertion of IV tubes and catheterization. She shared with the counselor that she wanted very much to be normal and to eat like her brother and sister. However, she could at most eat three goldfish crackers, two grapes, or one small cube of cheese at any one meal. She would sometimes chew the food for up to 15 minutes. As the counselor described this, many questions came to mind. Was her reluctance to eat physical or psychological? Did her disease just take her appetite away, or did the food make her sick? Was there some broken sensory synapse, so that her body was telling her that she was full when she was not. Maybe she was misinterpreting the signal.

To gain a basic understanding of her disease and a framework of how to proceed, the counselor and I Googled it. With this new knowledge, the counselor could ask more meaningful and targeted questions, and the two of them worked as a team to increase her ability to eat. The ultimate answers, of course, will come not from Google, but from the client. However, Google is a good place to start.

Stump the Therapist

Another "what-to-do?" moment comes, when you have tried numerous ideas for the client, and none of them works. I once worked with a crack cocaine addict who was about as likable a person as I had ever met. He was so sincere and motivated, but he was still binging every few weeks, putting his marriage, his job, and his relationship with his kids and parents in jeopardy. Each time he relapsed, they lost confidence in him, and he lost confidence in himself. It was not for lack of effort that he was relapsing. He had been to a 30-day residential rehab program, attended NA, had a sponsor, was working the steps, and was coming to see me. Yet I felt that I was missing something, and that he was looking desperately to me for an answer.

Finally, after we had tried several approaches, in frustration I said to him, "You know what? You have stumped the therapist. All of the things we have tried seem to work for a while, but nothing seems to work consistently enough for you to stay clean." We sat there for several minutes in silence, and then to my amazement he said, "I think I know what I have to do. I need to increase my efforts. I am not making the best use of my sponsor. I am too quiet at the meetings. I got stuck on the Fourth Step and need to finish that, and I need to be more honest with my family and let them know what I am going through." He proceeded for twenty minutes to critique his past efforts and came up with a variety of new things to do for his recovery.

At the end of the session, he thanked me profusely for having helped him, saying it was one of the best sessions ever. While I was tempted to say, "Hey, no problem; glad I could help; happens all the time." But instead, I acknowledged and praised him, since he was the one who came up with all the answers, not me. Clearly, he had done all the work, and my contribution was to be present and be an attentive listener.

Stump the therapist works when clients are looking to you for the answers and not taking the time to examine their own ideas and resources. Timing and the right kind of relationship are crucial to doing this ... otherwise, it is a great way to lose clients.

Keeping Fresh

> "In the beginner's mind there are many possibilities, but in the expert's there are few."
>
> *– Shuru Suzuki*

One of the programs I supervise is intensive in-home therapy. The children in this setting are among the most difficult to treat. They are at risk of home removal, hospitalization, or incarceration. Outpatient counseling is not adequate to meet their needs. It is ironic that these children need the most experienced counselors, yet most the counselors who are willing to work in an in-home setting are those just getting out of college and/or starting their careers. Surprisingly, however, this works rather well, because these neophytes are willing to go to extra lengths to help the clients and their families. They are not burned out or jaded, but rather have a beginner's fresh perspective. They do not back off difficult cases. Each case is a great learning experience, and they are willing to try things that are unique and quite effective.

Burn-out, unfortunately, is common in our field. It can be the result of compassion fatigue, losing our sharpness over time, or even feelings of boredom with a particular client. This is especially true with clients who have been coming for a long time and for whom there has been minimal progress. There is a tendency to get bogged down and eventually feel frustrated. The solution is to keep fresh—to reignite your curiosity, and approach the client with a new perspective. One way to do this is to cultivate a beginner's mind and excitement, as if you were seeing the client for the first time. You could also think of this client as a referral from a colleague who wants help with a tough case and has faith you can help this person. This involves cultivating an activate curiosity and a deep desire to know and understand the origins and dynamics of his/her difficulties.

Another way is to imagine that client is one of the first ones you are seeing starting your counseling career. You're excited, you're open for suggestions, and willing to try just about anything. New ideas come with this fresh perspective.

One can also keep fresh by taking a more clinical approach to understanding the psychodynamics of the problem:

- How did it start?
- Why did it start?
- What function does it serve?
- Does it offer any benefits?
- What reinforces it?
- What are the obstacles preventing it from being solved?
- Does it have any secondary benefits?
- What has worked so far, and why?

The goal is to get to the source, the very essence of the problem, looking for the "Achilles heel," that crack in the armor. We must become psychological detectives seeking out the reason behind the reason. If we find ourselves reluctant to do this, we must question ourselves:

- What do I need to do to activate my interest, determination, and desire to help this client?
- How can I keep my interest active?
- What bores me? Why?
- What interests and excites me about the counseling that I do?

In this mode, not knowing is not a roadblock, but merely a bump in the road, an opportunity to learn from the experience.

Research has shown that experience, in and of itself, is not a major factor in determining the successful outcome in therapy. Sometimes the more experience the therapist has, the more rigid he may have become. He can easily settle into an approach, which is then generalized to most his clients. The approach ends up dictating the direction of therapy, and not responding to the specific needs of the client.

Adopting a different mindset sends the client a meta-message of hope and optimism, which is therapeutic in and of itself. The therapist's ability, willingness, and perseverance become a model for how the client can approach his or her dilemma.

Dam Good Therapy

Many times, it may appear that things are not going well, and the client is not making any progress. The therapist puts a lot of effort into the client, who seems to be absorbing or processing it, but there is no change. What may be happening is all the work is building up and will reach a point where it will take effect.

It is like standing in front of a dam. Behind the dam, water is filling up, but you can't see it because you're in front of the dam. Eventually when it fills up and runs over, then you can see the effects.

The counselor may feel that no progress is being made, but with patience and perseverance, the client has a sudden breakthrough. This may be the result of the client moving through the stages of change, or it may be that not enough factors have come together in order for the client to make a significant change.

Walking into Tracy's home was like walking into mass chaos. Tracy, seven years old, was referred for treatment, because she was reported to have been suffering from symptoms of having been sexually abused. She was timid, fearful, easily broke down crying, and was very clingy, sometimes inappropriately, such as burying her face in the counselor's crotch when she greeted her.

The home was chaotic, the result of having five children, one with autism and all under the age of nine. Only one of the children, a one-year-old, was the product of the current marriage. The older four kids had just recently been placed back in the home after being in foster care with relatives, where sexual abuse allegedly happened, but which was "unfounded" by Social Services.

The mother spent most of her time and attention with the one-year-old in her bedroom, leaving the rest of the children to fend for themselves. Frequent arguments then erupted among the children leading to physical aggression. There were also indications of some sexual activity going on between the children.

Mother and father seemed totally overwhelmed having to deal with the children and the relatives' counter-claims that the parents were the sexual perpetrators. This resulted in several investigations by Social Services.

The mother, who had severe ADD, appeared to cope by withdrawing. The situation quickly escalated, since what the children wanted (and needed) most was attention from the mother. When the counselor would go to their home to meet with the child, the mother would retreat to her bedroom and usually fall asleep. Efforts to get her to be more involved with the children, set up a schedule, and even to feed the children all failed. For example, it would take her an hour to fix lunch for all the children, because she was so easily distracted. They would be sitting at the table waiting for her, while she would be off in another room doing something totally unrelated.

A whole phalanx of service providers was working with this family. Each of the four older children had an in-home counselor (some from different agencies); the parents were seeing a family counselor; social services had a caseworker working with the family; and several of the children worked with counselors at school.

Despite all these efforts, change did not come easily. One counselor told the mother that she would not continue providing services, because nothing was likely to significantly improve, unless the mother made some changes. Amazingly, this seemed to have some impact. After six months of concerted effort in the home, little glimmers of hope began to appear. The mother would take the kids outside into the yard to swing. Dad would call the counselor with parenting questions.

Finally, a meeting was held with all the service providers, parents and relatives, where everyone put forth their best guess of what was happening and what needed to happen. The meeting lasted for four hours.

After that, things changed dramatically. The mother started displaying genuine affection towards the children and actually began spending an hour each day doing arts and crafts with them. The level of chaos in the home began to ratchet down. The parents were more optimistic, and Tracy began to emerge from her shell. All the efforts of the previous six months had not been in vain. The effects were building almost imperceptibly, but were real, nonetheless. Efforts that had seemed to go nowhere, now looked as though they might be successful. Until the meeting was held and a coordinated effort was made, one could not see the family's subtle progress.

It is difficult to determine if therapy goes on with no change, whether what is happening is "water building up behind the dam" or therapy is just not working. Patience and perseverance, along with a touch of optimism, are needed in both situations. If the relationship is strong, the information is consistent, and the commitment from the therapist is strong, then there is a good chance the overflow to success will occur.

When to Stop. When to Give Up.

We are taught many ways to deliver therapy, but rarely how and when to terminate therapy. There are a variety of ways to determine this. One way previously mentioned is to have clients set specific goals and when they are reached, the client is ready to go. Another way is to ask the client if they got what they came for, and if the answer is "Yes," then therapy can be terminated. I often kid with clients (half-heartedly) that if they are faced with a situation, and they ask themselves, "What would Jon tell me?" and can answer the question, then they do not need me anymore. Often, too, there is just a "knowing." Clients often sense that they are ready, and the therapist also senses this. Sometimes they just fail to show up for appointments, or they will make a final appointment and then cancel. It is helpful to contact them and get feedback, either positive or negative, about why they stopped treatment.

Sometimes clients do not want to stop therapy, because some part of them has become dependent on meeting with the therapist. This can be addressed by reviewing and setting goals and stretching out time between sessions or frequency.

As for prematurely terminating treatment, no one likes to admit defeat, especially counselors working with clients. There are many, many suggestions in this book on how to avoid this. But is there a time to give up? These are some guidelines that we can us:

- Therapy is not a panacea for all illnesses.
- Some people are determined not to change.
- There are extra-therapeutic factors that have a much greater impact beyond our control.
- Clients are overly invested and immersed in their dysfunction with the payoff being too high or risky to change.

- Not everyone can benefit from counseling due to their capabilities, intellect, or abilities.
- We may not have all the right tools in our toolbox to help.

Stopping prematurely may create a strategic advantage. I tell parents of children who are very recalcitrant about therapy that unless the situation is an emergency, therapy should end on a positive note. That way, if in the future, clients have more serious problems, they can look back on the counseling experience as being positive and productive and thus be more likely to pursue it again. If clients are brow-beaten into coming to therapy they may think, "Therapy sucks. I am never going back to see another therapist."

There are counselors who give up too soon. In some cases, this may be due to not recognizing clients' failures in therapy as part of their psychopathology. In other cases, they may terminate if they are offended by a client who gets angry or abusive towards them. Another is the supposed lack of motivation, though as stated before, motivating the client is part of the therapeutic process, but that is not always possible. A final reason is the relationship just does not gel for whatever reason.

All terminations should include a review of what worked, the progress the client made, or perhaps what didn't work. It should also include a discharge plan that includes referrals for other services and/or states conditions under which the client should return to therapy as well as suggestions for managing future problems or crises. This can be done over the phone if the client does not schedule a final session and is willing to engage.

CHAPTER 11

Beyond Talk Therapy

Find a place inside where there's joy, and the joy will burn out the pain.

—Joseph Campbell

NOT ALL PROBLEMS CAN BE RESOLVED using talk therapy alone. While talk therapy is the mainstay of counseling, other avenues of exploring and healing can lead to quicker, often better results. Most all these therapies require specialized training, but knowledge of them is important for referrals and possibly to spur your interest in pursuing them. There have been numerous non-verbal traditional therapies around for years such as play therapy, biofeedback, bio-energetics and expressive therapies such as psycho-drama, dance, art, and music therapies.

Modern psychotherapy began as talk therapy—psychoanalysis developed by Sigmund Freud. Freud depended totally upon the use of verbalization, beginning with free association. For several generations psychoanalysis was synonymous with psychotherapy. It was not uncommon for patients to be in psychoanalysis for years with little results, since the reality is that not all problems can be resolved or healed by cognitive-verbal exploration alone. Eventually psychoanalysis gave way to more emotional, behavioral, and somatic focuses.

Times have changed, and perhaps there is no more exciting progress in the field of psychotherapy than what is happening in brain research coupled with new research into the effects of trauma on the body. Advances in scanning and imagery technology are revealing how, on a neurological level, the brain is impacted physiologically by various mental health conditions. Because of these advances, our ability to understand the interaction between the body and mind has increased our knowledge of how certain conditions develop and how they might be treated.

Researchers have learned, for example, that trauma exists not only as memory in the brain, but is stored in many other parts of the body. They also are learning which areas of the brain are affected. Most damage from trauma lies beneath the verbal spotlight. One reason is that the speech center often shuts down during traumatic events, and people cannot completely verbalize what happened to them. While words may point the direction to these difficulties, they cannot, in and of themselves, heal these non-verbal infections. These advances in brain science have spawned new therapies and at the same time given legitimacy to some ancient practices such as acupuncture, yoga, tai chi, qi gong, and meditation.

Somatic Therapies

In recent years, it has become increasingly clear that trauma resolution must include the body, not just the brain, as an essential part of the healing process. (To even differentiate the brain from the body makes no sense). Somatic psychotherapy is a term for several treatment techniques that integrate awareness of the mind and body to create new solutions. Though these approaches may look like *traditional* talk psychotherapies because talking is involved, the difference is that the client is simultaneously tracking his reactions on multiple levels: thoughts, emotions, and physical sensations. Somatic therapies incorporate *bottom-up* strategies as opposed to *top-down* strategies. Most cognitive-verbal approaches are a *top-down* strategy—meaning that if you can change the thinking, the body and emotions will change (i.e., motivation will increase, mood will improve, and stress levels will be lowered). Bottom-up is the opposite. The idea is if you can calm the body and modify internal processes, then thinking and feelings will change. This is more succinctly said, "Issues are in the tissues." When we feel stuck with a behavior or symptom, even though we may cognitively understand it, somatic psychotherapy can take it to a new level of resolution.

Somatic therapy differs from other approaches in its emphasizing the body-mind connection and the need for both the client and therapist to mindfully observe the self in the present moment with curiosity and without judgment.

Somatic Experiencing

Developed by Peter Levine, Ph.D, Somatic Experiencing is a naturalistic approach to resolving and healing trauma. It is based on Levine's observations that highly stressed animals recover from life-threatening situations through the completion of the "Fight, Flight, or Freeze" response without any remaining trauma symptoms. He gives the example of a cat catching a mouse. The mouse may freeze and shut down in this traumatic experience, and if the cat gets bored with the "dead" mouse, it will go off and leave the mouse. The mouse may lie dormant for several minutes, and when it senses the danger has passed, will literally shake off the trauma and run into its hole automatically recovering from the stress experience to live another day. Dr. Levine noted the same capacity in people, but this gets over-ridden by fear. The trauma becomes entrenched in the body/mind. However, by becoming aware of these bodily sensations, befriending and discharging them, one can overcome them and re-establish equilibrium.

One day Dr. Levine had an experience that would profoundly change his life and his understanding of the effects of trauma and how to ameliorate them. As he was walking in a crosswalk on his way to a friend's house for a birthday celebration, he was struck by a car. The impact left him numb, paralyzed, and in a fog of confusion, terror, and disbelief, not knowing whether he would live, die, or be crippled. He was soon approached by many people including a woman who said she was a pediatrician, and who kindly connected with him and comforted him with her presence. In his overwhelmed, frightened state, he went in and out of consciousness aware of the rescue squad's attempt to help him and the physical sensations that wracked his body as he tried to make sense of what was happening. His body began to shake, and he instinctively tried to protect himself to ward off the danger by striking with his arm. He actively discouraged any attempt to stop the shaking, intuitively understanding that this was his body way of helping him by "resetting his nervous system and bringing him back into his body." The combination of the caring presence of the woman and allowing his body to shake and tremble helped to stabilize his nervous system thereby minimizing the traumatic effect of the accident and the risk of developing post-traumatic stress disorder.

> Traumatic symptoms are not caused by the event itself. They arise when the activation, mobilized to meet an extreme or life threatening event, is not fully discharged and integrated. This energy remains trapped in the nervous system where it can wreak havoc on our bodies and our minds."
>
> —*Van Der Kolk, 2014.*

Through proper attention and support, Somatic Experiencing directs awareness to resource (healing) states, initiating "pendulation" between resourced and unresourced states. Clients must build up their inner resources before going back to dealing with the trauma experience. Once they can consciously and effectively access these resources, then elements of the trauma and inner sensations are slowly recalled, but only to the degree the client can tolerate the memories. Trauma *re-experienced* in this way is usually tolerable for the client, as it is done in small doses, called "titrations." Titrations are expanded and deepened only as the client's capacity expands. For this reason, trauma work often proceeds at a slow pace, and relief is experienced in increments. Nonetheless, these slow changes are significant for their long-lasting impact and promotion of overall health.

Sensorimotor Psychotherapy

Another well-known somatic therapy is Sensorimotor Psychotherapy developed by Pat Ogden. It is unique in that it emphasizes tuning into the body with a here-and-now awareness of the sensory experience to achieve mental well-being. The goal is not for clients to learn or remember the trauma they experienced, but rather how they experienced it. With this internal awareness, they gain access to new ways of healing as they process and integrate their experiences. Thus, they rediscover lost abilities to actively defend and protect themselves and create a new sense of self.

One of the major balancing acts in treating trauma is how to access traumatic experiences from the past without re-traumatizing the client. Avoiding the proverbial "opening Pandora's box" becomes a challenge of skill, timing, and trust. It is said, "The slower we go, the faster we will get there" (Klutz, 1996). The memory of the trauma is stored in the body and by focusing on the body's memory of the event(s) instead of the mental and emotional components, clients learn how to process events without retraumatization. Therefore, the therapist focuses on the body and the "somatic language" and not just the narrative and emotions. This can take the form of changes in posture, gesture, breathing rate, facial color, eye blink, stillness or agitation, stiffness or looseness. All these are part of the story.

Helping the client to tune into the physiology of what he is experiencing and become mindful of the sensations gives him a new avenue to explore. First, the client realizes a correlation between the emotions and the body—that the way they experience emotions is through inner sensations. For example, anger might be tightness in the chest; embarrassment might be a flushness in the face; sadness might be a choking up. The next step is to challenge the client's negative interpretation of those sensations. For example, "Maybe the knot you have in your stomach is not anxiety so much, but rather a warning to be careful." What causes many emotions to be overwhelming is the meaning we assign to them (the feeling about the feeling), so by placing a positive connotation on them and enhancing acceptance of them, the therapist helps the client to be less reactive and less challenged by their sensations. It is important, however, not to dismiss the client's interpretation and automatically override him with our "positive interpretation," but to merely suggest it, and see if he is receptive.

The next step is to learn ways to regulate and calm the sensations. This can be done by having the client experience these sensations, with the therapist being present in a loving way and observing how they unfold naturally. Additionally, the individual can be taught relaxation and self-soothing techniques, breathing exercises, or any number of other ways to calm the body.

If the sensations are still too formidable, the client can be taught to find a healing or safety resource. He can then be instructed to access the healing resource and "oscillate" between that resource and painful ones. This is like the titration in Somatic Experiencing. In this manner the client can mitigate the impact of the negative state and learn new ways to regulate his emotions related to the traumatic events.

Both Somatic Experiencing and Sensorimotor Psychotherapy have the same goal. Somatic Experiencing focuses on cultivating mindfulness, as the therapist assists the client in developing a "Witness" aspect, while Sensorimotor takes a more systematic educational approach to create mindfulness. Both focus on the five aspects of experiencing in the world, called the Five Elements:

1. Rational thinking/beliefs,
2. Meaning-making through inner images,
3. Body sensations,
4. Emotional feelings, and
5. Behavioral movement.

The goal is to develop awareness of and integrate the five. Both Levine and Ogden encourage therapists to teach clients how to overcome the high, intensive reactivity that often follows trauma. Both therapies are designed to develop a greater capacity for regulation of the nervous system. By building a connection to one's resources (internal and external), the body-mind can transition out of old dysfunctional patterns and into healing.

Yoga

Yoga is an ancient, oriental practice that has found great popularity in recent years. It focuses on different postures of the body, as well as breathing and meditation. Yoga helps individuals get in touch with their body and its functioning, thereby increasing their sensitivity to the body and gaining mastery of it. Most yoga taught today has been stripped of its religious and spiritual roots, and yet it has provided thousands of people new ways of discovering and experiencing their body leading to a healthier and more peaceful lifestyle. Therefore, its importance as a therapeutic tool cannot be overlooked.

There are several types of yoga. The most common, and what most people know of yoga, is hatha yoga, which is composed of moving the body into different positions, called asanas. These postures are designed to help the body to relax. While some of the more advanced postures, such as putting your leg over your head, look anything but relaxed, the goal is to create ease and limberness with all parts of the body. This is not meant to be strenuous, but rather take you to the threshold of your ability, and then relax into that position. This requires focus, awareness, and concentration. In that way, the person becomes attuned to his/her body and the ability to gain control certain aspects of the body. Clients who are traumatized often lose this connection, believing their bodies have betrayed them and are, therefore, a source of pain or numbness. After several sessions of yoga, however, most participants feel an improved sense of control over their bodies and, surprisingly, their emotions and thoughts as well. Yoga teaches individuals a way to access serenity, a major goal of yoga, and they are often surprised by not only how tense and uptight they have become, but also how quickly they can attain a sense of peace greater than anything they have previously experienced.

Yoga is gentle, but powerful process that teaches the student control of the body and the mind producing new vitality, balance, and improved health. Often as practitioners become more balanced and aware of their body, bad habits such as smoking, drinking, use of drugs (including the need for certain medicines) fall away, because the practitioner feels so positive and renewed from the practices that polluting his body with *chemicals* and disrupting the balance becomes undesirable.

Yoga also teaches breathing exercises. Breathing is the one physiological process that is both involuntary and voluntary, meaning that we can control consciously our breathing by slowing down or speeding up our breaths, or if we are not conscious of controlling our breathing, our body automatically takes over. Yogis for centuries have mastered these skills through a practice known as pranayama. "Prana" is a term for life force. Deep, slow breaths calm the body, and focusing on the process of breathing is a way to center ourselves and become mindful in the present. Normally, we inhale and exhale one pint of air. With normal deep breaths, we can inhale and exhale an additional three pints of air. With training one can also exhale an additional three pints. The lungs have the capacity of ten pints of air, so through deep breathing we can get seven times the amount of air that we normally breathe. This super-oxygenation enriches the blood and helps to focus the mind (Satchidananda, 1970).

So, by calming the body you calm the mind, and by calming the mind you calm the body. The body and mind work in tandem. Practitioners learn to become masters of their physiology and to transition from being hyper-aroused to feeling peaceful and, eventually, safe within their own bodies. Yoga does not necessarily make problems go away, rather it teaches practitioners to go away from their problems—to an inner space of stillness and balance, which becomes the *home base* from which they operate. This is in sharp contrast to the sense of impending doom that most trauma survivors experience daily. It helps to rewire the brain and balance between they sympathetic and parasympathetic system, so the body is not in a constant state of hyper-vigilance.

Yoga is not only valuable as a therapeutic resource in a psychotherapy setting, but research on the effects of yoga done extensively in a variety of settings, such as prisons and schools, have revealed remarkable changes in participants. For example, the Prison Yoga Project and the Satchidananda Prison Project sponsor volunteers teaching yoga in prison settings. Incidents of violence have dramatically subsided, and profound changes have occurred in the prisoners' lives, outlook, and temperament. The participants often earn the respect of the other inmates and staff. They become "model prisoners" and a much lower security risk. The yoga group creates a sharp contrast to the usual prison culture of every-man-for-himself by focusing on the attainment of self-control and a peaceful presence. It also creates a bond between members, who previously felt isolated and vulnerable.

Yoga in the classroom has been found to lower incidents of acting-out behaviors, increase students' ability to focus, and improve academic performance. Once these practices become embedded in the school, they become the norm, and disruptions are an anathema to the calm, peaceful classroom. Part of yoga is meditation/mindfulness practice. In schools where meditation has been implemented, there are noticeable benefits. Studies have shown suspensions decrease by 79 percent, attendance increases by over 98 percent, and academic performance is noticeably increased.[1]

Tapping and Energy Therapies

Jeffery Zeig once said, "The stranger the therapy, the more effective it is." Well, energy therapies probably take the prize. Tapping your body and humming Happy Birthday seem to be far from traditional therapies. Introducing this therapy to clients can seem almost apologetic. "I know this may seem strange,

---

1   NBC News, Jan. 1, 2015 http://www.nbcnews.com/nightly-news/san-francisco-schools-transformed-power-meditation-n276301

but what we are going to be doing is tapping certain parts of the body, and that will make your problems go away."

The technique draws from the tradition of acupuncture, the oriental treatment for physical conditions. The main idea of is that pain is caused by a blockage of energy in the body. According to this theory, there are certain lines of energy flow in the body called meridians. Each of these meridians is associated with a certain organ of the body. Along these meridians there are points where the energy gets blocked called acupuncture points. One way to think of it is that there are power lines in our body, and the acupuncture points are like transformers, which can either send the energy on or block it. When the energy is blocked, it is a source of pain. By placing a needle in these points, the energy breaks up and gets dispersed along the meridians. This dissolves the pain and increases the life force in the body.

There were two discoveries that led to the development of the energy therapies. One was that pain could be relieved by simply massaging the acupuncture points, and therefore needles were not always necessary. The second was that since all emotions have a physiological component, massaging or tapping points could ameliorate emotional pain.

As with many discoveries, this happened quite by accident. In 1979, Dr. Roger Callahan, a traditionally trained psychologist, was working with a lady named Mary who was extremely water phobic. She panicked at having to go out in the rain and could only bathe in a couple inches of water. Dr. Callahan tried many traditional therapies with her such as hypnosis, systematic- desensitization, relaxation therapy, etc., to no avail. One day at his house where he was doing therapy, she started to panic near the pool. He asked her where she felt that feeling in her body. She said she felt pain and nausea in her stomach. Callahan knew that the endpoint of the stomach meridian was under the eyes. He asked her to tap points under her eyes with her fingers. As soon as she did, she said the uncomfortableness diminished and then disappeared. She started walking quickly towards the pool, and Dr. Callahan tried to stop her, but she said that the fear had gone away, and she was no longer afraid of the water. Thirty years later she still has no fear of water.

Intrigued by this phenomenon, Dr. Callahan went on to explore whether there were points in the body that would alleviate other psychological difficulties such as anxiety, depression, and addiction. He developed numerous tapping sequences, which he called algorithms. He was amazed that nearly all mental illness conditions could be treated almost instantaneously by using these sequences.

Another one of his discoveries was that people could change their "negative energy" to "positive energy" just by tapping on the outer part of the side of hand that one would use to deliver a karate chop. He had them doing this while saying, "I deeply and completely accept myself." Predictably, he called this the "Karate Chop." So, if one is feeling despondent, critical, fearful, anxious, or overwhelmed, the first step is always to do the Karate Chop.

One of his students, Gary Craig, developed a further refinement. He reasoned that there were a finite number of points (around ten) that provided relief from mental health issues, and that by tapping all of them, the client could gain relief without having to remember which sequence went with each disorder. He then proceeded to freely communicate this to anyone interested. He called his approach EFT, Emotional Freedom Therapy. To date, thousands of people have benefitted from these techniques.

EFT Techniques

Basically, the approach is to first create what Craig called "a set-up statement" in which a problem is paired with the statement, "I deeply and completely accept myself." Then specific acupressure points are tapped. So, someone with anxiety would say, "Even though I am anxious, I deeply and completely accept myself," or someone who is having trouble with addiction would say, "Even though I am addicted to cocaine, I deeply and completely accept myself."

To measure how well the technique is working the clients are asked to think about the difficulty they are trying to change and feel it as strongly as possible. Then they are asked to measure the level of intensity from 1 to 10 with 10 being the most intense. This is called the SUD (Subjective Unit of Distress). It may sound counterintuitive to have clients feel very strongly the feeling that is causing them the most distress, but the greater the intensity of the feeling, the deeper it can it be neutralized or discharged. Once clients experience it at their highest tolerable level, then the tapping procedure can begin. The goal is to repeat the procedure until the SUD gets down to a tolerable level, hopefully 0.

Here is the sequence for this tapping: (The points to be tapped and suggestions for tapping come from *The Gold Standard EFT Tapping Tutorial*).

http://www.emofree.com/eft-tutorial/tapping-basics/how-to-do-eft.html

(See chart on next page for exact sites.)

KC: *The Karate Chop point (abbreviated KC) is located at the center of the fleshy part of the outside of your hand (either hand) between the top of the wrist and the base of the baby finger.*

TOH: *On the top of the head. If you were to draw a line from one ear, over the head, to the other ear, and another line from your nose to the back of your neck, the TOH point is where those two lines would intersect.*

EB: *At the beginning of the eyebrow, just above and to one side of the nose. This point is abbreviated EB for beginning of the Eye Brow.*

SE: *On the bone bordering the outside corner of the eye. This point is abbreviated SE for Side of the Eye.*

UE: *On the bone under an eye about 1 inch below your pupil. This point is abbreviated UE for Under the Eye.*

UN: *On the small area between the bottom of your nose and the top of your upper lip. This point is abbreviated UN for Under the Nose.*

Ch: *Midway between the point of your chin and the bottom of your lower lip. Even though it is not directly on the point of the chin, we call it the chin point because it is descriptive enough for people to understand easily. This point is abbreviated Ch for Chin.*

CB: *The junction where the sternum (breastbone), collarbone and the first rib meet. To locate it, first place your forefinger on the U-shaped notch at the top of the breastbone (about where a man would knot his tie). From the bottom of the U, move your forefinger down toward the navel 1 inch and then go to the left (or right) 1 inch. This point is abbreviated CB for Collar Bone even though it is not on the collarbone (or clavicle) per se. It is at the beginning of the collarbone and we call it the collarbone point because that is a lot easier to say than "the junction where the sternum (breastbone), collarbone and the first rib meet."*

UA: *On the side of the body, at a point even with the nipple (for men) or in the middle of the bra strap (for women). It is about 4 inches below the armpit. This point is abbreviated UA for Under the Arm.*

Tapping Tips

- Some of the tapping points have twin points on each side of the body. For example, the "eyebrow" point on the right side of the body has a twin point on the left side of the body. Years of experience have taught us that you only need to tap one of these twin points. However, if you have both hands free you can certainly tap on both sides for good measure.
- You can also switch sides when you tap these points. For example, during the same round of The EFT Tapping Basic Recipe, you can tap the "karate chop" point on your left hand and the eyebrow point on the right side of your body. This makes the tapping process more convenient to perform.

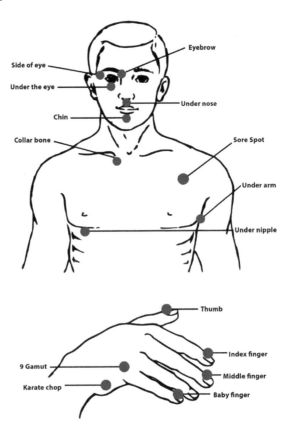

- The tapping is done with two or more fingertips. This is so you can cover a larger area and thereby insure that your tapping covers the correct point.
- While you can tap with the fingertips of either hand, most people use their dominant hand. For example, right handed people tap with the fingertips of their right hand while left handed people tap with the fingertips of their left hand.
- You tap approximately 5 times on each point. No need to count the taps because anywhere between 3 and 7 taps on each point is adequate. The only exception is during the Setup step (explained later) where the Karate Chop Point is tapped continuously while you repeat some standard wording.
- The process is easily memorized. After you have tapped the Karate Chop Point, the rest of the points go down the body. The Eyebrow point, for example, is below the Top of the Head point. The Side of the Eye point is below the Eyebrow point. And so on down the body.

My first experience with EFT was on myself. I was to testify in court in a divorce hearing, one of my least favorite things to do, but I felt my client needed my support and observations. As I was preparing to go the day of the hearing, my anxiety was high. I had just learned about tapping and thought, "What the heck, I'll give it a try." I tapped, and to my pleasant surprise, my anxiety lowered significantly. I had no idea it would have this effect. As I was driving to the courthouse, again some anxiety started to creep up and again the tapping helped. As I was in the ante room waiting to testify, I did it once more, so that by the time I took the stand I was calm, attentive, and confident. That was enough to convince me of its efficacy.

Soon after, another experience further sold me on this technique. My wife and I were scheduled to stay at a hotel in Washington. When we checked into the room, however, we immediately noted how fragrant it was. It was as though the staff had powdered the rug with carpet freshener and did not bother to clean up the excess—the odor was overwhelming. My wife immediately started having an allergic reaction to the chemicals, having trouble breathing, sweating, and feeling light-headed. We went to the front desk, told them we could not stay in the hotel, and immediately checked out. Outside the hotel, she was getting worse, and it looked like we would have to call 911. I suggested that she do the tapping, and in within several minutes her panic was gone, her breathing was easier, and she no longer was having a medical emergency. We were both so grateful to have learned about tapping and seeing how it helped.

EMDR and Brainspotting

While tapping may seem a strange therapy, EMDR (Eye Movement Desensitization and Reprocessing) runs a close second. This technique, discovered by Francine Shapiro, involves remembering traumatic experiences while moving the eyes in different directions. Apparently, she discovered this technique during a time when she was worried about being diagnosed with breast cancer. Feeling down and out about it, it is rumored that during a walk in the park, she stopped to watch some children in swings. As her eyes moved back and forth to follow the children, she noticed that the intensity of her feelings diminished. This spiked her curiosity and led to the development of EMDR, which is now practiced by 25,000 practitioners across the globe.

EMDR is utilized when a client is plagued by negative, intrusive memories. Eye movements (or other bilateral stimulation) are used during one part of the eight-phase treatment. When the clinician has determined which memory to target first, he asks the client to hold different aspects of that event or thought in mind and watch his finger as it moves back and forth across the client's field of vision. As this happens, for reasons believed to relate to the biological mechanisms involved in Rapid Eye Movement (REM) sleep, internal associations arise, and the client begins to consciously and unconsciously process the memory and disturbing feelings. In successful EMDR therapy, the meaning of painful events is transformed on an emotional level. For instance, a rape victim shifts from feeling horror and self-disgust to holding the firm belief that, "I survived it, and I am strong." Unlike talk therapy, the insights clients gain in EMDR result not from clinician interpretation, but from the client's own accelerated intellectual and emotional processes. The net effect is that clients finish EMDR therapy feeling empowered by the very experiences that once debased them. Their wounds have not just closed; they have transformed.

As a natural outcome of the EMDR therapeutic process, clients' thoughts, feelings, improve—all without speaking in detail or doing homework used in other therapies.

Brainspotting

"The eyes are the window to the soul."

—*William Shakespeare*

Brainspotting is variation of EMDR discovered by David Grand while working with an ice skater, who had a long history of trauma. Her mother had constantly berating her and criticizing her ice skating. One of the most significant time was when the client was six, her mother and father divorced. The mother blamed the breakup of the family on the client's ice skating, which devastated the client. Additionally, the client had suffered several traumatic falls during practice over the years.

Grand used a modified, slower version of EMDR having her move her eyes back and forth while processing her trauma. At one point, he noticed her eyes stopped moving and seemed to fixate as did his hand. He was transfixed by the process amazed by what he was witnessing. He described it as though someone took his hand and stopped it. He encouraged her to continuing looking from that point, and as she did, a barrage of traumatic memories began to emerge, which she described in detail. Equally surprising, was that she processed the trauma without being emotionally overcome by it. Additionally, other memories she had previously worked on in therapy, and both assumed had been neutralized, were resolved at a deeper level.

The next morning, she called Grand with great news that during her early morning practice, she had successfully done the triple loop, which she had never done before. In fact, she had done it several times, and now believed she could incorporate it into her routine quite easily. (Her inability to do the triple loop had been a major block in her progression as a champion ice skater.)

He realized he had come across something special. He soon discovered that there was a precise point in individuals' visual field, which if they focused on, would allow them to access and process situations not accessible by verbal means. In other words, they could resolve traumatic events without even having to talk about them. While he realized the importance of such a discovery, he also determined that, if he could learn the neuro-biological reason for this phenomenon, it would give more credibility to the therapy. With the help of brain researchers, he discovered that the fixed gaze helps the client access the sub-cortical brain where these traumatic, often non-verbal, or pre-verbal dissociated events were stored.

Further experience revealed that each person has his own unique eye position where the brainspot, as he called it, exists. Brainspots can be detected in two main ways, which Grand calls outside window and inside window. Outside window means the therapist can discover the spot by slowly moving a wand through the client's visual field watching for facial expressions or other reflexive reactions such as the blinking, sudden fixation of the eyes, or sighing. Inside window means clients can determine where the spot is by themselves. Further, he also realized that sometimes when clients seemed to be daydreaming and staring at a spot in the room, they may be accessing their brainspot.

While stressing the value of brainspotting, he also emphasized the importance of attunement to the client and the importance of learning from every client, whom he believes has something to teach us. The more mindful we are of who and how we are, the more mindful the client will be. Not surprisingly, this dynamic relationship contributes to the effectiveness of the technique.

Mindfulness for Clients

Chapter 9 addressed the subject of mindfulness as it relates to therapists. Mindfulness is also a powerful and effective treatment tool. It is now being used and studied in many settings and configurations. What about it is helpful in psychotherapy? The simplest answer is that it helps clients relax and reduce stress. When seeking out therapy, clients are usually in a state of agitation or suffering, whether from trauma, current stressors, a medical condition, or life style. One of the first steps in treatment is to help them relax. In a relaxed state, they are more receptive and able go beyond their situation. To facilitate this, the therapist must also be in a relaxed state. Just this presence alone can be reassuring and therefore relaxing. One reason for this is the discovery in neuro-science of mirror neurons in the brain. These neurons respond in the brain of the person witnessing another's action, as if he were performing the action himself. So being in a room with a calm person can automatically calm another person.

You may wonder what about mindfulness makes it relaxing. First, it is the process of being fully present i.e., aware of our internal and external processes. Stress comes from remembering the past or anxiety about the future. By focusing on the present, especially in the safety of our office, there is no cause for alarm. Second, in mindfulness when fully present, we suspend any judgments of ourselves or what we are experiencing. It invites us to witness our positive and negative patterns, perceptions, and reactions with curiosity. By engaging a "neutral" part of ourselves, we use different parts of the brain other than those occupied by habitual patterns and faulty perceptions. We allow ourselves simply to be aware and do nothing other than be conscious and observant. Thus, we learn to regulate our thoughts and emotions. For example, if our mind tends to wander, we can control this by focusing on our breathing or being conscious of what our mind is doing and then redirecting it back to the present.

Some clients are uncomfortable with the idea of mindfulness, though it rapidly is gaining broader acceptance. The easiest way to introduce them to the experience is through a guided relaxation. Here is an example that is easy to follow and gives client a taste of what mindfulness is:

Have the client lie down or get comfortable sitting up. Then give these following instructions:

> *Just get comfortable and turn your attention inward. Imagine your body feels very heavy...or light.*

Breathe

Take some deep breaths inhaling slowly. Be aware of the air coming in and out of the nostrils. Now breathe in to the count of seven, (1,2,3, etc.), hold for a count of three (1,2,3), breath out to a count of seven (1,2,3, etc.) and pause for a count of three (1,2,3).

Now continue with this breathing for five breaths. Breathe in to the count of seven, (1,2,3, etc.) ..., hold for a count of three (1,2,3) ..., breathe out to a count of seven (1,2,3, etc.)... and pause for a count of three (1,2,3)...

Surroundings

Now become aware of your surroundings... Be aware of all the sounds you hear...the music...my voice...any other sounds in the room. Now become aware of the physical sensations of being in the room... the weight of your body against the chair or sofa...the temperature of the room...any draft or breeze... Now become aware of the smell in the room... and the taste in your mouth... and even with your eyes closed you may notice the darkness on your eyelids... or perhaps some design or color...or maybe even no sensation...and that's okay. Just be aware that all these things are happening in the here and now.... You get so busy during the day that you do not even notice what is happening in each moment of your life.

Internal Awareness

And these are only the things that are happening outside of our body. Now turn your attention inward and be aware of the air going in and out as you breathe...filling and emptying the lungs. Now become aware of any place in your body where you are carrying tension or discomfort...just relax that place... imagine the air you are breathing in is going to that place...bringing in a sense of comfort and relaxation. Imagine as you breathe out, you are breathing out tension from that place. Just allow that place in your body to relax. Now do this again for any other place where you feel tension...just allow that part to relax and breathe in the relaxation sending it to that part. If you focus intently, you may even be aware of your heart beat or the pulse in your body.

Peace in the moment

As you become aware of the here and now, externally and internally... and as you relax your body, you can become aware that as your body is relaxed, your mind is relaxed... and as your mind is relaxed, your body is relaxed. You can also become aware of a sense of peacefulness in the moment...and in this moment...and in this moment. In each moment, we are surrounded by this peacefulness, but we get so caught up in the day-to-day activities that we don't experience the peace in every moment. Just imagine you are bathing in that peace...that peace is permeating you and you are soaking it up like soaking up the sun lying on the beach. Imagine each cell is being bathed in the peace... and that you become that peace. Allow yourself to experience that as fully and completely as you would like... If your mind begins to wander just notice where it takes you...to the future or the past... where does it take you? Bring it back to the now and just relax your neck and throat and your eyes and eye lids. And again re-discover the peace in the moment. Now we are going to be coming out of the relaxation. Just open your eyes when I count to ten and try to maintain that same sense of peace and awareness of the here and now that you have now. 1,2,3, etc.

Usually once clients go through this experience, they are open to further guidance. There are many books and techniques that can guide you in helping them. The most important factor, however, is that you have practiced and experienced mindfulness on your own.

Expressive Therapies

Expressive therapies take into consideration that different people have different ways of expressing themselves. Not everyone is proficient. I realized after working in a residential drug-treatment center that certain kinds of clients did not seem to thrive. After much observation, it was apparent that the program's therapeutic design was all verbal. There were movies, lectures, readings, group talk therapy, individual talk therapy, and many written assignments. These activities were neither giving these residents hope nor improving their self-esteem. Instead, the activities seemed to add to their burden. Often they did not understand what was being said or how to respond. Their lack of writing and spelling skills embarrassed and handicapped them further. I thought, "What if a drug treatment program was entirely centered around *physical* prowess and accomplishing certain physical feats, and I was a client, how would I feel?" Since I had asthma as a child, I never excelled nor developed my physical skills. If treatment was centered on accomplishing physical feats, I would feel frustrated, overwhelmed, and defeated. I would not like being in treatment, and probably would be a treatment failure or quit treatment thinking, "There is no way I can do this."

So, the staff and I decided to introduce other modalities into the treatment milieu. We had clients do collages, write rap songs, draw their hopes and dreams, listen to certain music and ask what they heard in the songs, participate in guided imagery, and perform some psychodrama. We even had them do drumming. All these "expressive" activities added breadth and depth to the program and gave some residents a way to shine that they did not have before.

Expressive therapies are designed to help clients explore and express themselves in a variety of ways. These include art and music therapy, dance and movement therapy, psychodrama, poetry therapy, play therapy and sand tray. While many therapists utilize some of these techniques in their therapy, to understand and be competent requires advanced training and certification. There are dangers in utilizing these techniques without proper training. One of the most common mistakes is when therapists misinterpret what clients are experiencing. There is a tendency to lead clients astray based on the therapist's interpretation of what is going on and not the client's. As a result, this can contaminate the process by forcing clients to focus on an aspect they may not consider relevant and, therefore, overlooks their meaning and interpretation, which are much more valid and critical for effective therapy. So, training is essential, and, therefore, each therapy has its own association, training, standards of practice, and certification procedures to ensure quality therapy.

Expressive therapies provide opportunities for clients to be creative and express themselves in new and fun ways by tapping into different parts of the brain. While these therapies can be incredibly useful, they too have their limitations. Some clients are not predisposed to these modalities, since they may see themselves as not being creative or artistic, or they are uncomfortable expressing themselves in this way. Some of their reticence goes back to childhood, when they were constantly being berated and criticized, or they never developed the motor control or specific talent to do such activities. With some gentle prodding, however, they may become interested and break through whatever barriers they have towards the activity. When this happens, it increases their self-confidence and opens new channels of communication.

Biofeedback and Neurofeedback

> Someday neurofeedback will be adopted and no one will remember they opposed it.
>
> —*Sigmund Othmer, Assoc. Editor of Clinical Electroencephalography*

In my opinion, if any medication had demonstrated such a wide spectrum of efficacy, it would be universally accepted and widely used.

—*Frank H. Duffy, Harvard Neurologist*

Much of psychotherapy is teaching coping strategies and mechanisms to deal with stress and emotional dysregulation. Given that these symptoms are created and exist in the realm of physiology, then it is not unreasonable to think that learning ways to control our physiology could be helpful. Unfortunately, this is not what most of us were taught.

Biofeedback is the process whereby a person learns to control certain physiological states such as blood pressure, heart rate, and muscle tension. Simply getting on the scales is to measure weight loss or gain is a form of feedback. Conditions such as migraine headaches, incontinence, high blood pressure, chronic stress, and chronic pain can be treated with biofeedback. Electrodes are attached to the skin to measure skin temperature, sweating, blood pressure, heart rate, and breathing rate. The results are displayed on a computer screen. By trying different relaxation techniques, such as deep breathing, progressive body relaxation, and guided imagery, the client can observe which activities help, and what he should do to relax. Once he learns this inner control, then the machine is no longer needed to give feedback. Biofeedback is not only used to treat disorders, but also to promote and increase performance in athletes, musicians, dancers, etc.

Neurofeedback is biofeedback applied to the brain using EEG's (electroencephalograms), to address brain dysregulation. Daniel Amen, a brain researcher, made an interesting observation: If you go to a doctor with heart problems, he looks at your heart; if you go for stomach problems, he looks at your stomach; and yet when people go with mental disorders, which are the result of brain dysfunction, their brain is never looked at or studied. Therapists end up treating the symptoms and not the biological cause of the problem. Neurofeedback provides a unique way to observe and heal certain dysfunctions in the brain.

The activity that goes on in the brain is both chemical and electrical. Psychiatrists deal with mental disorders by focusing on the chemical imbalance by prescribing psychotropic medications to help regulate the chemical brain activity, yet do not address the electrical brain imbalance. Neurofeedback is the therapy that measures and regulates the electrical brain activity. With the advent of new pharmacological medications in the last few decades, neurofeedback took a back seat. Now as some of the medications' limitations are being discovered, the pendulum is slowly swinging back towards neurofeedback, as its benefits become more known. "Once the brain has been trained to produce different patterns of electrical communication, no further treatment is necessary, in contrast to drugs, which do not change fundamental brain activity and work only as long as the patient keeps taking them" (Van Der Kolk, 2014).

During a neurofeedback session recipients' brain wave activity is measured by sensors, which are attached to specific meridian points on the scalp and forehead. Not all neurofeedback is the same, however, since there are at least a dozen or more different systems. What is considered "traditional" neurofeedback requires the client to either relax with earphones and create more pleasing sounds as the relaxed state increases or to watch a screen that will be responsive in interesting ways when the client can achieve focus and concentration. The client is not asked to try to do anything. The brain itself responds to the stimuli and directs the appropriate brain state. It seems a bit counterintuitive that one is rewarded for not trying, but letting go. In fact, the harder you try, the less successful you will be. Another form of neurofeedback, called LENS, gives the therapist information that analyzes brain wave patterns. Neural gridlocks created by stress and trauma are addressed using the brain's own electromagnetic language, allowing the brain to reboot and restores to normal functioning.

While these approaches are effective by themselves, they are enhanced when paired with talk therapy. They tend to enhance each other, i.e., neurofeedback aids talk therapy, and talk therapy enhances the effects of neurofeedback.

For example, neurofeedback has been very effective in treating trauma. Bessel Van Der Kolk, founder and director of the Trauma Center in Brookline, Massachusetts, has long been an advocate for the use of neuro-feedback. He wrote that people with histories of trauma have "…excessive activity in the right temporal lobe, the fear center, combined with too much frontal slow-wave activity. This means that their hyperarousal emotional brains dominate their mental life. Our research showed that calming the fear center decreases trauma-based problems and improves executive functioning" (Van Der Kolk

2014). These kinds of results are not easily achieved through talk therapy alone, if at all. But when the two are combined, there is a synergistic effect that relieves stress and promotes healing.

Neurofeedback also is used to reverse underlying conditions of ADHD and other learning disabilities, especially in children. The uses of neurofeedback are growing each year as practitioners and researchers learn new technology, and different disorders are addressed. Van Der Kolk lists some of these: "relieving tension headaches, improving cognitive functioning following traumatic brain injury, reducing anxiety and panic attacks, learning to deepen meditative states, treating autism, improving seizure control, self-regulation in mood disorders and more" (Van Der Kolk, 2014).

Neurofeedback is on the cutting edge of brain research and innovations based on scientific research. It has come a long way since the 1970's when it was first used, and it will continue to evolve as new information about the brain is discovered.

Nutrition

With all the research being done linking the body and the mind, we should consider the effects of nutrition, which profoundly affect the functioning of the body and the brain. I experienced a most dramatic example of this with a lady who exhibited the most severe symptoms of depression I had ever witnessed. She appeared in my office totally disheveled, slumped over during the whole session, picking at her shoes, making no eye contact, and barely able to talk above a whisper. She felt totally helpless, stuck, and hopeless. I recommended among other things that she see her primary physician. I did not hear back from her for nearly six weeks and my phone calls went unanswered. To my relief, she finally called back and agreed to come in for another appointment. When I saw her, I could not believe it was the same person. It seemed like a miracle. She was bright, lively, erect, and engaging. I immediately asked what had happened to her.

"Vitamin B-12," she replied, "My doctor started giving me Vitamin B-12 shots, and I feel like a new person."

The body needs proper nutrition to operate efficiently. Lack of nutrition is the cause or contributor to many mental illnesses or aspects of mental illness.

While psychotherapists are not expected to be nutritionists, having a working knowledge of the interplay between nutrition and mental health is a valuable, if not essential tool to have in one's toolbox. Any thorough assessment of a client's condition should include inquiry into the nature of their diet and eating habits, as well as any supplements they are taking. In this way, a vital component and possible direct cause of instability can be detected, in which case a referral should be made to a physician or nutritionist.

Clients should be encouraged to do research on their own as to what a proper diet is for them. Many clients who are averse to any psychotropic medications are often open to suggestions for diet change or supplements. Being able to lead them in the right direction without making specific recommendations can be critical. We must be careful not to operate outside the scope of our practice, but that does not mean we cannot educate them about the need for proper nutrition and help them make informed decisions about possibilities for further professional services.

However, getting people to change their eating habits can be difficult. One in-home counselor, who had a background as a chef, was appalled by the eating habits of the family with whom he was working. He decided to treat them to "a regular meal," which included meat loaf, green beans, mashed potatoes and gravy, and a salad. He decorated the table and had them all sit together (which was a first for this family). The children eagerly approached the table, and then a look of disappointment came over their faces. "What's wrong?" inquired the counselor. "Where are the McNuggets?" they asked. That was all that they cared about.

Even though this meal was a typical American meal, it still did not contain many of the nutrients we need daily, but it certainly was a step up for this family. If we think of food as the fuel to run our bodies and brain, we begin to see why some people have the problems they do. I recently saw in my practice a young man who drank power drinks during the day, took no vitamins or supplements, and ate no food until around midnight in a restaurant where he worked. He needed to smoke pot to bring him down so he could sleep. Along with this routine he admitted he did no exercise. Of course, he was very depressed and emaciated, and felt like his life was out of control, especially his emotions. On some level, he knew that his diet was "crap," but had little motivation or desire to change it. I knew that helping him with his depression would be very difficult until we could make some headway in changing his diet. I told him his diet was controlling him and not the other way around. It took some education, motivation, and a step-by-step process to help him—first, to cut down on his drinks and pot, and slowly introduce foods, vitamins, and supplements. Within six weeks along with his regular counseling, he turned a corner. His health and his outlook began to change as he started taking charge of his life.

The impact of a healthy diet with the right kinds of supplementation can work wonders. Ideally, all our nutritional needs would come from the food we eat, since this is the better way to absorb nutrition, but our diets do not necessarily provide the level and kinds that we need. With the right diet clients, who for years were on medications, can come off them. Obviously, this is not true for all clients, but it does offer an avenue of hope they may not know of or thought about.

While there are an incredible number of supplements and vitamins to choose from which may be helpful, I have chosen four that seem to be the most common to improve mental health:

1. Omega-3 Fatty Acids

Omega-3 plays a critical role in brain function, especially memory and mood. It has been shown to be effective in improving mood, especially unipolar depression. It also improves cognition. Some studies have indicated that it is more effective than Ritalin in treating ADHD. It is found naturally in fish such as tuna, salmon, and halibut and also walnuts and flaxseeds.

2. Vitamin D

Most Americans are deficient in Vitamin D, the sunshine vitamin. Lack of vitamin D is linked to depression, dementia, and autism. A partial reason for SAD (Seasonal Affective Disorder) is the diminished sunlight during the winter months, and as a result, less Vitamin D being produced in the body.

3. Magnesium

Magnesium is sometimes referred to as the stress antidote. It is the original "chill pill," which helps to reduce anxiety, apathy, depression, insecurity, and irritability. It is found in seafood, seaweed, greens, and beans.

4. B Complex

This set of vitamins are often called the mental-health vitamins.

Here are the B Vitamins that are essential for mental health:

B-1 Thiamine – *Necessary for the health of the nervous system.*

B-3 Niacin – *Prevention of mental confusion and memory loss*

B-6 Pyridoxine -*Coenzyme for the production of serotonin, dopamine, and GABA*

B-12 Cobalamin – *Helps in the prevention of depression*

To keep a balance of B vitamins in your system, medical professionals often suggest for healthy adults B-complex vitamins over individual B-supplements. The B-complex is also found in stress tabs.

If a nutritional assessment indicates a suspected problem, refer the client to a qualified nutritionist, or a medical doctor, who practices integrated medicine or functional medicine. They are excellent resources.

The Gut and the Brain

You got to have guts to do that.
I can hardly stomach that situation.
I felt like I had butterflies in my stomach.
I had a gut feeling about it.
My gut's telling me it's not right.
That was a gut-wrenching experience.
It makes me sick to my stomach to think about that.

These sayings are so common, they seldom give us pause to think about what they mean. Is there is a connection between the gut, which comprises the whole gastrointestinal tract, and the brain? Apparently, from such sayings, we tend to know this intuitively, but until recently it has not been well researched. What is it about our stomach-gut that affects our brain and vice-versa? Well, we have a whole population of bacteria in the stomach called the microbiome. There are said to be between 10,000 and 35,000 species totaling 100 trillion bacteria living in the stomach (Wahl, 2014) and if all gathered together would weigh about 4 to 5 pounds. These bacteria have a tremendous effect on our health, mentally and physically. The greater the variety of these bacteria, the better chance a person has of having a healthy brain, and the healthier the brain, the less likely a person will have gastrointestinal problems.

The microbiome is made up of good bacteria and bad bacteria (Perlmutter, 2015). One goal for optimum mental and physical health is to have a robust microbiome with lots of "good bacteria." How can we increase the number of good bacteria? The health of the microbiome is dependent on the quality of food we eat. There are prebiotics and probiotics. Prebiotics are specialized plant fibers that beneficially nourishes the good bacteria present in the large bowel or colon. While probiotics introduce good bacteria into the gut, prebiotics act as a fertilizer for the good bacteria. They help your good bacteria grow, improving the good-to-bad bacteria ratio. Recently, the popularity and production of different types of probiotics have exploded. Probiotics help to increase the overall health of the intestinal lining, the improvement of cognitive functioning, and increase energy level. If your client is having digestive problems, you may want to recommend they consider taking probiotics.

So how does the gut with a lot of good bacteria in it help the brain? The gut communicates to the brain through the vagus nerve (the main nerve that connects the brain and the stomach that sends messages both ways). It sends chemical messengers, which are produced in the gut. These messengers include growth hormones, various vitamins such as B12, and even neurotransmitters such as glutamate and GABA (Perlmutter, 2015). Amazingly, we have an estimated 100 million neurons in the stomach, not just the brain. (Interestingly, the heart contains more than 40,000 neurons.) In fact, 80-90% of the serotonin found in the body is manufactured by the neurons in the stomach. (Perlmutter, 2015) The stomach is often referred to as the "second brain" or more formally the enteric nervous system. It is also true that the brain affects the gut. Worry, mental stress, brain imbalance can all affect the digestive system and result in chronic constipation, irritable bowel syndrome, and poor digestion.

Scientists also have found that GABA, a chemical, that helps stabilize the nervous system and reduces anxiety, is produced in the digestive system. It is classified as an inhibitory neuro-transmitter, which calms down the neurons.

Lack of sufficient GABA may even cause ADHD and possibly Tourette's. Researchers are trying to discover which bacteria are essential to the productions of GABA, to treat the underlying cause of ADHD and replace Ritalin, which does not go into fixing brain tissue (Perlmutter, 2015).

One of the culprits of the brain that is only recently being recognized is inflammation. We are very familiar with inflammation when our ankles get swollen, or we sustain an injury or a burn. Inflammation within the body is much subtler and harder to detect. Some scientists, for example, are saying that depression is the result of inflammation in the stomach, and that Alzheimer's is the result of inflammation in the brain. This creates a topsy-turvy way of looking at mental illness. It may seem hard to believe in many cases, that if the gut is okay, the brain will be okay.

There are many threats to the microbiome including chlorinated water, the Standard American Diet (SAD), toxic personal-care products, and many medications, especially antibiotics. Antibiotics have been described as the atom bomb for the microbiome, destroying good bacteria as well as bad. So, there are many factors that affect our mental health. As we increase our knowledge of these factors, we are better able to serve our clients. Rarely in most conversations does the subject of food, diet, and digestive disorders arise. It is important to at least explore this, since it can be a significant factor that no talk therapy by itself will help.

Sandplay Therapy

> Often the hands will solve a mystery that the intellect has struggled with in vain.
>
> *—C. G. Jung*

Sandplay therapy is not *only* for children, but also adults. The therapy involves a client placing miniature figures, objects, and materials representing all aspects of life and fantasy into a sand tray, an elevated box filled with sand painted blue on the bottom (which, when the sand is swept away, can represent a body of water). Strategically placed in the sand tray, figures and objects create a three-dimensional picture, which is meaningful to the client as perhaps a story or a representation of inward feelings. In essence, the client is creating his own world.

Having its roots in Buddhism and Jungian therapy, sandplay therapy is a highly effective way to gain access to unconscious material, since it is all symbolic. The advantage is that the client can deal intra-psychically with situations in a representative way without having to resolve them in a literal way. For example, children can often work out their inner conflict independently without any direct intervention from the therapist. Most sandplay therapists act as passive observers not giving any interpretation of what is going on, but sometimes providing clarifying statements or posing curious questions such as, "Tell me about this figure," or "What is going on in that corner over there?" This process involves a strict respect for the sacred "knowing" of the client. Because of this process, the need for training is essential for the therapist to know how to guide the client through the process of opening the doorway to and connecting to the unconscious world.

The following is an interview with sandplay therapist, Katharine Knapp, who has a practice in Charlottesville, Virginia. We explore some of the subtler aspects of play therapy and how it can be used in conjunction with other therapies:

Kate, what is sandplay therapy?
Sandplay involves the use of objects placed in a tray of sand as the therapist elicits the welcomed opportunity to discover the client's hidden or silent material. The interpretation is the client's alone to discover in a "free and protected space."

While many play therapists utilize the sand tray with children, most people may not be aware of the wonderful benefits to its use with adults and couples. Projected experiential *play* offers fabulous ways of self-discovery and invites the curiosity needed for relational work. The big "aha" moments often come through inviting a client to explore the creative less-utilized part of the brain or the playful discovery of a world created within a tray of sand. These experiences can be profound. But even if not, there can be great benefit from them. The experiences build on themselves, providing a journey for the client or couple. This journey then has a beginning, middle, and end. It offers the pendulation (an exercise to develop a relationship between safe, authentic space and conflict that the client relates in the narrative). This pendulation then allows the client to move from a place of safety out into the challenging material and back to safety in a free and protected space, witnessed and guided by the guardian presence of the therapist.

I have heard you talk about a necessary part of sandplay therapy is the creation of a container. What does that mean? I know that the sand tray is a container, but it is much more than that.

It is, because there needs to be a sense of safety in the room. It's funny because I don't talk about this very often, but only occasionally with a client who has trauma do I use the word, "container" and in a sense this is like the womb or the "circle of security" that allows the client to delve into the deep material and return safely.

A container means a boundaried space, a place that has boundaries that is protected. So, I will speak of the walls in my room or the sides of the tray as though they are the four directions: the east, the west, the north and the south, the above and the below. This mirrors our relationship with the Universe. The client is free to explore anything and everything, things that society say are bad or wrong. He can explore shadow material here, and he is safe to do so without judgment. The important thing is the act of the hands-on building and the being *present* after having built the story, not speaking (as in traditional "talk therapy"). This allows the "builder" to integrate what was created with what gets reflected on during the time spent processing the experience with the clinician. Following the "building" process there is conscious silence, which provides space for curious awareness. This reflection period is where active questioning occurs, developing coherence or an awareness of the lack of coherence for the client or couple. Often, this process is a powerful tool for shifting patterns that seem stuck as clients view the narrative from a different perspective.

One of the things that impressed me when we had the training from you was how you use the sand tray to facilitate problem-solving with the children without direction from a therapist. It struck me so profoundly that they could work out their inner conflict in the sand tray without you explaining things to them. I wonder if you could speak a little about that.

Sure. Again, it is trusting in the process. Many clinicians believe that they have to have the answers. To do sand tray well, you should trust that the client has all that he or she needs.

That's a huge one.

Yes, and you have to trust they will discover it, because you are holding the container for them. When that is true, they are free to create in this free space. Then they will project themselves into this safely held container, and it will mirror back to them the self, and in the mirroring they will discover what they need. Most of what I do is to invite *curiosity*. To get their perspective changed I will have them walk around the tray. This is really, really important. People who do sand tray and only do it from the direction that the person created it, limit it. And the other thing I do is to NOT interpret their work. I will not tell them what it means. I might write down a lot in my notes about what I see, but I do NOT tell them my thoughts unless they ask me about it. And then, I usually respond with a question such as, "I'm curious... what do YOU notice, what intrigues your awareness here, and how do you feel about what is tickling your awareness right now?"

Do you ask any questions?

Yes, during the note taking I observe a lot. I may notice all kinds of things that the client may not be ready to receive or maybe doesn't notice. In my notes I write about what I observe that I want to be curious about with the client during the reflection time. This allows the client to delve a bit deeper. I lead with questions that are open-ended and that invite the client to explore "meaning-making." This is what you are doing—you are creating an environment to integrate the concrete meaning with the inferred meaning out of the context of their story (bring the unconscious into the conscious). By inviting a new perceptual meaning, I assist the client in integrating their experience into a broader context. I set this intentional goal energetically at the beginning. It is not through what I say; it is how I hold the intention in my body. It is how I set my desire or goal from the very beginning before they walk through the door. Then when they come in, there is this knowingness in my body that believes this client will in fact discover the Self. They always do.

I love that. Your intention creates the environment for them to open up. It sounds like a way to help develop mindfulness.

Yes, and without judgment. Most children don't have that experience. They live in a world where most adults have the power and they don't. So, I am providing them safety in a world where I can be a guardian who protects them, so they can look at their own story without the judgment of other adults. I am very careful how I invite parents into this space. I teach parents to only observe and say, "Thank you for sharing this with me." I want parents to be cautious as they often add their opinions, which communicate judgment. An example is a parent saying, "That dog looks happy playing over there." They don't know if that dog is supposed to be a dog or a boy pretending to be a dog, and they certainly don't know if the dog is happy.

That's fantastic. That's very powerful. I love that. Exactly.

Another example is a 5-year-old boy who came to me with lots of anger. He was acting out and very explosive in pre-school. His father had a rage problem. The mother and father were separated and in the process of divorcing. By the second year of seeing him every week and doing the sand tray or play therapy, I began to see a pattern emerge in the stories. The pattern led me to suspect abuse. I couldn't ask him directly about my suspicions. You can't ask that sort of thing as that would be "leading" the client. You must allow the child to get to a point where he can give voice to it. The container is not just the sand but the sacred space of the room. The sand tray is a concrete story of objects that manifest the inner story going on in the room. It holds the energetic pattern of the client. And I can be present in "eldering" the child in a way that gives him permission to tell his story without speaking his story, because he is too scared to speak it out loud. Eventually as he was playing, he took two objects—a monster object, which he laid on top of a little girl in the sand. He moved this object up and down repeatedly on the girl in the sand. I knew something was happening here that mirrored his life, so I just said, "I am curious about this part of your story. Is there more that Ms. Katharine can understand that what you are showing me? What else is happening?" He said, "That is me and my sister, and my dad is telling me what to do." He was six years old at that point.

It took a year to prepare for court; giving him room to express his emotions, memories, and questioning. Because of this work and of all the direct quotes and direct photos for court, I was able to protect the child. We went to court. The lawyer took my pictures and blew them up into huge poster sizes. The boy had also done drawings of himself and giant collages. All of those were shown in court. We could not prove the father was the perpetrator. We could absolutely prove that my client **believed** that his father was the perpetrator. In the end the child was granted protection until he turns 18.

The key here is note-taking and not making an assumption, not putting my suspicions in spoken words. I wrote in my notes what was in the tray and what the child said in quotes about his story. And when the father's lawyer said it was hearsay, my response was, "It is not my voice; it is the child's voice. I am simply representing the child. I am not giving you my voice, nor my judgment. It is up to you, the judge, to hear the child's voice. You have already heard that I am an expert witness, and all I am doing is witnessing the child's voice, since he cannot be here today." *That was awesome.*

It was awesome. It is very powerful work. So, this is the way to access the unconscious and deal with the situation on the unconscious level instead of trying to problem solve.

What I find is that when clients are stuck, it is because the bridge between the conscious and the unconscious blew up. It is not even that the bridge needs repair. The bridge blew up, and I have to build a bridge either from the conscious to the unconscious or the unconscious to the conscious. I can try several different ways. For instance, I talk to teenagers very directly about that. I had one client who had experienced significant trauma, and the teenager struggled with being present to her own body. She did not identify as male or female. She voiced wanting to be agender (no gender), saying she would rather be invisible than have to acknowledge any gender. We talked about what happens when this client feels overwhelmed, and the client said, "I think I am dissociating, because I feel separate from who I really am. My bridge is gone." So, we talk about how to get back. One of the ways to do that is through cultivating curiosity about these projections.

How do you present projections as a concept they can understand?

I don't use the word, first of all. Instead I give them an experience. The experience is everything. If I can give them the experience of the link, they will know it is possible. So, I contain it. I will do that by saying, "We'll look at one aspect." Let's say someone is having trouble in their relationships, and she can't seem to connect to the other person. She can't seem to problem-solve any more; she is absolutely stuck in this relationship without a bridge. She cares so much about what the other person thinks. I can see she is projecting all this stuff onto the other person, but cannot see that. I will ask them to find objects on my shelves that will represent the way she feels. I go to the feeling first, not the cognitive. Most of the time when people are stuck, they tell me they do not know how they feel. "I don't know what I feel. I don't know what to do." So instead of dialogue that is cognitive, I say, "Show me. Find me something that feels like how you are feeling." The bridge gets built as they slow down the process and experience the narrative through concrete objects that can hold the unconscious meaning associated with buried feelings.

That's exciting.

It is cool to see things unfold in the office, especially with adults who come in expecting to process very cognitively. They want solutions; they want you to give them the solutions and want their problems fixed in four sessions. They very quickly see that this is going to happen in a very different way.

So do you do that with everybody?

No, not everyone. It's in my toolbox. I draw on it when the basic modalities do not seem to be working. I don't always begin this way. I am pretty intuitive, and I get a feeling for where the client is starting from. If the client is really ready to jump on board and do some discovery work, I may not need it right away. I may only use it as a one or two-time experience. Men tend to be very cognitive. They tend to be solution-focused, so I don't always do it in the beginning. I want to develop the relationship first. I want them to feel comfortable in my room and in my space. My room looks different than most counseling offices. I need to develop that rapport first, then I will throw in something novel. When I see a couple, I will often ask them to introduce their families to me by utilizing the objects in the sand tray to express their "feel" for each family member. This can tell me lots and lots about a family.

I think it is interesting you have the curtains there. It's a big surprise! (She has curtains covering up all her figures and objects on shelves)

Well, I found that it was overwhelming, sometimes even to me sitting in the room.

A big distraction possibly.

The voices, … you know, they "speak." They have an awful lot of energy. I had clients, whom I worked with for years, who noticed when the curtain went up and they said, "It is so calm in your room now, what did you do?" I said, "I am in here all day every day, and I needed some space from all the energy in the archetypes surrounding me. Now I can breathe in here. It is not as loud in here as it used to be." There are not so many voices.

Each figure has a story or a variety of stories.

That's right. They hold the space for the archetype or the personality of the character represented.

One of the things I hear when you talk is what I call neutral language. You are not saying, "How did you feel?" or "What did you feel about that?" Rather, "What was that like for you?" or "What was your experience with that?" You have to learn to be very open-ended with all of your comments and questions.

Yes, I will ask them, "If you could be like anything in this world—a tree, a stone, a pond, an animal, or a person—what would you be like?" and then I will say, "Is there a guide here? Is there a stone that speaks? Is there a tree that has a voice? Is there a person who could be a guide and tell me about this world? Who speaks for this world?" So again, I am inviting their projections to speak, not them. By separating them, I am literally separating the psyche, so that it can mirror back to *them, not me,* the voice of the story.

The exciting moment happens when I invite them to come in a little closer; come closer to the tree. Peer around the tree. What does it look like from the back of this tree? What is that? I am curious about what is happening? What does this tree know that these participants don't know? That is a very different way of getting into the story. Most therapists are going to talk about the people and people's feelings, right? Well, what if the tree could speak, and the tree could tell us what the tree knows is happening here?" You are really projecting out.

You know the bad thing about this is that I see how inadequate other treatments are. How can you possibly do therapy effectively, if you are not doing what you are talking about?

I know, and for me it has been so intuitive. When I have a family and do a family therapy session, one of the things I do is set the energetic container immediately by saying to the family, "Everything that gets talked about in here is going to activate your own internal narrative. Each one of you have places in your own story that are going to respond differently than somebody else, so when you leave my room I want a commitment right here right now that you will not talk about what happened in this room for at least 48 hours. The reason for that is because your story (old stuff) is getting activated, and it may have nothing to do with what we are really talking about here right now."

Then I will say to the parents, who are usually nervous, and the child who is often shaking and sometimes crying, "There is too much emotion here; we are going to slow this down. We are going to learn how to communicate from a place of feelings instead of our reasoning thinking (cognition). We have to start with the feelings, because feelings always trump intellect. It doesn't matter how much you know. Your body is getting activated because of the emotional system that is trying to regulate itself. If we don't build a bridge from the reactive part of the brain to the thinking rational part of the brain, it won't matter how brilliant you are. When we are dysregulated, then we can't connect to our intelligence. You do this best by listening to your feelings first and then being aware of their sensation in the body. That means not being outside them and trying to fix them. It means being mindful, being present, and asking yourself, "How long can I tolerate those feelings before I am going to explode, before I am going to avoid, before I am going to try to fix them with my reason?"

So, if they say they don't want to get to that point, what do you do?

When they do that, I will say, "I invite you to be curious."

The voice of curiosity.

Yes, always lead with curiosity. "I invite you to be curious. Let's not make assumptions. Let's not make decisions about what this is going to be like at the end of an hour. Just be curious to have an experience."

Yes, you have to get outside yourself to mirror back to see yourself.

It's all in the mirroring back. So, the sand tray is a physical container to toggle back and forth between the conscious and the unconscious realm. It illuminates the soul. You can use a table without any sand and images. The important thing is resourcing someone using the concrete objects, because as soon as you do that, you have taken what is inside their head and projected it outside. Then it is bound in this concrete object. Then it is almost object-relations theory.

Another thing I use is psychodrama. I would use scarves and rope. I worked with a 46-year-old man who was so tied to his mother that he couldn't seem to separate. So, I gave him the rope and I held the rope and said, "Do you really want to let go of your mother or not? You are 46. You talk about her all the time and how bad it was. Do you really want to let go?" And he said, "Yes." Then I said, "Pull the rope out of my hand." He is a strong man, and I really had to put my feet down and really hold. I made it very difficult, and he kept pulling and pulling. Finally, I let go and he fell back into the sofa. I said, "Do you think you are free yet?" and he said, "Yes." I said, "No, the rope is still in your hands. What are you going to do with the rope?" It was concrete; what are we going to do with it? We went outside and burned it. He had to absolutely physiologically see that he was letting go, and he was the author of it. Do you know what I mean?

Yes, that was his story.

Again, it is using concrete objects to represent what is inside the psyche. You are taking it out of the psyche and making it concrete. I had one woman who used scarves and did a similar thing to let go of her mother. I think about a year later I forgot and brought the scarves back into the office, and she saw the one scarf. This was back in the days when I did not realize how important it was to "decloak" it when I was done. I just didn't know the importance of it. It had a visceral impact on her. She said, "What is my mother doing back in your office?" I just went, "What?" She said, "That scarf, get it out of here." The projection is that strong. So, what I do now is I decloak it. Before we leave we take off what we projected onto it and it returns to the wall. It is now simply a scarf, an object again, because if we don't do that, the attachment is too strong.

Is it a matter of just returning it to the wall? How do you neutralize it?

Well, it depends on whether I am working with a child or an adult. If I am working with a child, I don't worry about it. With adults, I do, because the attachments are so different in the adult world. Maybe it is because we are so much more cognitively based than children are. With an adult, I use very clear language. I say, "We really want to separate out your story from this object now. I want you to return it to the wall and in doing so we are returning it to the world of images. It no longer has that meaning." In that way, it can be used again in a different way, and they are cognitive about it. With the child, I never want them to be that cognitive about it. I want it to stay in that place.

You mentioned that you sometimes combine sandplay with other therapies.

Psychodrama is a nice coupling with the use of the sand tray. I overlap psychodrama and the use of sand tray. Often with adults I will not have the sand tray at all. I will have a table instead of the sand. In this way, the couple, a husband and a wife, will feel like I am treating them less like they are children. I still utilize all the objects. The objects become the projection. Defense mechanisms are often broken down when you have an object in front of you. The client's perception of the object may be distorted, but even if that happens, the clinician can see that right away, because you have a literal, concrete object in front of you, and that holds the container for the projection. What I do then as the clinician, through questioning, is to alter the client's perception of the projection. It employs guided dramatic action to facilitate problem-solving using methods such as sociometry, role theory, and group dynamics and integrates cognition, affect, and behavior. Psychodrama offers the use of objects and the social engagement of everyone in the room to intensify the metaphors and "experience." The use of the material world, such as scarves and larger costuming items serve as symbolic "place holders" for the psyche to project into and have mirrored back a greater experience and thus understanding.

For example, let's say a couple is stuck, and they are at opposite poles of understanding. She doesn't know why he won't clean up after himself; he doesn't understand why it should be important to her. She is talking about her emotions, and he is approaching it logically and thinking he doesn't have time. She is in her emotional mind, and he is in his logical mind. They are stuck, and the clinician is not able to bridge that gap. What I do is have them project it out, bring the objects into play, and often he can see her emotion, because they are projected out in the story in front of them. She can see where he is coming from easier when they are looking at a third place instead of looking directly at each other.

Another useful tool is to use some of the material from psychodrama to develop clients' resources and give them what they need to cross over that bridge to insight. A resource can be internal or external. When someone feels "stuck," then I might ask them, "Can you name me your five strengths?" He may say, "I am likeable and friendly; I have a big passionate heart; I am good at soccer; I am intellectual; and I am a good dad." Often when people are depressed, it is hard to come up with five positive qualities. That is the place where it takes time to develop questions like, "Do you have friends? What would they say about you?" to help them see what they can't see in terms of positives. Then I will have them go to my wall and pick five objects that represent those states. As soon as they do that, they have projected the strengths onto an object. Then I can ask them to play with the objects by asking them to put them together. "How do they work together? How does one help another?"

I have an actual example. I met with a woman who was having trouble with her adult son. She was in a new marriage, and her current husband didn't seem to understand how hard it was for her to parent her adult son, so there was friction. I suggested she bring her husband in to increase dialogue. She said, "I don't know if he will come. We are just really stuck, when it comes to parenting this 30-year-old. I said, "Well tell him to come in; we will have some fun." He came in and I said, "I don't really know you, and you don't know me. And I don't know how you guys work together. Would you pick objects from my wall that would give me a picture, a window into who you are? Pick an object that stands for everyone in your family."

Well, they picked objects that covered the whole floor. Most people only pick one or two objects. He went in and picked objects for his mother, his siblings, his father, his first wife, his kids, his second wife. It was wild! And she did the same thing on her spot on the floor. Then I said, "Tell me what happens when they meet. What does it look like? Show me." I have done this in the sand tray as well. Then they start moving the pieces together. Well, this was phenomenal. She picked Yoda as her husband. And he did a very similar thing where he put her as an angel very "big," and he was small underneath her. It was a golden moment. Then I could invite them to look at what they had put in front of themselves. What do they notice? How did it feel to look at it from the opposite side of the room? Walk around the room. Change your perspective. Get down on the floor and look directly at the objects instead of above. You see each of these positions change your perception. Then we can talk about it in a very intellectual adult way.

In terms of using this with adults, you are opening up their relationships with their projections. You are shifting their perspective. And if I am asking them to project their strengths, then I ask them, "What sabotages those strengths?" Then they will get an object to represent the saboteur (damager). Then I will say, "Show me. Put it on the table. Put it in the sand. Show me the relationship of what happens. Put it in front. Find something that represents you. You are passionate, and your anger gets in the way." Whatever that is, you see it in three-dimensional concrete form. It changes our relationship to the concept, the projection that we are focused on at the time. Does that make sense?

Yes, it is like narrative therapy except you are acting it out instead of telling about an event.

Yes, because you are using the narrative of their life. In a way, it is Jungian. We are looking at the symbology, and we are pulling from the transpersonal and transcultural, what the cultural voice is. There is the collective unconscious that Jung talks about, and then there is the very personal story. If I assume that for you a lion means Aslan, the lion from C.S. Lewis's *The Lion, the Witch and the Wardrobe*, which represents the loving God, and I don't ask you what the lion means to you, then I might miss an important detail in your story. I could miss the fact that a lion means something very different to you, because you came from a village where a lion killed your father. You see my point? Their personal narrative about those symbols is going to impact the story that emerges as much as the collective cultural symbols.

Thank you, this has been very enlightening.

CHAPTER 12

Responses to Questions

THE FOLLOWING ARE SOME OF THE QUESTIONS presented to me in *What to Do, When You Don't Know What to Do* workshops. Various questions and my responses are posted on my website, jonwindercounseling.com. You are welcome to submit questions there and/or your solutions for the situations submitted.

Cut Off from Feelings

Question: I have a client who "lives from the neck up," i.e., very little or brief emotions other than relaxed, peaceful, comfortable, "over it already." Mother was an abusive alcoholic, who broke the client's wrist at age 5. The setting is a residential substance-abuse facility for women. We have recently tried art therapy without emotive response.

Response: The woman has learned to survive in her life by cutting off her feelings. She will tend to avoid these feelings and situations at all costs, especially if her main life experiences were traumatic resulting in anger, criticism, blame, confusion, and cruelty. Her blocking should be validated and honored. First, she should feel secure in her coping mechanisms. Urging her to change can be just another force, telling her she is wrong, or she is living her life wrongly.

The question becomes is this your agenda for her?

The first step is to just reinforce her and her cognitive process, so that she can become more effective in mentally processing her problem. It may be that you see her stuckness as an inability to express or process what happened in her past, and this may be true. However, one way to think about expressing her feelings is like an unripe fruit. You cannot pick it, until it has matured enough to let go of the tree. A person will not let go of feelings, until they feel safe enough and develop trust with the therapist. This may be a long-term process, especially if she has had negative experiences in the past with a therapist. Also, if the person has not learned emotional regulation, getting in touch with feelings can be a downhill slope into a pit from which she is afraid she cannot emerge.

When the person's strength, trust, and faith increases, her emotions will emerge. So, then the question becomes how does one increase these qualities? Positive reinforcement, consistency, respect, forgiveness, genuineness, and compassion will all stimulate the ability to express feelings. Group therapy can be especially useful, when clients see others opening up and experiencing the relief, healing, and even joy from doing so.

Unmotivated Parents

Question: I have been working with a family with four children and a mom and dad. We have been together nearly 6 months, and when I work with the child things go well. But it seems like all my attempts to work with mom and dad have not been successful. They have not instituted any of the suggestions that I have given them, and they're continuing to treat the children in a way that's undermining the therapy and causing them to continue to have bad behavior.

Response: Many times parents are not ready to change. There are a lot of forces at work in their lives that cause them to be fearful and closed off including false pride. It is much easier to place the burden of blame on the children, rather than look at their role in the problem. It takes a lot of energy to change, and if they are in survival mode (and raising four children can do that), they have no energy to spare. An initial goal would be to provide positive support and energy to the parents and to lower their stress level. That may involve letting the parents complain about the children and the problems the children present.

This should not be done in front of the children, but in a special session.

At some point, it would be helpful to say, "Why do you think the children are having such problems?" This is usually a show-stopper in that for the first time the parents may have to look at their role. This does not always happen. They may still blame other forces (teachers, video games, relatives, etc.).

Next, would be to take time to have the parents discuss how they were parented and what they liked and disliked about the way they were raised. Use this as a springboard to talk about their own parenting style, i.e., how they are different or the same as their parents. This is a nonthreatening way to begin to bring up the subject of parenting with the least defensiveness. Once you get them talking about their parenting, you can praise them for the positive intentions and interventions, and then ask if they would like some further ideas. At this point you can begin parent training.

Unfortunately, however, there are parents who will drain you no matter how much time and energy you put into them. They are like an emotional black hole; they will eat up all the energy of the therapy. If it becomes obvious after much time, that the parents are not invested in treatment, as a last resort you should focus on giving the child whatever positive input and skill-building you can to build up his resilience, identify inner and outer resources, and increase his skills and ability to cope with the parents' ineffectiveness. For example, "I know that your mother has a mental illness that prevents her from being the kind of mother you would like and need. I will help you find new ways to deal with her and people who can help you."

Attachment Disorder

Question: I have a client who says she has an attachment disorder. I asked her where she got that "diagnosis," and she said she got it off the Internet and felt like it described her to a T. She is very vague about what she wants, saying just to care about people more. She is very cold in her presentation and appears to be very narcissistic, and at times, critical of me and my approach. I wonder whether she wants to change. And to be honest, I am not so sure I want to continue with her.

Response: You should get into her history to find out when and why she had to develop such emotional armor. That kind of bravado is often a cover for a very deep hurt. Somewhere along the line she needed to shut down her true feelings to keep from getting hurt. Her *best defense* now is a *good offense*. She has learned to "do it to them, before they do it to you," and you are one of the recipients. She is presenting you with an opportunity to check your own emotional strength and ability to not take things personally. If she is, however, being abusive, you must confront her empathically. "I know that somewhere along the line you found that kind of language to be acceptable, and perhaps you needed it to survive, but in here, it is neither necessary nor acceptable. We can find better ways to express what you are going through."

Also helpful is the metaphor of the wall. She has a wall of many bricks built up around her. Each one of those bricks is the result of being hurt and now exists as distrust. The wall serves one purpose—to keep people out, so she doesn't get hurt. But in the process, the wall has three unintended consequences: 1. The wall is blocking positive feelings from others coming in; 2. The wall prevents her negative feelings being shared with others; and 3. The wall blocks her positive feelings from getting out. The net effect is that being behind the wall may feel safe, but it is isolating and prevents meaningful relationships. Only by establishing trust can the wall come down, and you could be the first to provide the safety and security to allow that to happen. It may come down one brick at a time in the beginning, but as trust builds, the momentum increases, and the person can open up to newer, fuller relationships.

As far as her not wanting to change, I am sure she has some major trepidation. Her wall is her protection and stripping that away too soon may make her very vulnerable. Patience and perseverance will be necessary. The key is to keep her invested in therapy enough to continue. Play to her strengths, and redirect them to serve her instead of isolate her.

Not Open for Help

Question: What do I do when the client is not open for any suggestions?

Response: We must determine why the person is blocked. There may be many reasons why the person is not open. (Some of these are covered in Chapter

5.) If suggestions are made too early in the process, the client may not have the trust to proceed. This can be an indication he does not feel validated. Further work is needed to build the therapeutic relationship. He also may feel challenged, because he usually makes his own decisions, or it may be he doesn't see the validity of your suggestions.

When you venture out with the clients and get shot down, it is an indication that they are not ready to join the dance (see Chapter 6). The key is to back up and ask what they want and how they think they should go about it. Start with their ideas. If they say they have none, ask permission to give them suggestions. This often paves the way for more cooperation and receptivity. If there still is no response to your idea, you can reframe this as their being careful not to proceed too fast, and you appreciate their careful consideration of your proposals. This may be the point to ask the questions: "What works for you? How can I best serve you? What do you need from me?" They may say, "I don't know. You're the expert." You may respond, "But you are the expert on yourself, and I will work with you to define your needs and goals."

There are many less-threatening themes you may entice him to work on just to get the ball rolling. Subjects like stress reduction, self-esteem, self-disclosure, strength bombardment, and general coping skills are just some of the more neutral ways to get involved in the therapeutic process. Once he has experienced some success or self-discovery in any one of these areas, he may be willing to take on more serious or deeply-rooted issues.

Drug Addict Can't Stop

> **Question:** I am working with a young adult who is unable to stop using drugs despite jail and being homeless.

Response: There are many avenues to explore with this situation. One of the main questions to explore is what do the drugs do for him? And many times, the question is, what did the drugs do for him? Because addicts are often trying to recapture their original high but cannot do because of increased tolerance. Additionally, it is said that drugs are a solution that no longer work, but the addict does not realize it. Ironically, drugs have now become the cause of the problems (homelessness, isolation, depression, arrests, etc.). Addicts end up taking drugs to avoid the painful consequences of their neglect and/ or mishaps. This is the kind of a circular, self-defeating dilemma in which they get caught.

It can be summarized with this scenario. If the average person is involved in a situation causing pain, he/she will try to eliminate or change the situation, whereas, if the addict is in a situation that is causing him/her pain, he/she will try to eliminate the pain with drugs. That's why, for example, an addict, who is in debt, had his electricity turned off, and is suffering in the heat of the summer, will, if he gets some money, not pay off his electricity bill, but instead buy drugs so that he won't mind having the electricity off.

To fully answer your question would take a whole book, but the main focus is to build the kind of relationship with the person, so that you can explore his addiction with him and mutually come up with a solution. For example, when addicts come for outpatient counseling in the first session, I usually *forbid* them to stop using, which is a paradoxical intervention. Instead, I invite them to be curious about their use. One reason is that they expect me to tell them to stop, and they have built up all their defenses as to why they won't or can't. The second, and more important reason, is that I want them to explore their drug use and report back to me. These are the questions I want them to explore during the week and ask themselves:

- What do they like about their drug of choice?
- What is the feeling they get?
- Where in their body do they feel it?
- Is it the same every time?
- What is pleasant about it, if anything?
- How is the effect of one joint, pill, or drink different from two?
- How much does it take to attain the high they desire?
- Are they able to attain the high they desire?
- At what point do they lose to control (feel drunk, OD'd), if any?
- Do they still find the high satisfying, or does it just get them back to "normal"?

This approach takes them off the defensive and puts you in a position of being a person who is joining with them in the exploration, rather than being just another person trying to get them to stop using.

Another approach is to have them *play out the movie*. What this means is it is not uncommon for addicts to romanticize their drug use. They love the high, thinking they are doing the right thing, because the drug helps them feel confident and more outgoing, or helps them have great sex, but they do not consider the long-term consequences. Ask them to *play out the movie* of their drug fantasy by seeing themselves getting high but explore the after-effects. What are the possible consequences? How will they live with the consequences such as spending all their money, getting physically sick, embarrassing or neglecting the family, getting into legal trouble, etc.

Unfortunately, your client is willing to pay a high price for getting high, but you never know his breaking point when he will realize what drugs are doing to his life. You also should consider where he is in the Stages of Change (see Chapter 2). He is probably in pre-contemplative or contemplative stage of change. Having him play out the movie may break down some of his resistance.

The Butt of Jokes

> **Question:** I have a client who has difficulty with people taking him seriously. He looks a little strange, having a rather childish demeanor though he is 25. He has a pouty face and talks in a baby tone of voice when stressed. He was bullied in school and got beat up several times. Now he is wanting to find a companion and wants to be taken seriously, but his family and friends continue to play practical jokes on him, call him "mental," and never taking seriously anything he has to say. I can see the real person in him, but don't know how to help him bring this out and be more real.

Response: First of all, I would congratulate for seeing the good in him, and you should congratulate him for wanting to change and to be taken seriously.

You said that you see him in a different light, and I would talk to him about that. What is it that you see? How is it different from how others see him? You should do some strength bombardment by not only giving him positive feedback, but with his doing a self-inventory of his own strengths.

I would encourage him to be assertive with family and friends, and this could be done in role plays. Begin teaching him about the difference between being passive and assertive and why he has a right to be treated with respect. Teach him to say, when made fun of, "I don't appreciate that. It used to be funny, but to me it is not any more. I am serious about what I am saying." Now the first few times he says this, he may get some derogatory feedback like, "Who do you think you are?" or "You got something up your butt?" Help him respond to these comments in a non-reactive way. "No, I am just trying to be a better person and would like people to respect me and my efforts." If he doesn't react the way they want him to, that will soon extinguish their efforts.

Reluctant Addicts

> **Question:** How do you help others when they do not think they need help? I end up wanting recovery for them when they do not want it. I do not think this can be done, unless they want to work on recovery.

Response: What if I ask you to change everything in your life? How receptive would you be? This would mean making new friends, changing your daily routine, developing new habits, creating new ways of problem-solving, and giving up the one thing you can depend on to help you cope with life. This is often the challenge addicts face when entering counseling and contemplating recovery. Such a radical change is tremendously overwhelming to addicts, who generally have few resources inwardly or outwardly. There is a tendency among human beings, especially addicts, to stick with what is familiar, even though it may be tremendously uncomfortable or even destructive, rather than shift to something constructive and healing i.e., recovery and sobriety, because these are unfamiliar. The solution is to narrow down their situation to one or two aspects that changing would improve their lives.

The source of the addiction (drugs, alcohol, sex, gambling, eating, etc.) was originally seen as the solution or source of relief to the previous unbearable life or pain. If the addict's life has centered around addiction for a long time, the brain recreates the idea that abstinence and recovery will result in going back to the original situation he is trying to escape that fueled his addiction. And he may very well go through withdrawals, depending on the kind of addiction. Quitting makes him very vulnerable.

The therapist must understand that these dynamics underlie clients' reluctance and acknowledge and express the difficulty of the task of recovery. With support, understanding, caring, and love, they can begin to accept recovery as a viable and attainable alternative.

Elementary School Child and Gangs

Question: I'm a counselor at an elementary school, and we have students who as young as age 7 say they belong to a gang and even wear the colors. When I told the parents, they said. "I know; we are members of the gang." What can I do?

Response: This is a classic situation of having to deal with very strong cultural influences. Attempts to dissuade them, which seem the most logical thing to do, will go against the wishes of the parents. There are two approaches: one is to focus on reframing the positive aspects of being in the gang, such as a sense of belonging, protection, support, loyalty, and acceptance. These are universal values that can be discussed and promoted. The other approach is to provide cultural alternatives, expose them to other experiences such as field trips to the arts, TV stations, airports, and even college campuses. Many of these children and their parents may not have not been on a college campus, and exposing them to this experience may create a whole new outlook for them. Also, you may encourage them to get involved in sports such as T-ball or Little League.

Abusive Client

Question: I have a client who gets very angry and starts accusing me of not knowing what I'm doing. He will sometimes stand and berate me. Part of me is indignant about being treated this way, and another part tells me not to take it personally. What should I do?

Response: The first step is to evaluate your own interactions to be sure that you are not doing anything to provoke the client. We all have blind spots—

certain looks, gestures, tone of voice, or comments that seem innocuous to us but may hit a raw nerve in the client. Many clients are extremely sensitive and attuned to any such nuance that may be interpreted as condescending, whether intentional or not. Often they have been subjected to disrespect by many others in their life and therefore are always on hyper-alert to verbals or non-verbals that they considered a put-down.

Next, you may apologize for having "offended them," and this obviously was not your intention. You can welcome feedback even, but given in a respectful manner. Such apologies are not what these clients usually expect and can change the tone of the session. Or you can do the opposite, which is to tell them to sit down, calm down, and that you don't respect or deserve that kind of treatment, all in a very respectful tone of voice. While others in his life may tolerate such berating, it is not acceptable in the therapy room. Some clients, especially narcissistic clients, respect someone who will challenge them and not "roll over and take it."

More often than not, you need to see this kind of interaction as part of a pattern that has existed for a long time in the client's history and is not at all about you. So, your decision not to take it personally is always the better way to go. The bottom line, however, is that you do not have to take abuse from your clients. Being assertive and understanding are the most effective ways to manage the situation. In this situation, finding the proper balance between the two can be the greatest challenge.

Arguing Couple

> **Question:** I am working with a couple, and all they seem to want to do is come in and argue. I have tried a number of ways to engage them, and they will work for a few minutes, and then the couple is back bringing up old stuff and arguing.

Response: Counseling with couples can be extremely difficult for several reasons:

- Therapy is often the last resort before divorce.
- One or both may not want to be in therapy. They are only doing it to appease the other, or to prove that even

counseling will not save the relationship.

- There is a tendency for the couple to re-enact the negative dynamics of their relationship in front of the therapist. This includes yelling, accusations, innuendo, sarcasm, and even threats, which if allowed unabated, will only crystalize their enmity instead of dissolve it.

- The therapist has to walk a tight rope being careful to not side with one over the other. This is made more difficult when one partner is obviously more responsible than the other for the trouble.

The therapist needs to define the parameters of what she can do for them. Her goal is not to decide who is right and who is wrong, but to help them clarify their communication, which may or may not result in their staying together. The therapist may state her preference that people stay together, but sometimes the relationship is so toxic and the trust level so damaged that the parties may decide to go their separate ways.

While it is important for the therapist to see the psychodynamics of the couple's difficulty by allowing them to argue in the session, at some point these interactions must be contained. Tell them, "You don't need to pay me to watch you argue. My goal is to help you clarify your feelings and communicate without arguing." If sessions start to get out of hand, the therapist can ask one of them to step outside. That person can be either the one most out-of-control and needs to leave the room to calm down, or that person may be the one to stay in the room to work with the therapist to calm down.

Many times, when extreme emotions erupt, what you are seeing is an older version of their younger self. These emotional reactions may very well have originated in their childhood. You may say to them, "Wow, where did that part of you come from? It seems you are sabotaging yourself and the relationship, which means you are really hurting on a deeper level. What can we do to help that part of you feel more accepted or validated?"

Finally, if feelings are so explosive, individual sessions with each partner may be indicated. This may be crucial to build rapport with each person, so that when the therapist has to confront the offending party, the person is more receptive to hearing and receiving feedback. Once issues are clarified and the stress level is reduced, then the couple can be seen together again with the understanding that vitriolic outbursts are counter-productive and will not be tolerated.

Non-Responsive Mother

Question: I am working with a 13-year-old girl who was adopted along with her sister. The sister can do no wrong, and my client gets blamed for everything. Mom works in the evenings, does not provide any structure at home, and when my client hangs out at the neighbor's, which is a relatively stable family, mom yells and screams at her for not staying home. Mom will not accept that her actions play any part in the problem.

Response: You need to invite the mother in and hear her side of the story. If she continues to place all the blame on the daughter, you may have to agree with her at first. Then you can begin a subtle shift in how you address the issue from blaming everything on the 13-year-old to getting the mother to accept her responsibility. How do you create a situation in which you can shift the focus away from the client and get the mother to take responsibility?

The goal of working with the mother is to help her develop a new relationship with her daughter that will allow her to have a more positive impact and influence with her. To accomplish this, there needs to be a subtle shift in the mother's thinking through reframing using the following transitions:

- The child is the problem.
- I am having a problem with the child.
- There are problems within the family that need to be addressed.
- How can we work together to make the changes?
- What can I as a parent do to improve the situation?

For example, if the mother says that the client is totally disrespectful, you can shift the focus simply by saying,

"Sounds like you are having a difficult time getting her to respect you." You don't need to dwell on it the first time you say it, but you begin to sprinkle this kind of language in your responses to mom.

The response to "She won't do anything I ask her to do," becomes, "So you can't get her to cooperate with you."

Then you can begin to join with the mother and say, "What do we need to do to get her to cooperate?" and work cooperatively with the mother until she begins to accept ownership.

Then you can switch the focus back to her and say, "What do you need to do to get her to cooperate?"

Of course, this may take place over several sessions.

The goal is to take the onus off the child and spread the responsibility and solution to the parents and possibly other members of the family by supporting the stronger members and empowering the weaker members. The focus changes from "fixing the child" to "improving the relationship with the child," to "improving relationships with the parent/family" This is done by:

1. Building a trusting relationship with the mother.

First, establish rapport with her by discussing any issue such as her interests, concerns, job, childhood, and how she was raised. This will help her to be less defensive. Next, enhance feelings of love and commitment towards the child by identifying an age where there was strong bonding. This can often be done by looking at pictures of the child at a younger age when the mother felt positive towards the child.

You can also work with the mother to reduce her stress level. Administering an inventory like the Parental Stress Index can open the door to talking about the stress she is feeling not only from difficulty with the child, but from other aspects of her life. Once this connection is made by acknowledging and expressing understanding and empathy, you generate hope increasing the mother's locus of control and allying with her. At this point you can address what would *she* like help with. What are her personal needs? What changes is she willing to make?

You may need to de-escalate her by having her take some deep breaths, relax, lower her voice and respond softly. Praise the mother for any changes she makes and brag about any positive changes in the child's behavior. Help the mother to understand the child's behavior is a tip of the iceberg, and that there may be many other factors causing the problem, which should be taken into consideration. Emphasize the child needs encouragement instead of criticism.

2. Identify her parenting practices

You can validate the mother's past efforts by acknowledging her difficult past and present circumstances and praise her for her efforts. The next step is to help her identify specifically the changes she would like to see in her child. Consult with her about origins of the child's behavior and what her best guess is about why the child is the way she is. Try to pinpoint where things went wrong (trauma, developmental mishaps/delays, other events).

3. Give the mother feedback and new tools.

To increase cooperation, give help by asking if the mother would like some advice and/or feedback about parenting. If so, develop a "parenting prescription" (a set of actions she can do to manage the situation constructively). Then model ways to handle the child and ask the mother to observe. Invite the mother to do the same and observe her and give her feedback after asking how she could have handled the situation differently.

Infidelity

> **Question:** I have been seeing a couple for about 6 weeks. I sensed I was not getting anywhere and asked to see them separately. During my session with the husband, he disclosed that he was having an affair and was leaning towards leaving the marriage. I am not sure what to do at this point. Do I encourage him to tell the wife?

Response: It is important when working with couples to set out the rules for confidentiality at the beginning, especially if you will be seeing them separately, and what you would do in the event of an affair. In effect, you have three clients: the husband, the wife, and the couple. You should respect the confidentiality of all three. Some therapists are not willing to see a couple if there is an ongoing affair. Others are willing to go along for a set amount of time. You may want to suspend couples counseling, until you can clarify the intent of the person with the affair. This, however, could increase the suspicion of the wife. You can tell her that you need to work with him to help him clarify his true feelings about the marriage.

Ideally, you can encourage him to end the affair and be willing to help him through this process. At that point, the question becomes should he disclose this to the wife? This is very controversial. Many disclose their infidelity to assuage their guilt. Others do it, allegedly, to not hurt the other person, but in effect are trying to protect themselves from hurt. Affairs have two major impacts: the affair itself and the lying and deceit that goes along with it. Disclosure is like a bomb going off on the relationship. The shock of the betrayal is devastating, but if the other person should find out by some other means, this is even more devastating. Withholding and having a relationship built on lies and deceit is not a recipe for success.

You may be able to get him to rethink the whole situation. What is the attraction of the other person? Is it not possible his wife could develop these qualities? What is missing in his marriage? If things could change, would he be willing to reconsider? One way to assess this is a shortened version of the Miracle Question: "If you could choose today to stay in the marriage or leave it with minimal or no damage and have whatever you would like, which would you choose?" If he does agree to needed changes, that would be the preferred way to go (especially if children are involved). If he is not willing to end it and/ or he is determined to get out of the marriage, then you should tell him that there is no point in further marriage counseling, unless the goal is to amicably end the marriage. In the end, there are no easy solutions.

Trauma Treatment Worse

Question: I am working with a client who was sexually traumatized when she was 13. She is now 28 and just starting to talk about this situation. At first I thought we were making a lot of progress, but it seems like we hit a wall. Her depression had started to lift, but now the more we talk about any real meaningful events, the more she is getting more depressed and feels like she is losing all the good feelings she had from doing therapy.

Response: There is often an excitement and relief when a person first opens up and is able to share some of the pain they have experienced. It often takes a lot of courage and momentum to take that initial step. Once that step has been taken, it becomes easier to go on, but feelings are like the layers of an onion. The outer ones are easier to take off, but as the client progresses, the inner layers are more difficult to express, because they have more of a charge on them.

One way to look at this is that memories are stored in time capsules, and those memories will pop open when the person is ready to remember them. It is as though the body/mind has an innate wisdom to know when the person is ready to deal with these memories. So, as the deeper, more hurtful memories get revealed, the pain is greater and has more of a residual effect. Thus, it feels like a step backward, but the reality is that as a person gets stronger, they can remember more and more hurtful memories. Therefore, ironically one of the fruits of their progress is their remembering more painful situations.

Timing is important in these situations. It may be necessary to rotate sessions between doing deeper memory work and talking about more neutral, lighter situations at the next session. Or it is fine for the client to take some time off from therapy and let the natural process of healing take place without stirring up more feelings. The client needs to know that he/she is in control of the situation.

Abandonment Issues

Question: What can you do if a child doesn't like you as a woman because of abandonment issues?

Response: First, I would validate her not liking you as a legitimate feeling, and you can even reframe it as a positive "taking care of yourself, since no one else has ever been there for you consistently." You can acknowledge that she needs to do this to protect herself, and you can join her by saying, "If I were in your place, I probably wouldn't like me either."

Then you might state the conditions you would want a therapist to meet in order to trust and like them. "If I had a therapist, before I would accept her she would need to prove herself by..." and then list conditions you sincerely would expect and/or what you think the client might say. You might say things like:

- Leaving me alone when I want to be left alone.

- Not always be asking me a bunch of questions.
- Showing me that she truly cares about me as a person.
- She shouldn't tell me she cares, and then I can never contact her again after the therapy session is over.
- Taking an interest in me other than talking about how screwed up I am.

Then ask her what she would say.

Be aware, if and when she opens up and gets more personal with you, the scarier it may be for her for fear of losing you, and she may cut you off abruptly or turn on you with the unconscious attitude of, "Do it to her (reject her), before she does it to me." It takes a lot of patience and a willingness to be with her for the long run, but that is what she needs. (You can see how a borderline personality disorder might develop).

Finally, also be conscious of the fact that you may only be able to take her so far in the process. If you are kind and caring and consistent, that can mean a lot.

Our administrative assistant brought her newly, adopted dog to work each day. The dog was very timid, especially around men, and if you looked at her in a certain way would either bark or run at the drop of a hat. I saw her as a challenge. I bought her treats and within a week or two had her eating out of my hand. She would even come up and nudge me with her nose, but she never let me pet her. We never got to the point of being "best buds," but she was able to trust some—much more than she did at the beginning. And so it goes. This is analogous to how far you can take some clients in the process.

Teenage Anger Issue

Question: How do I handle a teenage girl with her anger issue, when she blames me for not helping her to change?

Response: Reframe the situation as one in which she trusts you, because she can express her feelings to you, and you are important to her, because if you were not so important to her, she wouldn't be so angry with you. People don't get angry at people they don't care about. This almost sets up a paradoxical situation, where the more she expresses her anger toward you, the more she is expressing how important you really are to her.

Other things I would suggest:

- Find ways to be in situations with her in a neutral way. This means doing something together that she obviously would have fun doing, and it has no charge on it.
- Find a way to give to her—not to win her over—but as a sincere expression of caring about her. This could be a card (maybe even one you made yourself), some candy, a plant, or even something like a picture of something special that she might like.
- Equally as important, give to her by finding positive ways in which she has changed and point them out to her. The idea is you don't want to have all your transactions dealing with the fact that she is angry with you.
- Finally, be aware that this is a pattern that she has had with others and probably developed it in childhood. It has become a way for her to hold onto her anger and express it without having to take responsibility for it—she can always blame others for it. Hopefully, you can point this out to her without her being defensive.

Unmotivated Child

Question: A child I am working with is unmotivated. Rewards and punishment don't work. She wants a great deal of attention and doesn't care if it's negative or positive. She is at a stalemate—school, relationships, family. She lies about everything, even when it is not consequential. I am pretty sure there has been some sexual abuse, but she will not talk about it. She will not take responsibility and see problems as always someone else's fault. She exhibits RAD (reactive attention disorder) tendencies. She is 11 and has been with us for 3 years (children's home).

Response: The first thing I would do would be to re-join with her in any way you can. Try to get the relationship on a different track. Start out with any neutral kinds of interactions totally unrelated to what she thinks is counseling.

Get into her world and find out what she is interested in. Talk about fun things or funny things. Look up some funny things on You Tube.

Once that happens, find any positives, even if it is in her negative behavior. If she is lying, rather than trying to stop it, go with it. If it is not consequential, encourage her to tell you more. The lying is not nearly as important as the reason for her lying. Her making up stories about everything is a way to get attention, and I would want to explore the possibility that she has learned that telling lies gets better results than telling the truth. Take on the onus of the lying, rather than putting it on her, by saying something like, "I feel like sometimes you tell me the truth and sometimes not." (Avoid the word, *lie*, since it is such a charged word.) "You must be pretty good at it, because I am not easily fooled. How can I know when you are telling me the truth and when not?" If she responds, "I always tell the truth," you can say, "See that's a prime example—I don't know if you are telling the truth or not." You can almost make it a game. Have her tell you some things, and you have to guess whether or not they are the truth. You are trying to de-stress the situation so that she will feel more comfortable telling you the truth. Tell her, "I would love to have the kind of relationship where you could feel free to tell me the truth about anything."

The part that stands out for me is her wanting a great deal of attention. I would reframe your statement to she "needs a great deal of attention." There is a saying in Transactional Analysis that a person will work for negative strokes rather than no strokes at all. Given that she is showing some tendencies of RAD, she may not know how to get "positive strokes." Some children become immune to positive statements such as "You're such a pretty girl," or "You do things that really make me happy," because whoever said them ended up take advantage of the child. Or she may reject these overtures, because in many ways she is using this as a test to see if you are sincere and can be trusted or can easily be pushed away.

When working with a child who is at a stalemate, the question that comes to my mind is "What can I offer that she would want?" I do not know what kinds of rewards you are offering. I might explore things that are less materialistic like hope, a new way of seeing herself, or ways to build on her positive characteristics. This may be rebuffed, if she feels that if she gets her hopes up, she will only end up getting disappointed, so it is better to have no hope. So, what you want to do is to create some little hopes, and make sure they can be accomplished. Give her some mini-goals related to her improving her self-esteem. Hopefully, this will get the ball rolling, and she will open up and have the courage to go forward.

Withdrawn Adolescent

Question: An adolescent was brought to me by his parents. He has been to two other therapists, and they could not work with him because he was so shut down. He came into the session, slumped down on the couch, arms crossed, and pulled down his hoodie to cover his eyes. Any attempt to engage him on any subject, however neutral or non-confrontational, was at best met with a one or two word answers, but mostly he gave me a glaring look and looked away. No amount of joking and lighthearted banter penetrated his stoic countenance. I don't know how to get through to him.

Response: Adolescents often present a unique set of problems:

- Rarely do adolescents come to therapy of their own volition. To the contrary, most come against their wishes.
- Given their reluctance towards therapy, their main goal is often to prove that therapy will not work or help them, thereby having a reason to quit.
- Therapy is seen as just another adult trying to tell them what to do, and they just want to be left alone.
- Grappling with parents, teens learn to engage in power struggles and often utilize these skills in negotiations with the therapist.
- Adolescents can be more explosive than other clients. Their brains are undergoing a transformation, and they literally lack the mechanism to control their emotions.
- Teens eschew tradition. They do not sit upright, quietly engaging in friendly conversation. They often speak freely, act disrespectfully, and profess to care less what the therapist thinks of them (though I think they do).

There is no hope of helping an adolescent without first developing a positive relationship. In the beginning, it may involve just getting into their world and putting aside any overt attempts to "help them." The goal of the relationship is to gain their respect and cooperation and not to be their best buddy. It is important to set limits, establish boundaries, and shape values in a way that are palatable for the client.

Have a sense of humor. Kids do a lot of crazy things and when they do, a sense of humor is vital. There is a time to be serious, but only after the stress level is down and humor helps to lower that level.

Accept his reluctance towards therapy and pledge to help him get out of it by working with him to convince whoever sent him that he doesn't need it. But to do that, certain things need to be accomplished.

Challenge him to grow and help him identify and build positive character traits instead of only focusing on the negative behaviors. One of the middle schools I work with decided to have a gang prevention group for students that the teachers identified as being high risk for gangs. To entice them to join the group, they touted it as a "leadership group," telling the students they had been specially chosen. This generated much excitement among them, but when the first group met and saw who all was in the group and that the focus was gang-prevention, they were immediately disappointed, discouraged, and felt betrayed. Talk about his leadership potential, if you can identify it.

I had a similar client situation, and there was a running dialogue in my mind as I witnessed his behavior. It went something like this:

> *What happened to this poor boy that he would be so shut down?*
> *How can he be so rude?*
> *I should be able to get through to him with my clinical prowess.*
> *Okay, you win. You can stonewall me, but you will lose in the end.*
> *Why torture this poor kid by making him stay here and be interrogated by me?*
> *We are just getting started, don't give up too soon.*
> *I am really at a loss. I have nothing to offer the kid he will respond to.*
> *My time is too precious to spend trying to get him to open up and then convince him he has a problem.*

CHAPTER 12: RESPONSES TO QUESTIONS

I need to help him. What is the key to open this person up? There must be some chink in his armor.

He is showing signs of major depressive disorder.

And finally, how can I gracefully end the session that seems to be going nowhere?

I kept trying to come up with conversational topics that he could respond to (favorite group, song, TV shows, sports, pets, etc.). There were times where we had long periods of silence which seemed to strengthen his resolve.

After all these mental gyrations, I settled on just being peaceful and mindful of myself and interject my presence into this situation in whatever way I could, even if it was silence, without any desire for a specific outcome. I convinced myself to just be compassionate and accepting while trying to understand him. The bottom line, however, is not to make yourself and the client miserable, so if the deadlock cannot be broken, discharge the client and tell him you are available should he ever want to come back to counseling. You don't want to burn any bridges by being overly confrontational, and even more important not leave him with the feeling that counseling sucks, and he will never seek counseling again.

EPILOGUE

COUNSELING IS A SACRED AND CHALLENGING PROFESSION. It can be a fascinating journey into the frontier of the human mind. Gifted therapists, such as Marsha Linehan, Bessel Van der Kolk, Peter Levine, Pat Ogden, and many more, the ones who developed new approaches, were inquisitive, introspective, and possessed an insatiable curiosity. They were also not geared to settle for the status quo; they saw a glimmer and they pursued it. They were not limited by existing models and protocol. In fact, they even went beyond the logical, traditional models to pursue their approach, and in doing so, showed courage and perseverance in postulating new ideas and introducing them to their colleagues. But even beyond all of that, they showed a concern for and commitment to the well-being of humanity and the need to end suffering. So, this is no less a sacred challenge for all of us.

We too must get outside of our comfort zone if we are to be truly effective. We must allow ourselves to be fascinated by the mysteries of the human psyche. As therapists, we help clients go from the known to the unknown. In other words, clients have a problem that is known, but they do not know how to solve it, what underlies it, or what caused it. These are all aspects of the unknown that may be revealed. What is needed, that both the clients and the therapist have to explore the unknown, which is a leap of faith. This requires courage, curiosity, and creativity, especially when uncovering the wounds of trauma. We do not know what we will find when we begin to explore the pain. We have to be able to reach out to the clients and join with them—in effect, we are building a bridge from the known to the unknown, a bridge over troubled waters.

As stated earlier, it is okay to not know what to do. The benefit of just being fully present with another human with their pain and suffering should not be under-estimated. Two souls earnestly searching for healing and health can lead to solutions, and not only solutions to problems but to help clients to enjoy and celebrate life and discover a deeper and richer meaning to life. Does this sound Pollyannaish? Once you have experienced the rewards of helping another person heal, it all seems both very doable, and at the same time, quite miraculous. The challenge is to join the with the client to promote recovery and healing by providing solace, companionship, a positive spirit, and hope.

Ultimately, doing therapy is self-discovery. We are bound to benefit, if we develop the qualities listed above keeping an open and present mind and a calm, loving presence with a commitment to easing the suffering and promoting the healing of others. If we are mindful and learn from our mistakes not afraid to search out our own shortcomings, we not only bring the reward of that to each of our clients, we will not panic if we don't know what to do. Hopefully, this will spur us to increase our knowledge and skills and develop our character. We are then humbled by the enigma of their lives and their innate ability to overcome their tribulations. And in the long run, as each one of us helps a person to overcome stress and/or tragedy and reach their God-given potential as humane human beings, we are creating a more tolerant, kinder, understanding, and peaceful world.

REFERENCES & SUGGESTED READINGS

Abblett, M. (2013). *The Heat of the Moment in Treatment*. New York: W.W. Norton & Company

American Counseling Association (2014). *ACA Code of Ethics 2014* Alexandria, Va.

Anonymous, (2001). *Alcoholics Anonymous*. USA: Alcoholics Anonymous World Services, Inc.

Beatty, M.(1992). *Codependent No More: How to Stop Controlling Others and Start Caring for Yourself*. Center City, Missouri: Hazelden

Caby, A. & F. (2014). *The Therapist's Treasure Chest: Solution-Oriented Tips and Tricks for Everyday Practice*. New York: W.W. Norton & Company

Castenadas, C. (1968). *The Teachings of Don Juan: A Yaqui Way of Knowledge*. New York: Washington Square Press

Doherty, W. Ph.D. (1995). *Soul Searching*. New York: Basic Books

Dougherty, P. (2007). *Qigong in Psychotherapy*. USA: Spring Forest Publishing

Duncan, B. L., Hubble, M. A. and Miller, S. D. (1997). *Psychotherapy with "Impossible" Cases*. New York: W.W. Norton & Company.

Duncan, B., Miller, S., and Hubble, M. (1999). *The Heart and Soul of Change*. Washington, DC: American Psychological Association

Edgette, J. S. (2006). *Adolescent Therapy That Really Works*. New York: W.W. Norton & Company

Ecker, B.Ticic, R.,Hulley, L. (2012*). Unlocking the Emotional Brain*, New York: Routledge

Frankl, V. (2006). *Man's Search for Meaning*. Boston, Massachusetts: Beacon Press

Figley,C (1995*). Compassion Fatigue: Coping With Secondary Traumatic Stress Disorder In Those Who Treat the Traumatized*. New York: Brunnel Mazel

Furman, B. (2004). *Kids Skills*. Kangaroo Flat: Victoria. St. Luke's Innovative Resources

Gladwell, M. (2008). *Outliers*. New York: Little, Brown, and Company

Gottman Ph.D., J. (2015). *The Seven Principles of Making Marriage Work*. New York: Harmony Books.

Grand, D. (2013*). Brainspotting: The Revolutionary New Therapy for Rapid and Effective Change*. Boulder, CO: Sounds True

Grove,David (1989).*Resolving Traumatic Memories: Metaphors and Symbolism in Psychotherapy*. New York: Irvington Publishers

Jampolsky, G. (2011). *Love is Letting Go of Fear*. Berkley, CA: Celestial Arts.

Kabat-Zinn, J. (2012). *Mindfulness for Beginners: Reclaiming the Present Moment and Your Life*. Boulder, CO.: Sounds True

Karasu, T. B. (1992). *Wisdom in the Practice of Psychotherapy*. USA: BasicBooks

Kottler, J. (1992). *Compassionate Therapy*. San Francisco, CA: Jossey-Bass Inc.

Kottler, J. (2015). *The Therapist in the Real World*. New York: W.W. Norton

Levine, P. Ph.D. (2010). *In an Unspoken Voice*. Berkeley, CA: North Atlantic Books

REFERENCES & SUGGESTED READINGS

Meier, S. T., Davis, S. R. (2005). *The Elements of Counseling*. Belmont CA: Brooks/Cole

Mitchell, C. W. Ph.D.(2012). *Effective Techniques for Dealing with Highly Resistant Clients 2nd Edition*. USA: Clifton W. Mitchell Publisher

Mollica, R. (2006). *Healing Invisible Wounds: Paths to Hope and Recovery in a Violent World*. San Diego: Harcourt

O'Hanlon, B. and Beadle, S. (1997). *Guide to Possibility Land*. New York: W.W. Norton

O'Hanlon, W. H. (1987). *Taproots*. New York: W. W. Norton

O'Hanlon, W. H. (2006). *Change 101*. New York: W. W. Norton

Ogden, P., Minton, K., Pain, C. (2006). *Trauma and the Body*. New York: W. W. Norton

Orman, S. (2012). *The 9 Steps to Financial Freedom*. New York: Three River Press

Ortner, N. (2013). *The Tapping Solution*. Carlsbad, CA: Hay House

Perlmutter, D. (2015). *Brain Maker*. New York: Little, Brown, and Company

Post, B. B. (2010). *From Fear to Love*. Palmyra, Virginia: Post Institute and Associates

Reik, T. (1983). *Listening with the Third Ear*. New York: Viking Press

Robins, T (2008). *Unlimited Power: The New Source of Personal Achievement*. New York: Free Press

Satchidananda, S. (2002). *Integral Hatha Yoga*. Yogaville, VA: Integral Yoga Publications

Wahls, T. (2014). *The Wahls Protocol*. New York: The Penguin Group

Van Der Kolk, B.(2014). *The Body Keeps Score: Brain, Mind, and Body in the Healing of Trauma*. New York: Viking

Yalom, I. D. M.D. (2009). *The Gift of Therapy*. New York: Harper Perennial

INDEX

ABOUT THE AUTHOR

J ON WINDER IS A CLINICIAN, author, consultant, and lecturer. He is recognized for his practical and sensitive approach to counseling.

He graduated from the University of Florida, where he got his Masters Degree in Rehabilitation Counseling. He is a Licensed Professional Counselor and a Licensed Substance Abuse Practitioner and has been in private practice for over thirty years. He has been a clinician and consultant in addictions and mental health for over forty years. Previously, he was Clinical Coordinator of the Adolescent Drug Treatment Program for Central Virginia Community Services and is past director of the Arise Residential Center, a residential drug treatment program.

Mr. Winder has given many seminars to other professionals on addiction, families, childhood trauma, and clinical practices and supervised over 40 people for licensure. He has presented workshops and training locally, nationally and internationally. In 2001 he presented at the American Counseling Association Conference in New Orleans. In 2012 he conducted a 3-day workshop in Mauritania Africa on "High Risk Youth and Resiliency."